Signs for the Times

Signs for the Times

Symbolic Realism in the Mid-Victorian World

CHRIS BROOKS

London
GEORGE ALLEN & UNWIN
Boston   Sydney

George Allen & Unwin (Publishers) Ltd,
40 Museum Street, London WC1A 1LU, UK

George Allen & Unwin (Publishers) Ltd,
Park Lane, Hemel Hempstead, Herts HP2 4TE, UK

Allen & Unwin, Inc.,
9 Winchester Terrace, Winchester, Mass. 01890, USA

George Allen & Unwin Australia Pty Ltd,
8 Napier Street, North Sydney, NSW 2060, Australia

First published in 1984

British Library Cataloguing in Publication Data

Brooks, Chris
 Signs for the times.
 1. Symbolism (Art movement)—England—
History   2. Arts, English
 I. Title
 700   NX600.S95
 ISBN 0-04-800030-2

Library of Congress Cataloging in Publication Data

Brooks, Chris.
 Signs for the times.
 Includes bibliographical references and index.
 1. Arts, British. 2. Arts, Victorian—Great Britain.
 3. Realism in art—Great Britain. 4. Symbolism in art—
Great Britain. I. Title.
 NX543.B76 1984   700'.941   84-6277
 ISBN 0-04-800030-2

Set in 10 on 11 point Plantin by Grove Graphics, Tring, Hertfordshire
and printed in Great Britain
by Biddles Ltd, Guildford, Surrey

For Joanna

Meanwhile, we too admit that the present is an important time; as all present time necessarily is. The poorest Day that passes over us is the conflux of two Eternities; it is made up of currents that issue from the remotest Past, and flow onwards into the remotest Future. We were wise indeed, could we discern truly the signs of our own time . . .

Thomas Carlyle, 'Signs of the Times' (1829)

Contents

Part Three

List of Illustrations

Acknowledgements

For their permission to reproduce some of the illustrations in this book, acknowledgements are due to the Tate Gallery, London; the City Art Gallery, Manchester; the City Art Gallery, Birmingham; the Walker Art Gallery, Liverpool; the Royal Commission on Historical Monuments (England). I would also like to thank Mr and Mrs Badman of Alfington House, Devon, and the incumbents of the churches I have illustrated.

For their personal help and encouragement I owe thanks to Stephen Gill and to Martin Cherry, and to my colleagues in the school of English at Exeter University, in particular Peter Faulkner, Myrddin Jones, Michael Wood and Peter Corbin. Thanks also go to my typists, Lyn Longridge and Sandi de Solla, to the staff of the Graphics Section of the Exeter University Teaching Services Centre and, for their help in putting everything into perspective, to John and Sylvia Knight.

Finally, but above all, I want to thank Jo Cox, with whom I have discussed every idea in this book, and a few others beside.

Prefatory Note

In my discussion of Dickens's novels I have used throughout the text of the New Oxford Illustrated Dickens, 21 vols (London, 1948–58). Page references, given in brackets after quotations, are to this edition; chapter numbers and, where applicable, book numbers are also given. Volume and page references given in brackets after quotations from Carlyle and Ruskin are to the texts of the Centenary edition of *The Works of Thomas Carlyle*, 30 vols (London, 1897–9), and to *The Complete Works of John Ruskin*, edited by E. T. Cook and A. Wedderburn, 38 vols (London, 1903–9). Where there is any possibility of ambiguity, references are given in the notes; in the case of all three writers, as of others discussed in the book, full bibliographical details are also given in the notes. In the chapters dealing with Pre-Raphaelite painting and Butterfield's architecture, figures in brackets in the text refer to plates.

Signs for the Times

1

Introductory

Each word was at first a stroke of genius, and obtained currency, because for the moment it symbolized the world to the first speaker and to the hearer.

Emerson, 'The Poet', *Essays: Second Series*

If one were to compose a list of the half-dozen most vexed words in the English language, 'real' would have to be included. Yet there is no escape from it, or from its use. The difficulties lie, primarily, in the fact that the word straddles the two halves of that basic philosophical and psychological dichotomy, the separation of the self and the non-self, the dichotomy between 'the real' of individual consciousness − basis of *cogito ergo sum* − and 'the real' of the world outside that consciousness. We try to resolve this dichotomy every time we ask any one of the numberless questions that evolve from inquiring 'What is real?' There is no shortage of answers, but a remarkable absence of conclusiveness. Against Plato and the Socratic ascent to absolutes, there is Fichte's assertion of the autonomous will as sole arbiter of reality; against Thomist 'proof' are the 'proofs' of Ayer and the logical positivists. Cartesian rationalism, Bergsonian life-force, Existentialist alienation, all the succession of Western European philosophies have laid claim − if not siege − to reality; while poets, political economists and nuclear physicists all have their say as well. And the problems remain. Yet the very diversity of possible − and impossible − solutions suggests a workable hypothesis: because externality is inaccessible to an ultimate formulation, we must regard the real not as a 'something' with necessarily predicable qualities, but as open-ended, as an 'essentially contested concept'.[1] At the centre of the contest of argument and counter-argument is the necessity to make one of two decisions: either to say, solipsistically with Carroll, 'Life, what is it but a dream?', or to say that, although one cannot lock reality into a definition, it is, nevertheless, emphatically there, beyond the self. Dr Johnson's refutation of Berkeley is a quite adequate common-sense technique, and one followed, in the present century, by − with delightful appropriateness − Professor Wisdom, among others. A real world is there, but our knowledge of it can only be partial; this does not mean that we can dispense with the philosopher's formulations − or even with the solipsist's. What it does mean is that we can never regard the real as, in some sense, 'pure'; in order for there to be a definition there must be a definer. The philosopher's world-view must be seen, not as a definitive statement, but as the working hypothesis the self adopts in its attempt to construe the non-self. To say that Leibniz's Monadology is untrue as an explanation of reality exhausts neither its imaginative potential nor its relevance to the debate.

Such processes, the constuction of working hypotheses, are not, of course, the sole prerogative of philosophers. The primary means of their construction are linguistic, and all discourse both presupposes and embodies an interpretation of the real. As such, all discourse partakes of the nature of fiction: the order in which statements are made, what is included, what omitted, what stressed, not only determines precisely what is being said but also what is being talked about. We cannot 'tell the truth' about the world because there is ultimately too much of it for us to encompass linguistically. In any but the most restricted linguistic contexts 'right' and 'wrong' thus cease to have an absolute valency and become relative, for there is no final solution to reality to which they are referable, and reality, as we perceive it, has no necessary *a priori* order.

> Just as, in the existential view, man is confronted in his search for ethical order by the indifference of the universe, man is his search for perceptual order faces a chaotic world-stuff which gives no hints as to the proper method of sorting.[2]

The fictions we construct by means of language are, as was suggested earlier, the primary tool that we use to sort reality. Through language the myriad components of the real are labelled and, thus, discriminated: through the organisation of labels, reality becomes manageable. The process is not one of simply imposing labels, like the tagging of so much external lumber. We take the external into ourselves in the act of talking about it, for linguistic organisation is, necessarily, organisation in the very fabric of experience. We continually make and remake our world:

> . . . the object . . . in the world beyond individual consciousness . . . is not ready-made but results from a way of taking the world. The making of a picture commonly participates in making what is to be pictured. The object and its aspects depend upon organisation; and labels of all sorts are the tools of organisation.[3]

There is no unequivocal 'way of taking the world', and, in the end, the process of structuring – of fictionalising – is as important as the structure – the fiction – that is its product, for it is through the most profound acts of language that we reach the most profound acts of interpretation. In this sense, the historical phenomenon of literary realism may be seen as a concentrated development, an intensification perhaps, of our habitual modes of language-use. A realist fiction – whether that fiction is a history of the French Revolution or a novel about the Court of Chancery – always implies that its linguistic structure, the way it organises labels, has a precise correlation to the world of direct experience. This is well put by David Lodge.

> The circumstantial particularity of the novel is . . . a kind of anti-convention. It attempts to disguise the ·fact that the novel is discontinuous with real life. It suggests that the life of a novel is a bit of real life which we happen not to have heard about before, but which somewhere is or was going on . . . The novelist moves cautiously from the real to the fictional world, and takes pains to conceal the movement. Fictional characters are therefore provided with a context of particularity much like that with which we define ourselves and others in the real world; they have names, parents, possessions, occupations, etc., ordered in such a way as not to violate our sense of probability derived from the empirical world.[4]

This does not mean that we experience the medium of realism as in some way transparent: the medium itself is, after all, our primary experience and 'our sense of probability' will depend as much on the consistency with which the medium is structured as it will upon its imputed relationship to the empirical world. The languages by means of which we sort reality are not, of course, exclusively verbal, and this book, in dealing with a period in which realism was a major creative mode, will also consider the visual language of painting and the tactile, three-dimensional language of architecture. The different relationship of these languages to the reality of the empiric world will be explored when the arts that use them are discussed.

The enterprise of realism is an attempt to capture what the *being* of the real world is like. The distinctive character of the artists discussed in this book is that, for them, such an enterprise was co-extensive with an attempt to capture the *meaning* of the real world as well. In this, Dickens is the dominant figure – as he must, indeed, be a dominant figure in any discussion of the creative and imaginative life of the nineteenth century. What his novels hold in common with the world of Carlyle, with Ruskin and Pre-Raphaelite realist painting, with the theorists of the Gothic Revival and the architecture of Butterfield is a concern to give to the interpretative structures by means of which we understand reality a phenomenal existence within the fabric of that reality: in other words, to give to the semantic connotations of the real a tangibility like that of physical reality itself. In practice this results in a conflation of the immediate nature of direct experience with the mediate nature of our experience of symbolism, in which the sign mediates between ourselves and the reality it signifies. This is the process I have called symbolic realism and it is, in my view, a fundamental mode of the Victorian imagination. Its nature varies with different arts and different artists, and the further definition and examination of symbolic realism must wait their detailed discussion.

Terms like 'real' and 'symbolic', phrases like 'the meaning of the real world' are large indeed and can seem unwieldy and faintly embarrassing to us now. But they are the terms that we must use in talking about the Victorian creative achievement, for the writers, painters and architects who made that achievement possible were not frightened, as we so often are, by large thoughts and larger imaginations. In writing about them, about Carlyle and Ruskin, the Pre-Raphaelite painters, Pugin and Butterfield, Dickens above all, I am conscious of how limited critical commentary and exposition looks when set beside the imaginative and creative scope and quality of their work. *Nunc ubi sunt?* What Katherine Mansfield said about Dickens could well be extended to include them all: 'How little they make our little men look – mere pencil-sharpeners!'

PART ONE

2

'Flame-Images':
Carlyle and the Symbolic Reading of History

Brought up in the rural isolation of Annandale and the austerity of Calvinism, Thomas Carlyle saw early nineteenth-century Britain not only as chaotic, but as increasingly and inescapably so. As an undergraduate in Edinburgh, the fundamentalist piety of his upbringing was challenged and permanently affected by the uneasy scepticism of post-Humean rationalism. The excitement of London, which he first visited in 1824 and where he moved ten years later, was both imaginatively invigorating and psychically disorienting. Acutely aware of a current climate of moral and intellectual conflict, Carlyle also experienced the physical world with a distressing intensity – most evident in a pathological aversion to noise which lasted throughout his life. Dissociation, both mental and physical, was aggravated by what seemed an unprecedented proliferation in the very substance of the surrounding conflict: ever more ideas, ever more objects seemed to crowd upon the consciousness until the mind became incapable of ordering or even grasping the sheer multiplicity of things. In 'On History Again', speaking through the persona of Professor Diogenes Teufelsdröckh, Carlyle expresses just such a sense – half-fascinated, half-horrified – of the unmanageable density of contemporary experience, and of the sheer mass of unsorted data with which the modern mind is every day confronted.[1]

> Consider, now, two things: first, that one Tongue, of average velocity, will publish at the rate of a thick octavo volume per day; and then how many nimble-enough Tongues may be supposed to be at work on this Planet Earth, in this City London, at this hour! Secondly, that a Literary Contributor, if in good heart and urged by hunger, will many times, as we are credibly informed, accomplish his two Magazine sheets within the four-and-twenty hours; such Contributors being now numerable not by the thousand, but by the million . . . Allow even the thousandth part of human publishing for the emission of thought . . . we still have the nine hundred and ninety-nine employed in History proper, in relating occurrences, or conjecturing probabilities of such . . . Courage reader! Never can the historical inquirer want pabulum, better or worse: are there not forty-eight longitudinal feet of small-printed History in thy Daily Newspaper? (28, pp. 170–1)

The passage, with its unstable irony and its odd mix of the conceptual with the minutely physical, is typical of Carlyle in the guise of Teufelsdröckh. Indeed, in *Sartor Resartus*, Teufelsdröckh, as *'Professor der Allerley-Wissenschaft* . . . "Professor of Things in General" ' (1, p. 13) at the University of Weissnichtswo – Don't-know-where – is not only the perfect investigator of the complexity of experience, but also its primary exemplar.[2] His volume on the Philosophy of Clothes, with its 'almost total want of arrangement' and with many of its parts 'quite nondescript and unnameable' (1, pp. 26–7), suggests an analogy to the world itself, at least as it appears to the consciousness of the anonymous editor. Certainly, Ohmann's remark – quoted in the previous chapter – about the undifferentiated 'world-stuff' that confronts the individual in his quest for perceptual order could be applied directly to *Sartor Resartus*. In a similar fashion, Teufelsdröckh's life-story is contained in a collection of waste paper bundled into bags, 'a universal medley of high and low, of hot, cold, moist and dry' (1, p. 62), which constantly frustrates the editor's attempts at arrangement.

The experience of the world – and particularly the man-made world – as unmanageable, ungovernably diverse, is a familiar feature of Romanticism, occurring most centrally perhaps in Wordsworth's poetry. In *The Prelude*, his description of Bartholomew Fair becomes a fragmented series of isolated impressions, syntactic control threatening to disintegrate into a mere catalogue of dissociated phrases.

> – All moveables of wonders from all parts,
> Are here, Albinos, painted Indians, Dwarfs,
> The Horse of Knowledge, and the learned Pig,
> The Stone-eater, the Man that swallows fire,
> Giants, Ventriloquists, the Invisible Girl,
> The Bust that speaks, and moves its goggling eyes,
> The Wax-work, Clock-work, all the marvellous craft
> Of modern Merlins, wild Beasts, Puppet-shows,
> All out-o'-the-way, far fetch'd, perverted things,
> All freaks of Nature, all Promethean thoughts
> Of Man; his dulness, madness, and their feats,
> All jumbled up together to make up
> This Parliament of Monsters.[3]

Such disjunction precludes any apprehension of significant order in the phenomenal world, reducing perceived reality to 'the same perpetual flow/Of trivial objects, melted and reduced/To one identity, by differences/That have no law, no meaning, and no end'.[4] The effect upon Wordsworth is one of profound alienation, not only from the people who throng the London scene but also from any sense of substantial reality; perceptual confusion becomes a radical crisis of identity that threatens a loss of selfhood.

> Thus have I look'd, nor ceas'd to look, oppress'd
> By thoughts of what, and whither, when and how
> Until the shapes before my eyes became
> A second-sight procession, such as glides
> Over still mountains, or appears in dreams;
> And all the ballast of familiar life,
> All laws of acting, thinking, speaking man
> Went from me, neither knowing me nor known.[5]

Wordsworth's experience is strikingly paralleled in a passage from Carlyle's journal written in 1835.

> The world looks often quite spectral to me; sometimes, as in Regent Street the other night (my nerves being all shattered), quite hideous, discordant, almost infernal. I had been at Mrs. Austin's, heard Sydney Smith for the first time guffawing, other persons prating, jargoning.[6]

The remedy for Wordsworth lay in a reassertion of the creative nature of perception itself, and in the healing process whereby the imagination remakes reality through a dynamic synthesis of self and non-self. Such a process, subjective in origin, was not available to Carlyle. Despite the influence of German Idealism upon his thinking, it was precisely in the subjectivity of contemporary literature that Carlyle located what he believed to be its crucial flaw, unreality.

> How is it that of all these countless [authors], no one can attain to the smallest mark of excellence, or produce aught that shall endure longer than 'snow-flake on the river', or the foam of penny-beer? We answer: Because they *are* foam; because there is no *Reality* in them . . . Nothing but a pitiful Image of their own pitiful Self, with its vanities, and grudgings, and ravenous hunger of all kinds, hangs forever painted in the retina of these unfortunate persons; so that the starry ALL, with whatsoever it embraces, does but appear as some expanded magic-lantern shadow of that same Image, – and naturally looks pitiful enough. (28, p. 58)[7]

As Carlyle asserts earlier in the same essay, it is only 'by working more and more on REALITY, and evolving more and more wisely *its* inexhaustible meanings' (28, p. 53), that imaginative literature can find a future.

Carlyle's argument implicitly asserts the existence of a reality independent of the perceiver that is not only objectively *there*, but also objectively knowable. Such a reality is, moreover, qualitatively superior to any creative effort mounted by the subjective. It is vanity, the lack of '*an open loving heart*' (28, p. 57), that locks the soul into the self and denies access to an authentically real existence. The peculiarity of Carlyle's argument, however, and its significance in terms of so much subsequent Victorian literature and art, lies in the fact that his rejection of the subjective is balanced by an equally strenuous rejection of any simply materialist definition of reality. Materialism, for Carlyle, was the product of Newtonian physics and eighteenth-century scepticism, and the materialist cosmos, as seen by Teufelsdröckh in *Sartor Resartus*, nothing but a soulless and hopeless machine.

> 'To me the Universe was all void of Life, of Purpose, of Volition, even of Hostility: it was one huge, dead, immeasurable Steam-engine, rolling on, in its dead indifference, to grind me limb from limb. O, the vast, gloomy, solitary Golgotha, and Mill of Death!' (1, p. 133)

If a materialist explanation of the world is unthinkable, and if subjectivity is a delusory arbiter of the real, in what can reality inhere? Carlyle's answer lay in a redefinition of phenomena, a restatement — to risk tautology — of the reality of reality.

Carlyle set out the terms of his ontology in the early essay 'State of German Literature' as part of his discussion of Romantic German mysticism.[8]

> In the field of human investigation there are objects of two sorts: First, the visible including no only such as are material, and may be seen by the bodily eye; but all such, likewise, as may be represented in a *shape*, before the mind's eye, or in any way pictured there: And, secondly, the *invisible*, or such as are not only unseen by human eyes, but as cannot be seen by any eye; not objects of sense at all; not capable, in short, of being *pictured* or imaged in the mind . . . (27, pp. 70–1)

This was, in many ways, conventional enough — gleaned, rather unmethodically it is true, from Kant, Fichte and Novalis. Where Carlyle was far less conventional, however, was in the relationship he sought to establish between the everyday world of the visible and the numinous — not to say nebulous — existence of the invisible. It was in order to explicate this relationship that Carlyle developed the theory of symbolism that forms so substantial a part of *Sartor Resartus*. One calls it a 'theory', but Carlyle's pronouncements are so ambiguously and ironically presented, so mediated through Teufelsdröckh and the anonymous editor, that one looks in vain for any straightforward formulation. Indeed, it would be a misrepresentation to think of the book as fundamentally a work on semiotics, for it is primarily a work of the imagination that in its sometimes bewildering shifts of mode — fictive, autobiographical, philosophical, rhapsodic, satiric — is akin to the 'universal medley' of Teufelsdröckh's own biographical paper-bags. Granted such qualification, the outlines of a theory are, however, clear enough. Through Teufelsdröckh's Philosophy of Clothes, Carlyle argues — or, rather, asserts — that clothes are the external manifestations of more or less abstract forces — of social hierarchy, of political and religious power, of moral belief. Precisely because such forces are abstract they cannot be directly represented, '*pictured* or imaged in the mind': clothes, therefore, are symbols of such forces – the judge's red robe symbolises the agency of justice, and so forth. But the idea of clothing extends, metaphorically and by analogy, to any external covering, and thence to external appearance itself. Thus, throughout *Sartor Resartus*, the symbolic nature of clothes is presented as an epitome of the symbolic nature of the whole of material reality.

> 'All visible things are emblems; what thou seest is not there on its own account; strictly taken, is not there at all: Matter exists only spiritually, and to represent some Idea, and *body* it forth. Hence Clothes, as despicable as we think them, are so unspeakably significant.' (1, p. 57)

The visible and the invisible are not, therefore, mutually independent systems. Phenomenal reality is not – as it is in other forms of mysticism – merely a painted veil or dark glass obscuring the higher reality beyond, but an emblematic scheme articulating that reality. Symbolic meaning resides in the very stuff of the physical world. Such a redefinition of the metaphysical status of phenomena enables Carlyle to repudiate the world-view of the subjectivist on the one hand and of the materialist on the other. The one is wrong because he construes the physical world only in terms of himself rather than as a system of signs – if the external is symbolic at all, it can therefore only symbolise his state of mind. The other is wrong because he construes the world only in terms of its physical substance and thus denies any emblematic dimension whatever. Given the existence of some kind of transcendent actuality, of ' "the higher, celestial, Invisible" ' (1, p. 52), both the subjectivist and the materialist are condemned, as Carlyle sees it, to inhabit a universe that they have robbed of half its reality. Nevertheless, the passion with which Carlyle puts his case never quite gets over one's feeling that both the subjective commitment to the self and the materialist commitment to the concrete and tangible have a definiteness rather less than apparent in appeals to the sublime Invisible. To affirm that the material world is an emblematic structure denoting a higher spiritual reality may certainly be considered comforting; but as long as the constituent terms remain generalised the subsequent formulation – that the natural world is ' "*the living visible Garment of God*" ' (1, p. 43), that ' "the Universe is but one vast Symbol of God" ' (1, p. 175) – are semantically elusive. One wants to ask which elements in the phenomenal world denote which attributes of deity. What symbolises what? The semantic juggling of terms at once so imprecise and so all-encompassing as 'the Universe' and 'God' can result in the dishonest replacement of specific meaning by vague spiritual uplift. That Carlyle avoids this is a result not of any further refinement of theory, but of the intensity of his religious conviction and the imaginative force with which he conceives the agency of time.

To Carlyle, religious doubt was the special curse of early nineteenth-century intellectual and moral life. 'Belief, Faith has well-nigh vanished from the world. The youth on awakening in this wondrous Universe no longer finds a competent theory of its wonders' (28, p. 29).[9] Carlyle's own conception of Deity was orthodoxly derived from Judaeo-Christian and, particularly, biblical tradition, but apprehended with an intensity that metamorphosed the image of the Christian life into a vivid, even violent, spiritual drama. In the opening chapter of 'The Diamond Necklace', Carlyle is himself both the principal actor in and witness to such a drama.[10]

> In our own poor Nineteenth Century the Writer of these lines has been fortunate enough to see not a few glimpses of Romance . . . He has witnessed overhead the infinite Deep, with greater and lesser lights, bright-rolling, silent-beaming, hurled forth by the Hand of God: around him and under his feet, the wonderfulest Earth, with her winter snow-storms and her summer spice-airs; and, unaccountablest of all, *himself* standing there. He stood in the lapse of Time; he saw Eternity behind him, and before him. The all-encircling mysterious tide of FORCE, thousandfold . . . billowed shoreless on; bore him too along with it, – he too was part of it . . . O Brother! is *that* what thou callest prosaic; of small interest? Of small interest and for *thee*? Awake, poor troubled sleeper: shake off thy torpid nightmare-dream; look, see, behold it, the Flame-image; splendours high as Heaven, terrors deep as Hell: this is God's Creation; this is Man's Life! (28, pp. 328–9)

Such a dramatic transformation of a traditional body of belief is primarily an act of the creative imagination. This indeed was how Carlyle perceived the function of imagination: to rework traditional myth and story in order to achieve a new revelation of divine truth, a rediscovery of the spiritual reality that is emblematised by the phenomenal world. As he wrote in 'Biography', 'the highest exercise of Invention has, in very deed, nothing to do with Fiction; but is an invention of new Truth, what we call a Revelation' (28, pp. 53–4). For Carlyle, the prime area in which the imagination could discover new truth, and thus reveal the divine reality behind the mortal show, was in human history.

Time itself is God's creation and, through its processes, the inspired historian can read the agency of Providence. Such a view of history is described in *Sartor Resartus*, as also is the historical role of the hero – mercifully free, at this early stage, of the element of crude power-worship that disfigures Carlyle's later work.

> 'For great Men I have ever had the warmest predilection; and can perhaps boast that few such in this era have wholly escaped me. Great Men are the inspired (speaking and acting) Texts of that divine BOOK

OF REVELATIONS, whereof a Chapter is completed from epoch to epoch, and by some named HISTORY; to which inspired Texts your numerous talented men, and your innumerable untalented men, are the better or worse exegetic Commentaries, and wagonload of too-stupid heretical or orthodox, weekly Sermons. For my study, the inspired Texts themselves!' (1, p. 142)

Human history, then, is a process of progressive revelation, the working out through time of the ' "God-written Apocalypse" ' (1, p. 41). This is to set the role of the social commentator, studying the society of the present, and of the historian, studying that of the past, very high indeed: both are interpreting the ways of God to man. Moreover, as history is to be read with heroic lives as the primary texts, Carlyle's argument neatly relocates Christ as the greatest hero and his life, therefore, as the central text for the understanding of man's history. The point is most clearly made – as one would expect – in *Heroes and Hero-Worship*.[11]

Hero-worship, heartfelt prostrate admiration, submission, burning, boundless, for a noblest godlike Form of Man, – is not that the germ of Christianity itself? The greatest of all Heroes is One – whom we do not name here! Let sacred silence meditate that sacred matter; you will find it the ultimate perfection of a principle extant throughout man's whole history on earth. (5, p. 11)

Such a Christocentric view of history necessarily involves a new stress upon the significance of the Bible, which Teufelsdröckh places in terms of all other books in precisely the same relationship that Christ holds to all other heroes. ' "One BIBLE I know, of whose Plenary Inspiration doubt is not so much as possible; nay with by own eyes I saw Gods-Hand writing it: thereof all other Bibles are but Leaves, – say, in Picture-Writing to assist the weaker faculty!" ' (1, p. 155). The idiosyncrasy of Carlyle's argument, in fact, serves a position of impeccable theological orthodoxy: for the Christian, the life of Christ is the pivotal event in the whole of human history. But it is also precisely this idiosyncrasy which enables Carlyle to restate orthodoxy with new force and to relocate, for the nineteenth century, Christ and – with typical Protestant emphasis – the Bible at the very core of human experience, past, present and – by inference – future. Moreover, and as a corollary, the very orthodoxy of Carlyle's stance became for him and, presumably, for his audience a guarantee of objectivity. Interpretation of history, centred in the life of Christ and the study of the Bible, could be seen by an audience of believers as being authenticated by the highest authority of all – the revealed word of God. The perils of subjective distortion in the interpretation of events are thus avoided at the same time as materialism is rejected as an inadequate interpretative model. What results, if one follows the imaginative logic of Carlyle's argument, is a reading of the mortal, visible world in terms of the immortal and invisible as the only way of restoring to mankind a proper understanding of the totality of reality. This is both a way of construing existence and a literary manifesto; in its understanding of the everyday world as at once substantially real and emblematic it is a form of symbolic realism. That Carlyle's argument is not logically watertight, that it is based on assertion rather than on argument, often covering flaws in reasoning by rhetorical diversions, could hardly be disputed. But this is not what counts: Carlyle's symbolic realism is an imaginative strategy not a philosophical system. What matters is that Carlyle's beliefs about the make-up of reality, about the visible and the invisible, about the emblematic nature of phenomena and the centrality of God, Christ and the Bible to all human experience, gave him the basis for a new and creative apprehension of the world and, in particular, of history. The result was the writing of *The French Revolution*.[12]

Carlyle's particular view of history as progressive revelation, with a basis in the Bible, offers immediate parallels to typology – that is, to the technique of biblical exegesis, Patristic in origin, whereby events and persons in the Old Testament are interpreted both as historically real and as divinely ordained prefigurations of events in the New Testament, most centrally, of the life of Christ. That which prefigures is the type; that which is prefigured, the antitype. Thus, the story of Moses leading the Children of Israel out of Egypt to the Promised Land is a historical account of an actual sequence of events; but it is also, and simultaneously, a type of Christ's spiritual salvation of mankind, which thus becomes the antitype. Typology, therefore, allows events to be read as simultaneously real and symbolic. In other words, typology is a particular version of symbolic realism. The importance of typology in the Victorian arts has been the subject of a number of recent studies.[13] The reasons for that importance have been well described by G. P. Landow, as also have the peculiar qualities of typology that distinguish it from other forms of symbolism.

> Whenever spirituality is equated with reality, the historical, the literal, the here and now will seem of less importance – will appear to be less real – than the world of the spirit and idea. What is perhaps unique about Victorian typology is that it comes into being during an age when men have increasingly come to accept that reality inheres in present fact and not in a realm of ideas, forms, or spirituality. In fact, it is about the middle of the nineteenth century when 'realism', a term formerly employed to designate philosophies which propounded that ideas are most real, becomes used to designate aesthetic and other philosophies which hold that reality inheres in present fact. As should be obvious, a theory of symbolism and biblical interpretation like typology which purports to locate reality in both spheres is well suited to Victorian times.[14]

In the hands of biblical commentators, typology has quite specific limits. What appealed to Carlyle – and indeed to subsequent Victorian artists – was an extension of the technique into a broadly understood typological method. Such a method offered Carlyle a way of writing about the past that could both capture the concrete actuality of events and assert – by the assiduous use of biblical parallel and prefiguration – the spiritual verities inherent in those events. The symbolic relationship between the visible and the invisible could thus be precisely located and the message of their co-extensive reality be enforced. For Carlyle, the Bible was history, literally true, the patterns of which established the defining forms of all subsequent historical process; reciprocally, that process re-enacted and, indeed, remade biblical history in and through the phenomenal texture of the modern world.

In *The French Revolution* the people of France are constantly seen as the Children of Israel in the Old Testament, their history, like that of their biblical precursors, one of captivity and the struggle towards freedom, of frequent pursuits after strange gods and of violent physical conflict. The enemies of France are Israel's biblical foes – Egypt, the Philistines, Babylon. Specific episodes in the Revolution are repeatedly presented in Old Testament terms: the Parlement of Paris has a 'jargon as of Babel, in the hour when they were first smitten (as here) with mutual unintelligibility' (2, p. 100); the revolutionary vision of freedom is the 'first vision as of flame-girt Sinai, in this our waste Pilgrimage' (2, p. 184); the Bastille falls 'like the City of Jericho . . . overturned by miraculous *sound*' (2, p. 210); the Constituent Assembly is filled by a 'Noah's Deluge of vociferous commonplace' (2, p. 222), and so forth. The progress of the Revolution as a whole is divinely ordained.

> For as Hierarchies and Dynasties of all kinds, Theocracies, Aristocracies, Autocracies, Strumpetocracies, have ruled over the world; so it was appointed in the decrees of Providence, that this same victorious Anarchy, Jacobinism, Sansculottism, French Revolution, or what else mortals name it, should have its turn. (2, p. 212)

The overall moral pattern is one of divine vengeance upon the corruption, irresponsibility and human indifference of the *ancien régime*. The vengeance is just and inevitable, and Carlyle announces the biblical basis for the process early in the work.

> Manifold, bright-tinted, glittering with gold; all through the Bois de Boulogne, in longdrawn variegated rows . . . pleasure of the eye, and pride of life! So rolls and dances the Procession . . . Dance on, ye foolish ones; ye sought not wisdom, neither have ye found it. Ye and your fathers have sown the wind, ye shall reap the whirlwind. Was it not, from of old, written: *The wages of sin is death*? (2, p. 48)

The passage well exemplifies the density of Carlyle's use of biblical reference. The spititual nature of the Court's dereliction is indicated by the ironic reference to Proverbs, 14: 6, 'A scorner seeketh wisdom, and findeth it not'. The consequence of such dereliction is stated in the quotation from Hosea, 8: 7, 'For they have sown the wind and they shall reap the whirlwind', where 'they' refers to the people of Israel who have idolatrously abandoned the true God. The fourth verse of the same chapter of Hosea makes the appropriateness of the parallel with France even clearer: 'They have set up kings, but not by me: they have made princes and I knew it not: of their silver and their gold they have made them idols, that they may be cut off.' The image of reaping the whirlwind undergoes significant development in parallel biblical texts: these parallels are available through traditional commentaries, in particular through that of Thomas Scott, whose annotated edition of the Bible was probably the most widely known in the early nineteenth century.[15] Thus the passage from Hosea relates to prophecies of the punishment of Israel for the denial of God, and the fall of Jerusalem, in Jeremiah, 12: 13, and Isaiah, 17: 11; in the latter passage, 'the harvest shall be a heap in the day of grief and of desperate sorrow'. This, with the Hosea passage, relates forward to the New Testament, to Galatians, 6: 7, 'whatsoever a man soweth that shall he also reap', and it is through this passage that we reach the quotation from Romans, 6: 23, that concludes Carlyle's paragraph, 'For the wages of sin is death'. The tightness with which Carlyle handles his biblical source material is at once obvious. Moreover, by tracing specific quotations through parallel and related passages, one becomes aware of the complex of references which, though not a part of Carlyle's surface text, actually underpins the whole. Examples could be multiplied from throughout the work.

The passage discussed above, which establishes the central moral and religious dynamic of *The French Revolution*, also establishes the group of images that comes to form the work's vertebrate symbolic structure. The image of the whirlwind goes through an astonishing number of variations. The Versailles government is 'Wholly a vortex' (2, p. 118) and, at the court, 'loud-sounding inanity whirled in that distracted vortex' (2, p. 155); the people cry for arms 'as with the throat of the whirlwind' (2, p. 175); the heroes of the Bastille are forced asunder by 'the whirlpool of things' (2, p. 210); the bodyguards at Versailles are 'Whirled down . . . suddenly to the abyss' (2, p. 281); Princess de Lamballe is 'whirled down . . . against grim rocks' by 'the black World-tornado' (3, p. 227); Chevalier de Grave 'in this whirl of things . . . merely whirls with them' (3, p. 251), whereas General Bouillé is 'the son of the whirlwind' (3, p. 185); the army of the Revolution learns to 'whirl and whirl . . . swiftly like the wind or the whirlwind' (4, p. 53); the National Assembly sits amidst the 'wild piping of the whirlwind of human passions' (4, p. 70); in the conflict between Jacobins and Girondins, 'Frenzy meets Frenzy, like dark clashing whirlwinds' (4, p. 151). Most powerfully, Carlyle uses the image of the maelstrom three times, at the storming of the Bastille (2, p. 191), the execution of Louis (4, p. 110), and at the fall of Robespierre, when the whole of Paris is 'a huge Mahlstrom, sounding there, under cloud of night' (4, p. 283). Similar variations characterise Carlyle's handling of the images of wind and harvest, the former linking with a pattern of fire imagery that develops from the end of the first volume. Thus France in 1789 is 'wind-parched' and 'at the right inflammable point' (2, p. 176); by the following year her army, in an image ironically derived from Matthew, 12, and the parable of the faithful servant, is 'a whole continent of smoking flax; which blown on here and there by an angry wind, might so easily start into a blaze, into a continent of fire' (3, p. 82). Armed risings and pitched battles result, a 'whirlwind of military fire' (3, p. 170), a 'fire-whirlwind' (3, p. 222) in Santo-Domingo, 'a red blazing whirlwind' (3, p. 299) at the Tuileries. Associated fire images proliferate as the Revolution progresses, becoming increasingly infernal in association – a process epitomised in the development of the Jacobin Club, which becomes 'more and more lurid, more sulphurous, distracted . . . like a Tartarean Portent, and lurid-burning Prison of Spirits in Pain' (3, p. 32). In his description of the trial of Marie-Antoinette, Carlyle brilliantly evokes the Revolutionary Court as a demonic tribunal with Tinville presiding in hell's half-light.

> Dim, dim, as if in disastrous eclipse; like the pale kingdoms of Dis! Plutonic Judges, Plutonic Tinville; encircled, nine times, with Styx and Lethe, with Fire-Phlegethon, and Cocytus named of Lamentation! The very witnesses summoned are like Ghosts: exculpatory, inculpatory, they themselves are all hovering over death and doom; they are known, in our imagination, as the prey of the Guillotine.' (4, pp. 194–5)

Finally, the Republic becomes, under Robespierre and the Terror, 'the newest Birth of Nature's waste inorganic Deep, which men name Orcus, Chaos, primeval Night' (4, p. 223).

Throughout the whole of his history of the Revolution, not excluding the ultimate return to Chaos and Old Night, Carlyle never allows the reader to forget that the process is inevitable, the judgement of God. The Old Testament history of Israel, of Babylon and Egypt, is present throughout the narrative; images of wind, whirlwind and harvest constantly return the reader to the retributive pattern of the whole. Indeed, Carlyle calculatedly recapitulates his central image from Hosea in the opening paragraphs of his account of the Terror.

> The harvest of long centuries was ripening and whitening so rapidly of late; and now it is grown *white*, and is reaped rapidly, as it were, in one day. Reaped, in this Reign of Terror; and carried home, to Hades and the Pit! – Unhappy sons of Adam: it is ever so; and never do they know it, nor will they know it. With cheerfully smoothed countenances, day after day, and generation after generation, they, calling cheerfully to one another, Well-speed-ye, are at work, *sowing the wind*. And yet, as God lives, they *shall reap the whirlwind*: no other thing, we say, is possible – since God is a Truth, and this World is a Truth. (4, p. 203)

The movement of the whole towards a final and cataclysmic reckoning is not only apocalyptic in kind but specifically prefigurative of the Apocalypse itself. The anger and violence of the latter phases of the Revolution are 'as consuming fire' (4, p. 119): the phrase is a telling one. Moses, in Deuteronomy, 4: 24, warns Israel that 'the Lord thy God is a consuming fire', which anticipates Paul's monition in Hebrews, 12: 29 – again, significantly, a direct address to Israel – 'For our God is a consuming fire'. But Paul, commending the New Testament dispensation, specifically relates the concept to God's word that earth's corruptions shall be consumed in order that the New Jerusalem shall be created: 'And this word, Yet once more, signifieth the removing of those things that are shaken, as of things that are made, that those things which cannot be shaken may remain' (verse 27). The fulfilment of the process described by Paul is, of course, the Last Judgement, the fulfilment of the Apocalypse as foretold in the final book of the New Testament, Revelation; Carlyle's revolutionaries, 'removing those things that are shaken', are specifically depicted in terms drawn from Revelation. The National Convention, presiding over the Terror, is 'a kind of Apocalyptic Convention, or black *Dream become real* . . . and from its bosom there went forth Death on the pale Horse' (4, pp. 70–1); the image derives from the opening of the fourth seal in Revelation, 6: 8: 'And I looked, and behold a pale horse: and his name that sat upon him was Death, and Hell followed with him.' The retributive 'Sword of Sharpness; a weapon magical' (4, p. 141) into which the Revolutionary Tribunal is forged relates figuratively to 'the sharp sword with two edges' of Revelation, 2: 12. It is, with more exact reference, the weapon wielded by Death, as the agent of the Convention, against the fugitive Girondins – 'pale Death, waving his revolutionary Sword of Sharpness' (4, p. 189) – as it is one of the weapons of Death the horseman and of Hell, again in Revelation, 6: 8: 'And power was given unto them over the fourth part of the earth, to kill with sword . . .' The instrument of the Tribunal's vengeance is the guillotine, a concretisation of the metaphoric 'Sword of Sharpness', which is also the sansculottes' 'guillotine-sickle' (4, p. 215). With the triumph of the Jacobins 'the sickle of the Guillotine reaps the Girondins all away' (4, p. 199) and, to refer again to the passage quoted at length above, it is the principal tool in the 'harvest of long centuries . . . ripening and whitening so rapidly of late' which 'is grown *white* and is reaped rapidly . . . in this Reign of Terror'. The references to Revelation are, once more, conscious and precise.

> And I looked, and behold a white cloud, and upon the cloud one sat like unto the Son of man, having on his head a golden crown, and in his hand a sharp sickle.
>
> And another angel came out of the temple, crying with a loud voice to him that sat on the cloud, Thrust in thy sickle, and reap: for the time is come for thee to reap; for the harvest of the earth is ripe.
>
> And he that sat on the cloud thrust in his sickle on the earth; and the earth was reaped. (Revelation, 14: 14–16)

In his apocalyptic presentation of the Terror one can see the flexibility of Carlyle's typological method. The history of the Revolution, as Carlyle writes it, derives its patterns of significance and its symbolic status from reference to the biblical past. Events in France are, broadly speaking, antitypes that may be seen as fulfilling both historical and moral types derived largely from the Old Testament. In the presentation of the Terror, however, the temporal relationship between the Carlylean text and the biblical source is, in terms of its typology, reversed. By using Revelation so precisely to depict the Terror as apocalyptic, and precisely because the events described in Revelation are future events, Carlyle creates out of the Reign of Terror an authentic type of the Day of Judgement itself.

In a world like that of *The French Revolution* man's need is for salvation, for some hope of reprieve from the inevitability of condemnation. The force of redemption is not missing from Carlyle's overall picture, but it must be sought for in a France full of false prophets and parody Messiahs. The principal sin of pre-Revolutionary France, as of Israel before her, is, in Carlyle's eyes, the denial of her God. In the wake of Enlightenment scepticism Rousseau's *Contrat social* replaces Christianity: 'a new young generation has exchanged the Sceptic Creed, *What shall I believe?* for passionate Faith in this Gospel according to Jean Jacques' (2, p. 54). The Gospel of Rousseau not only replaces Christian faith, it also propagates what is for Carlyle a denial of the true nature of man. Men are – to use the phrase Carlyle employs again and again – the 'Sons of Adam', and he means the phrase to bear its full theological weight. It is for this reason that he finds Anacharsis Clootz' celebration of 'mankind' and the Assembly's abolition of titles so richly ironic: 'let extreme Patriotism rejoice, and chiefly Anacharsis and Mankind; for now it seems to be taken for granted that one Adam is father to us all!' (3, p. 53).[16] Far from a cause for celebration, the consequences of our descent from Adam are, to Carlyle's pessimistic conservatism, obvious enough: 'Sin had come into the world, and Misery by Sin' (3, p. 68). By denying God and – perhaps more important, imaginatively, for Carlyle – by denying Original Sin, the religion of Rousseau produces the false patriarchs and delusory hopes of Revolutionary France. The enlightened Controller-General Calonne for a time appears to remedy the hopelessly bankrupt French economy: 'Men name him "*the* Minister"; as indeed, when was there another such? Crooked things are become straight by him, rough places plain' (2, p. 67). In the following year Loménie-Brienne invites plans for a States-General – an invitation, as Carlyle sarcastically comments, 'to Chaos to be so kind as build, out of its tumultuous drift-wood, an Ark of Escape for him!' (2, p. 108). The States-General, when it is called, 'is there as a thing high and lifted up. Hope, jubilating, cries aloud that it will prove a miraculous Brazen Serpent in the Wilderness' (2, p. 151). These three examples are enough to indicate the general pattern: in each case Carlyle employs an Old Testament prefiguration of the New Testament Christ. 'The crooked shall be made straight and the rough plain' from Isaiah, 40: 4, is a direct prophecy of John the Baptist's words about Christ in Luke, 3: 5; Noah, in building an 'Ark of Escape' and rescuing the family of man is a type of Christ as saviour, as the Brazen Serpent from Numbers, 21, is a type of the Crucifixion and humanity's subsequent redemption. This technique of what might be called burlesque typology serves more than the purpose of local parody, for Carlyle's pre-revolutionary types do, in fact, prefigure Revolutionary antitypes, just as their original Old Testament types prefigure Christ. After Marat's death the Jacobins 'parallel him to One, whom they think it honour to call "the good Sansculotte", – whom we name not here' (4, pp. 169–70). Camille Desmoulins, asked at his trial to give his age, replies ' "My age is that of the *bon Sansculotte Jésus*; an age fatal to Revolutionists" ' (4, p. 257). Catherine Théot 'poring over the Book of Revelations, with an eye to Robespierre; finds that this astonishing thrice-potent Maximilien really is the Man spoken of by Prophets, who is to make the Earth young again'; Robespierre himself, meanwhile, having decreed the existence of the Supreme Being, is surrounded by Jacobins, 'kissing the hem of his garment' (4, p. 268). Many other parodies of Christ and of Christian salvation occur in the final stages of the narrative. Throughout *The French Revolution*, in fact, Carlyle presents the religion of Rousseau and its developments precisely as a religion, treating its history, therefore, as a text for exegesis and using typology as a major interpretative tool. The result has great and disturbing imaginative coherence: the gospel of the brotherhood of man is fulfilled in and through the organisers of murder and mass-execution, parody saviours who offer eternal sleep rather than eternal life. With the presentation of the Terror as a type of the Apocalypse it becomes possible to identify its agents as types of Antichrist.

Within this structure of burlesque salvation, however, Carlyle does affirm an orthodox Christian position. Indeed, however parodically Carlyle employs typology, the very registration of Noah, Aaron or whoever as types necessarily implies their orthodox fulfilment in the New Testament Christ. More overtly, Carlyle represents the Christian mythos – suitably enough – in terms of sacrifice and the need for mercy, setting its humility against the swagger and self-aggrandisement of the Revolution. Thus he contrasts the Rousseauesque celebration of the Feast of Pikes to 'those Thirteen most poor mean-dressed men, at frugal Supper, in a mean Jewish dwelling, with no symbol but hearts god-initiated into the "Divine depth of Sorrow" and a *Do this in remembrance of me*' (3, p. 49). The chapter in which this occurs is appropriately entitled 'Symbolic', focusing attention upon the bread and wine of the Last Supper as the pivotal emblems in any Christian view of history, simultaneously symbols of sacrifice and pledges of salvation. However, compared with the way in which the historical, moral and figural patterns of the Old Testament or Revelation are so consistently presented in the actual events of the Revolution, the similar patterns of the Gospels have relatively little place in Carlyle's narrative. There is, however, a significant, if somewhat ambiguous, exception to this: the execution of Louis XVI. At the time of his trial, his meal with

Chaumette suggests the Last Supper: 'Chaumette breaks his half-loaf; the King eats of the crust' (4, p. 93). He is betrayed by Philippe Egalité, to whom Carlyle later gives the name 'Iscariot Egalité' (4, p. 323). Struggling with his executioners on the guillotine, he is counselled to remember 'how the Saviour, whom men trust, submitted to be bound' (4, p. 110). Above all, as Carlyle says, 'Innocent Louis bears the sins of many generations' (4, p. 107). Carlyle in no way presents Louis as a Christ-figure: rather, he shows him to be weak and vacillating. Nor does Louis's death in any way effect the redemption of France, for his role is more that of simple scapegoat. Nevertheless, the Crucifixion is – given a Christian context – the type of all subsequent Christian sacrifice, and the last words Louis hears are those spoken by his confessor, ' "Son of Saint Louis, ascend to Heaven" ' (4, p. 110). The incorporation of elements from the Gospel narrative of the Crucifixion in Carlyle's narrative of Louis's execution movingly relocates that execution and gives to it the imaginative status of an antitype – even if only partial – of the Passion.

That the beheading of Louis should be presented in such terms is entirely consistent with the imaginative character of *The French Revolution* as a whole. Carlyle's viewpoint is eschatological: Original Sin, the perennial patterns of biblical myth and history, divine vengeance and the mystery of salvation, the certainty of the Last Judgement are, for him, not only the permanent realities in terms of which human history has to be read, but also the permanent realities which human history continually exemplifies. The historian is bound by two duties: one to the higher reality of spiritual truth, the other to the details of action and character whereby that truth is bodied forth. As Teufelsdröckh says in *Sartor Resartus*, ' "no meanest object is insignificant" ' (1, p. 57). Thus, in *The French Revolution*, a complex of actual historical events, documented, real in time and place, is consistently interpreted as a symbolic structure – moreover, a structure in which, because of the typological method in operation, the symbolic nature of an event is part of what defines that event's reality. It is in this way, referring back to the broad definition of symbolic realism given in the previous chapter, that Carlyle seeks to give to the interpretative structures by means of which he understands historical reality a tangible existence within the fabric of that reality. In practice, however, the figural representation of events and their literal representation always tend to remain distinguishable: in Carlyle's particular sort of symbolic realism, the mediating symbol never quite takes on the immediacy that distinguishes the real. To call Revolutionary France a whirlwind remains a figurative usage no matter how thoroughly that usage is incorporated into an overall strategy that identifies the patterns of contemporary history with those of the Bible, for the original formula of sowing the wind and reaping the whirlwind is itself figurative. Even when one considers Carlyle's continual identification of France with the biblical Israel, both in general and through the use of specific Old Testament episodes, there must always be a tendency for the reader to think of France as being *like* Israel rather than actually *being* Israel. the sheer density of events in the history of the Revolution necessarily precludes their being consistently identified with biblical events. Generally speaking, the most usual relationship between realist terms and symbolic terms in *The French Revolution* remains similetic, a union that, despite the intensity of the verbal pressure, never quite achieves a full amalgamation of its constituent parts.

There are, however, imaginative constructs in *The French Revolution* in which Carlyle's symbolic realism does achieve a fusion of what is symbolically true with what is literally true. As was suggested earlier, the blade of the guillotine is the concrete embodiment of the 'Sword of Sharpness': as a tangible and terrible reality it gives physical form to the Terror's prefiguration of the Apocalypse. The Carmagnole, triumphantly danced by the avenging sansculottes, ' "whirling and spinning" ' (4, p. 228) in ' "whirlblasts of rags" ' (4, p. 293), actualises the figural whirlwind that is at the core of the book's symbolic structure. The typological relationship that Carlyle establishes between Revolutionary France led on by an ideal of freedom and Israel in the desert is given ironic reality in the slaves' revolt in Santo-Domingo, where 'thick clouds of smoke girdle our horizon, smoke in the day, in the night fire' (3, p. 222). In each case fact and figure move into identity: there is an amalgamation of what is symbolically true with what is literally true. With the enactment of symbolic patterns in and through the phenomena that make up what we normally think of as reality, symbolism loses its mediatory nature and becomes directly apprehensible, the Invisible — to use Carlyle's own terms — becomes legible through the Visible.

Carlyle's influence on Dickens — as moralist, satirist, social critic — has long been recognised and was, of course, acknowledged by Dickens himself. Yet his debt to Carlyle may well have been on a level of creative consciousness deeper than that of ideas. A fully synthesised form of symbolic realism, both as a means of narrative organisation and as a strategy for understanding the contemporary world, emerges in Dickens's novels from the 1840s and comes to assume an increasingly central position in his imagination and his fiction. It is with the development of Dickens's symbolic realism and its expression in the novels of the 1840s and 1850s that the following chapters will be concerned.

3

'The Magic Reel':
Metaphor and Reality in
The Old Curiosity Shop

The vision of the world that Master Humphrey introduces at the beginning of *The Old Curiosity Shop* centres in the experience of a sick man listening to the restlessness of the city.[1]

> . . . think of the hum and noise being always present to his senses, and of the stream of life that will not stop, pouring on, on, on, through all his restless dreams, as if he were condemned to lie, dead but conscious, in a noisy churchyard, and had no hope of rest for centuries to come. (1, p. 1)

London has no longer the infinite variety that fascinated Pickwick and satisfied Tim Linkinwater in *Nicholas Nickleby*. Life's continuity has no longer the optimism of renewal, but simply the empty repetition of nightmare – the mood of the beginning of *In Memoriam*, 'The noise of life begins again'.[2] Such directionless continuity is immediately associated with death, as the vision of a sick man is changed into an experience of life-in-death. The ungovernable flow of reality is thus imaginatively linked with a movement towards death, a movement that becomes a dominant motif in the rest of the novel.

> 'I should have a son pretty near as old as you if he'd lived . . .' (15, p. 119)

> The clergyman's horse stumbling with a dull, blunt sound among the graves, was cropping the grass . . . enforcing last Sunday's text that this was what all flesh came to . . . (16, p. 122)

> The poor schoolmaster sat in the same place, holding the small cold hand in his, and chafing it. It was but the hand of a dead child. (25, p. 193)

Nell may be able to dream of the little scholar 'not coffined and covered up, but mingling with angels . . . ' (26, p. 194), but the fact of death not only refers forward, towards hope of immortality, but also back, to the quality of life, to its context in human terms. With such reference, we return to the reality of the life-in-death vision of London, to a pessimistic sense of life's futility set against Nell's Christian optimism.

> It was a very quiet place, as such a place should be, save for the cawing of the rooks ... First, one sleek bird ... uttered his hoarse cry ... Another answered . . . then another spoke and then another . . . Other voices . . . and others . . . joined the clamour which rose and fell, and swelled and dropped again, and still went on; and all this noisy contention amidst a skimming to and fro, and lighting on fresh branches, and frequent change of place, which satirised the old restlessness of those who lay so still beneath the moss and turf below, and the strife in which they had worn away their lives. (17, p. 128)

The contemplation of death is more than a *memento mori*, for in *The Old Curiosity Shop* the sheer fact of mortality is caught in tension between a concentration of life and a hope of heaven. A fundamentally anthropocentric vision of reality meets a deocentric morality at the point of death, and the attempt to understand death necessarily includes an attempt to grasp the significances of the two systems. Thus, the concerns of the novel necessitate also an emphasis upon time. A purely human view of time will see the past as limited by the moment of birth, and the future by the moment of death. A transcendental view will see temporal linearity merely as the condition of mortal existence, locating the moments of birth and death in the context of the infinite. Thus, the double vision of the fact of mortality necessarily involves the problematic antithesis of two time-scales: indeed, the phrase 'not coffined and covered up, but mingling with angels' is the most succinct statement of the paradox. But, whether one sees time in transcendental terms or not, personal reality is still caught in the present, and it is in the present that Nell must try to exist.

The present world that confronts Nell is, seemingly, in the control of her moral antithesis, Daniel Quilp, a control comically epitomised in the game of cribbage he plays with his wife, his mother-in-law and Dick Swiveller. Quilp cheats, he signals his partner, interrupts and confuses signals of the opposition, pinches and kicks his wife, prevents Mrs Jinwin from taking a drink, 'And in any one of these many cares, from first to last, Quilp never flagged nor faltered' (23, p. 177). He even takes his physical surroundings into himself, swallowing everything around him as a means of controlling it: he eats shrimps with heads on, hard-boiled eggs, shells and all, drinks prodigious quantities of scalding rum, smokes endlessly; his very perception is a kind of monomaniac consumption.

> With that he bowed and leered at me, and with a keen glance around which seemed to comprehend every object within the range of vision, however small or trivial, went his way. (3, p. 26)

Quilp retains and returns everything to himself; creator and deity of his world, his return after the supposed drowning is a grotesque travesty of resurrection. But Quilp's world – despite the efficiency with which he controls it – is the antithesis of any sort of human organisation, finding its logical extension, not in the context of human discourse and relationship, but in the world of inanimate objects.

From *Sketches by Boz* onwards, Dickens's work exhibits an acute awareness of the physical and inanimate world; of, more particularly, the sheer amount of matter that goes to make up the urban environment. This kind of heightened awareness suggests interesting parallels to the similar characteristics that are evident in Carlyle's work and that were discussed at the beginning of the previous chapter. Indeed, this quality of Dickens's imagination would seem to have had its origin, as it did for Carlyle, in the unique mechanics of the man's perception, in the very way that he saw and registered the world he lived in. Walter Bagehot remarked its primacy in Dickens's fiction.

> The *bizarrerie* of Mr. Dickens' genius is rendered more remarkable by the inordinate measure of his special excellences. The first of these is his power of observation in detail. We have heard . . . that he can go down a crowded street, and tell you all that is in it, what each shop was, what the grocer's name was, how many scraps of orange-peel there were on the pavement. His works give you exactly the same idea. The amount of detail which there is in them is something amazing – to an ordinary writer something incredible.[3]

In *The Old Curiosity Shop*, for the first time in Dickens's *œuvre*, this registration of material detail has an intensity so insistent as to become disturbing. Quilp's world-view finds its expression in a physical environment, epitomised by the wharf and 'The Wilderness', where all coherent structure seems to have collapsed, leaving in its place an anarchy of dissociated and decaying bits and pieces.

> The house stood – if anything so old and feeble could be said to stand – on a piece of waste ground, blighted with the unwholesome smoke of factory chimneys, and echoing the clang of iron wheels and rush of troubled water. The internal accommodation amply fulfilled the promise of the outside. The rooms were low and damp, the clammy walls were pierced with chinks and holes, the rotten floors had sunk from their level, the very beams started from their places and warned the timid stranger from their neighbourhood. (21, p. 162)

External physicality, however, is not simply a panorama of passively decaying rubbish, but an alternative to human reality in which deterioration has become positively aggressive, threatening the security of the individual, implicitly bidding to transform him into just another reified victim of decay. The menace of the physical world encloses and traps Little Nell.

There was a crooked stack of chimneys on one of the roofs, in which, by
often looking at them, she had fancied ugly faces that were frowning over
at her and trying to peer into the room. (9, p. 69)

Nell's vision of the external, like Quilp's world of rotting fragments, is far more
than an exercise in pathetic fallacy, for whatever seems to be vital in the world
of things hold its vitality without reference to the consciousness of the human
agent. Quilp's use of people as if they were objects is an extreme, but Sally
Brass's unmotivated onslaughts upon the Marchioness, Frederick Trent's
proposed manipulation of Dick and Nell, and the grandfather's subordination
of human happiness to financial acquisition are all only different in degree,
not in kind. It seems as if the collapse of mutual relationship in the human
world has given the world of physical objects its chance. People become things,
and things begin to usurp what, upon empiric grounds, we normally assume
to be human prerogatives: they take on faces, peer into rooms, threaten, and
seek to disrupt whatever security the individual may hold to. Dickens's
language systematically breaks down the usual restrictions upon semantic
attribution: attributes that one would normally apply only to the animate
become equally applicable to the inanimate. The barges by Quilp's wharf move
'in a wrong-headed, dogged, obstinate way, bumping up against the larger
craft, running under the bows of steam-boats' (5, p. 40). The world of the novel
becomes a battlefield in a struggle for existential *lebensraum*, with objects
constantly shouldering people out of the way. Dickens's 'predictions about
persons and objects' habitually 'tend to be statements of metabolic conversions
of one into the other'.[4] A world thus changed is not, in any familiar sense of
the phrase, empiric reality. Our experience of everyday is automatically sorted,
categorised, remembered or discarded, and it is this process of subconscious
selection that is obviated by Dickens's almost morbidly acute sensibility. A
kind of hyper-reality obtrudes itself upon our awareness. The empiric world
is the basis, but Dickens's imaginary world holds a tense existence between
the sane, familiar order, accepted in and through the organisation that we
impose upon the everday, and the anarchy of the insane unfamiliar. Everything
we know is *there* in the Dickens world but, recurrently, not in the way we know
it. Accustomed categories disintegrate, and the familiar, out of context, eludes
our mental grasp. Things and people have become estranged, transmuted into
the components of a world both continuous and discontinuous with our own.
Certain potentials, inherent in the familiar elements of day-to-day experience,
are dynamically realised. That which was inert becomes totally alive, that
which was animate becomes inanimate.

On the Surrey side of the river was a small rat-infested dreary yard called
'Quilp's Wharf', in which was a little wooden counting-house burrowing
all awry in the dust . . . (4, p. 29)

. . . a bookcase, which occupied a prominent situation in his chamber, and seemed to defy suspicion and challenge inquiry. (7, p. 53)

Nothing seemed to be going on but the clocks, and they had such drowsy faces, such heavy lazy hands, and such cracked voices that they surely must have been too slow. (28, p. 211)

The grandfather changes identity with the shopful of junk he has collected: 'There was nothing in the whole collection but was in keeping with himself; nothing that looked older or more worn than he' (1, p. 5). Miss Monflathers, with unconscious ambiguity, reduces Nell to a ' "wax-work child" ' (31, p. 235), and Samuel Brass, asleep in the Curiosity Shop itself, becomes 'the ugliest piece of goods in all the stock' (12, p. 96). But it is Quilp, the agent of the world of disintegrating objects, who most often seems to exchange any human identity he may have with the weird, alternative reality of the non-human. His wife and her mother begin 'to doubt if he really were a human creature' (5, p. 40); he is 'like a dismounted nightmare' (49, p. 369). It is, appropriately enough, in a dream that Nell recognises this absurd and disturbing mechanism of fluctuating identity and reality:

... Quilp, who throughout her uneasy dreams was somehow connected with the wax-works, or was a wax-work himself, or was Mrs. Jarley and wax-work too, or was himself, Mrs. Jarley, wax-work, and a barrel organ all in one ... (27, p. 209)

In the context of such dislocation, the structures and strategies of our organisation of the everyday are rendered inapplicable, and their inoperancy releases a metaphysical free-for-all. The parallel reality which Dickens creates takes its being from our world but estranges what it takes, dramatically asserting 'the inner world underlying actuality'[5] and alienating the human agent, who is discovered in a world of which he is ignorant, within which communication becomes increasingly impossible, and which seems indifferent or even hostile to his very existence.

The structure of reality that Dickens evolves in *The Old Curiosity Shop* is focused by and through the novel's dominant structural motif, the pilgrimage of Nell and her grandfather. The world through which they journey is radically fragmented. People live in the tight enclaves of their own concerns, relationships, professions. They structure their experience of reality in radically different ways and the contexts that they thus create for themselves are insistently and inescapably enclosed. The peregrination progresses by a series of irruptions into other people's worlds, each mutually dissociated. Short and Codlin exist in one long round of Punch and Judy shows, and Codlin, in particular, is comically alienated by what is called his 'false position in society' (17, p. 132). Similarly, Mrs Jarley and George are defined by their immersion in the private world of the wax-works: George's estimate of the weight of Nell and her grandfather as ' "a trifle under that of Oliver Cromwell" ' (26, p. 199)

only makes sense in that world. To read the novel is to be initiated into a series
of discrete realities, each with its own history and structures, and its own ways
of thinking about the world at large: the widow in the graveyard, the first
family they meet on the road, the poor schoolmaster and the little scholar, the
bargees on their way to the Midlands. The first confrontation with the
industrial city epitomises the whole.

> The throng of people hurried by, in two opposite streams, with no
> symptom of cessation or exhaustion; intent upon their own affairs . . .
> while the two poor strangers, stunned and bewildered by the hurry they
> beheld and had no part in, looked mournfully on . . . (44, p. 326)

Just as the pilgrimage focuses human solitude, so also does it focus the
imaginative corollary of such isolation, the accumulating oppressiveness of
the world of physical objects. The journey begins in the claustrophobic
atmosphere of the Curiosity Shop and ends amidst the equally claustrophobic
ruins of the village and the old church. The industrial city, again, epitomises
the subordination of the human world to the world of objects.

> On mounds of ashes by the wayside, sheltered only by a few rough boards,
> or rotten penthouse roofs, strange engines spun and writhed like tortured
> creatures; clanking their iron chains, shrieking in their rapid whirl from
> time to time as though in torment unendurable, and making the ground
> tremble with their agonies. (45, p. 335)

The man-made mechanisms have moved out of human control and set up life
on their own account. The consequences of such a world of alienated people
and aggressive objects are shown in the microcosm of Miss Monflathers's
Academy. The Academy is imprisoned in its own illusions, its moral and
emotional enclosure expressed by its high wall and the gate, 'More obdurate
than gate of adamant or brass' (31, p. 234). Threats to the school's
exclusiveness, outsiders must be reductively dismissed as mere things:
' "You're the wax-work child, are you not?" ' (31, p. 235). Within the school,
human connection is reduced to jealousy ('two smiling teachers, each mortally
envious of the other': 31, p. 234) and sycophancy ('each considered herself
smiler-in-ordinary to Miss Monflathers': 31, p. 235). Just as any human
contact from without threatens a system founded upon human dissociation,
so also any internal attempt to form mutual relationships is subversive. The
offender must be attacked ('verbally fell upon and maltreated': 31, p. 238),
deprived of human status ('set down as something immeasurably less than
nothing': 31, p. 237), and punished by being forced back into the prison of the
system (' "You will not take the air today, Miss Edwards . . ." ': 31, p. 238).
'Miss Monflathers's Day and Boarding Establishment' is Quilp's Wharf with
a genteel façade.

Such a world desperately needs the qualities of love, selflessness and
reponsibility so consistently shown by Nell. But Nell's role cannot adequately
be defined in ethical terms alone.

She raised her eyes to the bright stars, looking down so mildly from the wide worlds of air, and, gazing on them, found new stars burst upon her view, and more beyond, and more beyond again, until the whole great expanse sparkled with shining spheres, rising higher and higher in immeasurable space, eternal in their numbers as in their changeless and incorruptible existence. She bent over the calm river, and saw them shining in the same majestic order as when the dove beheld them gleaming through the swollen waters, upon the mountain-tops down far below, and dead mankind, a million fathoms deep. (32, p. 310)

The passage is of central importance, not only in *The Old Curiosity Shop*, but also in the history of the development of Dickens's fiction.[6] It is the first fully realised example of the way in which Dickens's central characters begin to assume the attributes of actors in a drama the terms of which are fundamentally spiritual and metaphysical. The passage focuses the novel's two time systems discussed earlier in this chapter. Nell's experience is seen in terms of a shift from a transcendental to an anthropocentric concept of time, from the stars, 'changeless and incorruptible' – the emblem of a divine infinity – to 'dead mankind, a million fathoms deep', with its insistent emphasis upon the overwhelming fact of human mortality. In the visual architecture of the image, the surface of the water is seen as the line of demarcation between the two systems; this visual structuring establishes a conceptual order in which that line becomes the hypothetical division between a reality suspended almost in the very moment of mortality and a world under the regimen of eternity. In the one, the ultimate reality is that of existence beyond change or corruption; in the other, the only permanency is that of death. But Dickens qualifies the absolutism of this visual and conceptual antithesis. If one imagines the whole metaphor in terms of a vertical cross-section, then the reflection becomes a point of stasis, with reference upwards to the stars which the surface mirrors, and downwards to the world of dead mankind, to where the reflection gleams 'upon the mountain-tops down far below'. A line of access is thus drawn on our conceptual map of the image, linking the opposited realities of death and eternity; the stars themselves remain inviolate and inaccessible, but man does have access to the faintly reflected image of their eternal state, to intimations of immortality. In its transcendentalism, its sense of the mortal world as shadow and reflection, parallels to the image can be found in Plato's metaphor of the cave and Shelley's 'dome of many-coloured glass'.[7] But, more important, one recognises the influence of Carlyle, not only in terms of the general conception of higher and lower realities, distinct but related, but also in the typological basis of the role assigned to Nell. Nell's vision is from the point neither of the stars nor of 'dead mankind', but from a point halfway between the regimen of mortality and the regimen of eternity. She sees as the dove saw, traditionally the image of peace and innocence, and, after the Flood, the messenger of hope and of new life. The typological relationship between Nell and the biblical dove identifies her as a harbinger of salvation.

It is precisely because of Nell's spiritual identity as, in part at least, a divine agent that her death carries such imaginative significance, for with it the world of the novel loses its primary access to redemption. Nell's potential as the messenger of salvation is never realised and her death, although it resolves the narrative, resolves nothing else. Rather, it seems to subordinate all else to itself. Reality, as imaged by the novel, alters in a way not dissimilar to that imagined by Sartre in *Nausea*: 'no appreciable change will take place, but one morning when people open their blinds they will be surprised by a sort of horrible feeling brooding heavily over things'.[8] Like Sartre's 'feeling', the change in *The Old Curiosity Shop* is one of total experience; it is easy to identify the stimulus as Nell's death, but almost impossible to define the experienced 'feel' of the change. Kit's journey to the village is a movement from one kind of reality to another, and the snowfall signals the point of transition.

> The flakes fell fast and thick, soon covering the ground some inches deep, and spreading abroad a solemn stillness. The rolling wheels were noiseless, and the sharp ring and clatter of the horses' hoofs, became a dull, muffled tramp. The life of their progress seemed to be slowly hushed, and something death-like to usurp its place. (70, p. 526)

The categories of visual organisation no longer hold true.

> He could descry objects enough . . . but none correctly. Now, a tall church spire appeared in view, which presently became a tree, a barn, a shadow on the ground, thrown on it by their own bright lamps. (70, p. 527)

Reality becomes a series of 'dim illusions'.[9] In the village, life has been suspended: 'Time itself seems to have grown dull and old, as if no day were ever to displace the melancholy night' (70, p. 528). Dickens manipulates the reader's expectations and responses until the village, in Eliot's phrase, is 'not in time's covenant',[10] and, in moving through it, Kit moves through a new kind of reality towards the centre of the mystery, the body of Little Nell. With this shift in the make-up of the real comes a corresponding dislocation of perception. Nell's grandfather tries to grasp the new reality that comes with Nell's death through a new and alien language.

> 'Angels hands have strewn the ground deep with snow, that the lightest footstep be lighter yet; and the very birds are dead, that they may not wake her.'

'Why dost thou lie so idle there, dear Nell . . . when there are bright
red berries out of door waiting for thee to pluck them?'

'Shut the door. Quick! – Have we not enough to do to drive away
that marble cold and keep her warm?' (71, pp. 534–5)

The change in the experienced 'feel' of reality that comes with Nell's death
is, however, prepared for in the novel by the whole way in which Dickens
registers the world. The clue to what is essentially a way of looking is given,
appropriately enough, by the showman, Vuffin, in conversation at the Jolly
Sandboys: ' "Once make a giant common and giants will never draw again.
Look at wooden legs. If there was only one man with a wooden leg what
a property *he'd* be!" ' (19, p. 143). Vuffin, and through him Dickens, is
talking about perceptual complacency. Familiarity breeds bluntness of
vision, a contempt for the essential mystery of reality. Eliot saw, as a central
feature of Andrew Marvell's poetry, 'the making of the familiar strange,
and the strange familiar'.[11] It is precisely this quality that informs the
depiction of the real in *The Old Curiosity Shop*. The 'strangeness' of the
novel is obvious enough: the Punch and Judy, the Wax-work, the Shop
itself – all unfamiliar, oddly isolated from the apparent normality of our
everyday experience. But, as Forster recognised, the strangeness is not
indulged for its own sake. 'Without the show-people and their blended
fictions and realities, their waxworks, dwarfs, giants, and performing dogs,
the picture would have wanted some part of its significance.'[12] Codlin and
Short, Vuffin and Mrs Jarley are all 'show-people', and what they show
are images of the larger reality of which they form a part: the puppets in
their archetypal roles; the dogs that walk upright like man himself; the wax-
works, the most life-like of all, advertised in a handbill claiming, suggestively
enough, that they 'enlarged the sphere of the human understanding' (28,
p. 215). They epitomise the novel's method, for Dickens is the greatest
show-man of them all, the winder of 'the magic reel' (Chapter the Last,
p. 547) that shows the real as magically strange.

  The Old Curiosity Shop is a mimetic show, offering an examination of
reality through an interpretative imitation of it. That is, of course, to state
the obvious – the same may be said of almost any work of literature from
Sophocles to James Joyce. What is important here is Dickens's extreme
consciousness of what he is doing – his awareness of the dual role of the
literary showman as both entertainer and as 'shower' – and his location
of mimesis and experience of mimesis at the centre of human awareness
and development. Dickens's reflections upon Kit's state of mind after the
pantomime at Astley's may be seen as a highly suggestive elaboration of
Aristotle's deceptively simple statement that people 'enjoy seeing likenesses
because in doing so they acquire information'.[13]

He had already had a misgiving that the inconstant actors in the

dazzling vision had been doing the same thing the night before last,
and would do it again that night, and the next, and for weeks and
months to come, though he would not be there. Such is the difference
between yesterday and to-day. We are all going to the play, or coming
home from it. (40, p. 296)

Dickens is not just talking about the familiar sense of anticlimax that follows
any personally important event, but about the whole Aristotelian process
of acquiring information through mimesis, and the problematic doubts and
misgivings implicit in that process. We are involved here in a whole tissue
of problems concerning the reality of reality: anticipation and direct
experience are real enough for the individual, but how real is what is
anticipated or experienced, and how does that reality change with time and
recollection? Kit's misgivings about Astley's are anticipated in *Sketches by
Boz*.

Some years ago we used to stand looking, open-mouthed, at these men,
with a feeling of mysterious curiosity, the very recollection of which
provokes a smile at the moment we are writing. We could not believe
that the beings of light and elegance, in milk-white tunics, salmon-
coloured legs, and blue scarfs, who flitted on sleek, cream-coloured
horses before our eyes at night, with all the aid of lights, music and
artificial flowers, could be the pale, dissipated-looking creatures we
beheld day by day.
We can hardly believe it now. ('Scenes', 'Astley's', pp. 109–10)

By the time of *The Old Curiosity Shop*, this kind of subjective experience
has become a central feature of Dickens's whole theory of perception –
'We are all going to the play, or coming home from it' – and, because
he is a showman himself, a central feature of the show he puts on. Where
do we draw the line between imitation and actuality in a novel that not
only offers an interpretative representation of the real, but also contains
a succession of parallel, though subordinate, representations and imitations,
a mimetic series within a mimetic whole? *The Old Curiosity Shop* images
the real world as a series of receding planes of representation and illusion,
in which subjective realities can find no guarantee of objective validity.
In *Pickwick Papers* there is a sense that anything might happen in the
narrative: in *The Old Curiosity Shop* such a sense pervades the very fabric
of experienced reality.

Vuffin's comic directive, ' "Look at wooden legs" ', is Dickens's demand
for a change in the perceiver's attitude to perception itself. Such a change
effects a radical alteration in the potential of the empirical world, an
alteration that becomes the basis for the special kind of realism evolved
in Dickens's later novels. Descriptions, in *The Old Curiosity Shop*, are
realistic enough, but there is more than realist reportage.

The streets were very clean, very sunny, very empty, and very dull.
A few idle men lounged about the two inns, and the empty market-
place, and the tradesmen's doors, and some old people were dozing
in chairs outside the alms-house wall; but scarcely any passengers who
seemed bent on going anywhere, or to have any object in view, went
by; and if perchance some straggler did, his footsteps echoed on the
hot bright pavements for minutes afterwards. Nothing seemed to be
going on but the clocks, and they had such drowsy faces, such heavy
lazy hands, and such cracked voices that they surely must have
been too slow. The very dogs were all asleep, and the flies,
drunk with moist sugar in the grocer's shop, forgot their wings
and briskness, and baked to death in dusty corners of the window.
(28, p. 211)

The realist impact of the passage is powerful: the repeated constructions
– 'very . . . very . . . very', 'such drowsy faces, such . . . hands . . . such
. . . voices' – create an echoic monotony in the linguistic structure; verbs
and adjectives chime together to negate any sense of activity, 'dull',
'lounged', 'dozing', 'drowsy', 'lazy'. All the 'felt life' of direct experience
is there; the terms of the description place the town in a world that we
can recognise easily enough as ours. But there is more. Such is the
cumulative effect of suspended animation in the passage that the attribution
of some kind of consciousness to the clocks comes as a shock – the clocks
take up the functioning of animate life as people lose their distinguishing
vitality. The focus of the passage moves from the human to the non-human
without any apparent change of terms. The mechanical operation of the
clocks and, implicitly, the more abstract movement of time itself come to
seem of greater imaginative significance than any signs of life in the human
world. As we realise this, the suggestion implicit in such a transference
of dramatic and conceptual focus becomes part of the structure of explication
that we have built up from our experience of the novel, and part of the
overall thematic emphasis upon time, transience, the physical world and
'dead mankind'. We are thus drawn inevitably towards a recognition of
parallels between the human inhabitants of the town and the flies, dying
in the grocer's window – the same drowsiness, the same loss of animation,
the same sense of entrapment and, pessimistically, the same sense of
approaching death. The description of the dying flies is more than a realistic
detail, and more than simply echoic of human life in the town: it is
emblematic, at once epitomising, paralleling and making explicit the
thematic architecture of the passage as a whole, and setting it within the
conceptual structure of the novel. The death of the flies is a symbolic
correlative to the death of man. But the status and signification of this kind
of Dickensian symbol are peculiar: it would be untrue to say that the flies
simply 'stand for' mankind, for their realist identity is retained; nor is it
true that the death of the flies is 'like' the death of man, for the relationship

between the two terms is far closer. In his discussion of symbolism,
W. K. Wimsatt quotes Stanford's definition of metaphor:

> [Metaphor is] . . . the process and result of using a term (X) normally
> signifying an object or concept (A) in such a context that it must refer
> to another object or concept (B) which is distinct enough in
> characteristics from A to ensure that in the composite idea formed
> by the synthesis of the concepts A and B and now symbolized in the
> word X, the factors A and B retain their conceptual independence even
> while they merge in the unity symbolized by X.[14]

Stanford's definition and notation provide a useful tool for an analysis of
Dickens's image. If we take X to be the string of terms signifying the death
of the flies, the concept A, and B to be the other concept, which I have
loosely termed the death of man, then we can fit the overall image into
Stanford's schema. The key word in his account of the role of X is
'normally', for he goes on to suggest that, even as X retains some of its
reference to A, its role is changed by reference to B: in the context of the
metaphor the 'normal' signification is subordinated. In Dickens's symbol,
however, this normal signification is completely retained. The signification
of A by X remains unimpaired, the flies in the window remain part of the
realist scene: the dying flies *are* dying flies. Yet, as we have seen, the
reference to B *is* made, even as B retains its independence in the passage's
structure of ideas. Dickens presents us with an essential ambivalence in
what Stanford calls 'the unity symbolized by X'. Whilst there is never any
doubt that the description is realistic, something has been added. By
retaining realism, but, at the same time, forcing us to recognise meaning
as an integral part of that reality, Dickens establishes a symbolic dimension
in the very stuff of the real world. The description functions, simultaneously, in the mimetic and conceptual structures of the novel. The flies,
I have said, neither 'stand for' man nor are they 'like' man; a different
principle of imaginative organisation has taken over. The distinct elements
are amalgamated in a composite concept; correlations between them are
immediate – grasped in a single movement of the imagination – because
their composite identity is presented as part of the novel's registration of
an empirically real world, not as an imposition upon it, nor even as an
interpretation of it. What we have, of course, is Dickens's own form of
symbolic realism. Similarities to Carlyle are clear enough, but the differences
are perhaps more important. Even in those images from *The French
Revolution*, discussed at the end of the previous chapter, where symbolic
truth and literal truth coalesce – the Carmagnole, the guillotine and so
forth – the significance of the image ultimately depends upon a conceptual
structure that is outside the text. Although we identify the Carmagnole
as an actualisation of the wind/whirlwind figure, the significance of *that*
figure is drawn from the Bible. Carlylean symbolic realism, partly because

of its typological basis, always depends upon the Bible as a semantic key. In the passage from *The Old Curiosity Shop*, however, the symbolic dimension of what is described is generated from the immediate context of the central image and from its place in the conceptual organisation of the novel as a whole. In comparison to Carlyle, Dickensian symbolic realism is semantically self-sufficient. Within the terms of the fiction, conceptual elements and realist elements cease to be distinct: the external world, in all its detailed succession of empirically recognisable entities – houses, shops, people, dogs in the street – has come to *mean* rather than simply to *be*. In Dickens's conception of reality, the symbolic and the actual are co-extensive. Examples could be multiplied from throughout *The Old Curiosity Shop*: the wasteland on the edge of London; Mr Punch as hero, 'slack and drooping in a dark box' (18, p. 132); Mrs Jarley's wax-works, 'staring with extraordinary earnestness at nothing' (28, p. 124); the whole context of Nell's death. In his insistence upon revising and realigning attitudes to reality, Dickens has remade the external world and rewritten its potential significance. The thematic material that *The Old Curiosity Shop* brings together – the oppressiveness of the material world, the sense of human solitude, the constriction of positive moral action, the emphasis upon transience and death, the incipient social disintegration – is of fundamental importance to the novels that follow. But fundamental also is the novel's synthesis of symbolic and realist values. In *Dombey and Son* and, even more, in *David Copperfield*, symbolic realism becomes a principle of both imaginative and structural organisation.

4

'What the Waves Were Always Saying':
Symbolic Realism in *Dombey and Son* and *David Copperfield*

In *Dombey and Son*, the unifying symbol is that of the sea.[1] As was suggested in the previous chapter, Dickens's use of symbolism cannot be considered in terms of a relatively simple one-for-one relationship between symbol and referent. Indeed, it is doubtful whether any truly metaphoric relationship could be so considered. There is a constant effect of interanimation between the constituent terms of a metaphor, and, even as those terms retain their individual identities, their specific areas of application, they are reciprocally qualified so that a third reality is generated through their relationship. Disparate meanings are not sunk without trace in a metaphor, to re-emerge, indissolubly united, in a pristine, new reality.[2] All figurative language is an integration of meanings in which the act of integrating remains a current part of the final metaphoric product. The amalgamation of terms is not an accomplished fact of the metaphor – in Crocean terms, a mental act of the writer prior to the figure's commitment to the page – but a continuing process: metaphor is fundamentally dynamic. Just as mass, in Einsteinian physics, can never be simply destroyed, so meaning is never entirely lost in its subordination to a new figurative schema. Goodman's definition of metaphor as 'an affair between a predicate with a past and an object that yields while protesting' nicely catches this enigmatic movement of metaphoric terms between the retention of old meaning and the adoption of new significance.[3] It is in precisely this area that Dickens's symbolic realism operates and that his presentation of the sea as both emblem and actuality in *Dombey and Son* attains its richest meanings.

The initial identification of the sea as an image of time and death is overt. The sound of the waves carries a message of mortality to Paul; Florence's mother 'drifted out upon the dark and unknown sea that rolls round all the world' (1, p. 10). The change in tense in the brief figurative account of Mrs Dombey's death is important. Whereas her death is conceived in temporal terms, as a completed event in the past – 'drifted' – the existence of the sea is a fact outside the limits of individual consciousness; its movement is continuous – 'rolls round all the world'. The sea is death in its non-human aspect. The novel's recurrent image of the river in its progress to the sea, however, locates death as a human event.

'How fast the river runs, between its green banks and the rushes, Floy!
But it's very near the sea. I hear the waves!' (16, p. 225)

. . . and often when she looked upon the darker river rippling at her
feet, she thought with awful wonder, but not of terror, of that river
which her brother had so often said was bearing him away. (24, p. 350)

The double time-scale of *The Old Curiosity Shop* recurs in the symbolic
structure of *Dombey and Son*. Time is seen in two ways: as a transcendental
reality, 'an unknown sea', and as a linear progression, the river-like motion
of personal time. These dual metaphors anticipate the imagery of 'The Dry
Salvages' by more than ninety years: 'The river is within us, the sea is all
about us.'[4] But there is, of course, a paradox in the first of these aspects.
To conceive time as transcendental is, necessarily, to contradict its nature
as a linear progression. Dickens is confronting the familiar theological
problem of eternity, outside of linear time but comprehending it. The
solution lies in a synthesis of the two aspects of time in the novel, a synthesis
that develops quite naturally from the imaginative logic of the imagery.
The entry of the river into the sea at the moment of death translates the
symbol of individual transience into the symbol of eternity. Dickens's
concept of death is thus temporally ambiguous, a concept again closely
paralleled by Eliot in his identification of the occurrence within time and
yet outside of it, 'the intersection of the timeless moment'.[5] The
significance of individual action is measured within two frames of reference:
in terms of what we empirically regard as time, and in terms of a
transcendental concept of eternity. Time is, in this sense, two-dimensional.
But this temporal ambiguity is never allowed to harden into a rigid dualism;
everything exists in eternity as – and, indeed, because – it exists in time.
Thus the sea comes to symbolise not only time in its aspect of eternity,
but also eternity in its aspect of time, eternity seen within the terms of
a human temporal structure. This wider figurative perspective contextualises
the development of character and action throughout the novel.

[Captain Cuttle] . . . felt almost kindly towards the boy as if they
had been shipwrecked and cast upon a desert place together. (39,
p. 549)

[Florence] . . . wringing her hands and weeping bitterly . . . like the
lone survivor on a lonely shore from the wreck of a great vessel
. . . (48, p. 667)

[John and Harriet Carker] sat conversing by the fireside . . . made
sleepless by this glimpse of the new world that opened before them,

and feeling like two people shipwrecked long ago, upon a solitary coast, to whom a ship had come at last, when they were old in resignation, and had lost all thought of any home. (53, p. 750)

Echoic images establish an objective framework for narrative development, allowing the reader to stand back from local significance and to see the specific in terms of overall conceptual and expressive patterns. But the repeated imagery of shipwreck is a part of the novel's structure of ideas, as well as a means towards aesthetic unity. What we might call 'total reality' is only perceivable, in the novel's terms, by an understanding of the different dimensions of significance implicit in any particular occurrence. Movement on the stream of subjective time is simultaneously, and necessarily, an event upon the sea of eternity; the transcendental is implicit in the mundane. Reality *a posteriori* and reality *a priori* are not seen as discrete but as complementary, and only by understanding both can we understand either.

The most fully developed example of this metaphoric and conceptual 'double-take' is the career of Walter Gay. Whereas for Florence, John Carker and the rest the imagery of voyage and shipwreck is a metaphorical extension of their situation, Walter actually goes to sea, and for him shipwreck is an actual experience. The wandering sailor is a familiar figure of romance, but in Dickens's novel Walter takes on a significance beyond his role as a stock figure out of the popular tradition. The figurative structure of *Dombey and Son* necessarily directs our attention to a further symbolic dimension beyond the narrative and dramatic importance of Walter's career. His voyage upon the *Son and Heir* is a voyage upon 'the unknown sea'. Given the symbolic identification of the sea, Walter's voyage becomes a type of peregrination. The shipwreck is an imitative enactment of death, a narrative realisation of the shipwreck metaphor, and Walter, like the other virtuous characters, comes successfully through hardships and setbacks. But that is only upon one level. Walter, the young hero, is sent on a quest, suffers an apparent death by water, returns from the sea to marry the princess and, eventually, to lift the curse on Dombey's kingdom.[6] The sterile London house is a *laissez-faire* castle in a nineteenth-century version of *Sleeping Beauty*: 'The spell upon it was more wasting than the spell that used to set enchanted houses sleeping' (23, p. 318). But the story is more, even, than a Victorian version of a fairy story, for in it Dickens seems to be responding, instinctively and imaginatively, to the folk tradition of fertility myth, later explored by Frazer and Weston.[7] Gay is transformed, by the pressure of his imaginative and figurative context, from the conventional hero to the central figure of a regeneration myth. Walter's whole status in the novel changes as a result of his experience: he reveals a new awareness of himself and of his role. When he tells Florence ' "I am but a wanderer . . . making journeys to live across the sea" ' (50, p. 713), he makes what is tantamount to a metaphysical judgement upon the state of man. He looks upon Florence quite differently, 'from a new and far-off place' (49, p. 694). This change in viewpoint results from more than a change in personal relationship. If we see the shipwreck as the central passage of a regeneration cycle, then it must be identified as the moment of spiritual awakening, the moment at which Walter is initiated into the perspective of eternity. Mr Morfin describes a parallel process:

> '. . . how will many things that are familiar, and quite matters of course to us now, look when we come to see them from that new and distant point of view which we must all take up, one day or other?' (53, p. 747)

The ' "new and distant point of view" ' significantly echoes Walter's 'new and far-off place'. But Morfin – in a conventionally Christian attitude – specifically locates this wider spiritual perspective in death and immortality: 'For now we see through a glass, darkly; but then face to face.' Shipwreck, death and eternity thus form a conceptual and metaphoric continuity; or, rather, perhaps, a cluster of ideas and images, in a constant flux of inter-related meanings, revolving around the nuclear problem of reality and its perception.

These distinctions, however, are too clear-cut. The shift between metaphor and narrative affects the whole make-up of reality in *Dombey and Son*. Walter's journey, with all its metaphoric implications, is an experienced reality within the novel. Within the terms of the fiction the voyage has a literal existence. Similarly, the figurative structures of the novel are palpable realities, matters of fact in the everyday world.

> His fancy had a strange tendency to wander to the river, which he knew was flowing through the great city; and now he thought how black it was, and how deep it would look, reflecting the hosts of stars – and more than all, how steadily it rolled away to meet the sea. (16, p. 221)

> All is going on as it was wont. The waves hoarse with repetition of their mystery; the dust lies piled upon the shore; the sea-birds soar and hover; the winds and clouds go forth upon their trackless flight; the white arms beckon, in the moonlight, to the invisible country far away. (41, p. 577)

The river really *does* flow through the city, the waves really *do* sound hoarse upon the seashore. Their significance is not imposed upon them by the experiencer of them, nor is there a separate conceptual structure into which the realist images of sea and waves are in some way fitted. The meaning and signification of the waves or the river are facts even as their simple existence is a fact. Realist structure cannot be distinguished from metaphoric structure. The more or less abstract problems of what I have called total reality and its perception are both set out and solved in the very texture of the novel. The two scales of reality, the one temporal and human, the other transcendental, are brought together. The *a priori* nature of metaphor, an imaginative structuring of experience that goes beyond experience as such, and the *a posteriori* nature of prose realism, become complementary and co-extensive. The same processes that were at work in *The Old Curiosity Shop* form, in *Dombey and Son*, a central technique of Dickens's creative imagination. Florence's insistent reminiscence of the sea, her awareness of transience and individual mortality, is thus seen as a species of higher understanding, a type of vision that is inaccessible and incomprehensible to her father. She 'sees' more of reality, literally and figuratively, than does Dombey.

Precisely because of her greater contact with what the novel establishes as superordinate moral and spiritual realities, she becomes the focus for the novel's insistence upon the power of human love. In rejecting her, Dombey rejects not only human commitment, but also the wider realities of time and eternity to which she has access. In Dombey's moral order, with its entire ignorance of spiritual values, with no kind of perspective upon eternity, death is a simple finality. For Dickens, as for Florence, such a system is untenable because it denies the reality of love. On the seashore at Brighton, the conversation between Paul and his sister presents love and death in a stark antithesis.

> 'If you were in India, Floy,' said Paul, after being silent for a minute, 'I should – what is it that Mama did? I forget.'
> 'Loved me!' answered Florence.
> 'No, no, Don't I love you now, Floy? What is it? – Died. If you were in India, I should die, Floy.' (8, p. 108)

For Florence, the fact of her mother's death is subordinate to the fact of her love. Florence denies, not death, but death's finality, and, because of this faith in transcendence, Florence is allowed her vision of total reality. Florence, ultimately, is the realist, and Dombey, with all his commitment to 'the world' and to the facts of business, is the victim of chronic self-deception. The ethical conflict in *Dombey and Son* is presented as a problem of reality, of what is real and what is not, a problem that forces itself upon the reader by means of the synthesis of realism and metaphor within the very structure of the novel. Thus, at a fundamental philosophical and aesthetic level, Dickens enforces what is, basically, a New Testament morality: a correlation of love and eternity, and an identification of human existence without love with moral and spiritual death. In such a context it would be difficult to overstate the importance of Paul's question to Florence, ' "Floy, are we *all* dead, except you?" ' (16, p. 224).

Criticism has largely ignored the significance of the opening sentence of *David Copperfield*: 'Whether I shall turn out to be the hero of my own life, or whether the station will be held by anybody else, these pages must show' (1, p. 1).[8] Doubting his own heroic status in the drama of his own life, David implicitly asks the question, what is a hero? Traditionally defined, heroism takes its basis in right action. In *Dombey and Son* right action depends upon right seeing, upon the proper understanding, against all obscurantist odds, of the world in which the individual lives. Thus, Florence's understanding of the emblematic meaning of experienced reality, and the moral initiative she derives from that understanding, defines her as the heroine. Similarly, Walter's heroism is endorsed by his active engagement in the co-extensively real and symbolic voyage in *Son and Heir*. Antithetically, Dombey's ignorance of the semantic that pervades the real precisely locates his moral dereliction, the sin of spiritual illiteracy. In *David Copperfield* the adoption of first-person narration gives Dickens the opportunity of tracing these defining processes of learning and understanding through the growing experience of the learner/narrator himself. The quests for right action and for right seeing coalesce in the growth of David's consciousness – the process, that is, of the novel itself. It is a critical commonplace that *David Copperfield* is a novel of education. But it is more than that – it is a novel about the heroism of learning.

Teaching and being taught are paradigmatic in the novel. David is subjected to the Murdstonian educational regime and to the brutal indifference of Salem House, against which is set Dr Strong's Academy, 'as different from Mr. Creakle's as good is from evil' (16, p. 237). He is initiated into the dubious mysteries of Doctors' Commons, teaches himself shorthand and, in his turn, assumes the role of teacher in his abortive attempt 'to form Dora's mind' (48, p. 694). Uriah Heep sits up at night ' "going through Tidd's Practice" ' (16, p. 234); Steerforth goes up to Oxford, coming down, significantly, without having taken his degree; Traddles reads for the Bar; Agnes becomes a schoolteacher. The paraphernalia of learning fills the novel: Peggotty's crocodile book, David's eighteenth-century novels, Mr Dick's Memorial, Dr Strong's Dictionary, Traddles's endless copying and Dora's hopeless account-book. Rosa Dartle's ' "I only ask for information" ' (20, p. 293) and David's ' "We have . . . a great deal to learn" ' (44, p. 637) stand almost as mottoes for the educational enterprise of the whole.

By the 1840s, Dickens's concern for education was not primarily that of a social reformer or reporter, but had become a focus for his central concern with man's understanding of the world he inhabits. To learn is to structure; the end of education an interpretative model through which the real can be approached. Thus the progressive stages of David's education are registered through a changing series of world-constructs which, by defining external reality through the relationship between self and non-self, provide also a developing definition of personal identity. Thus 'the natural result' of the Murdstonian system is not only to make David 'sullen, dull, and dogged' but also to enforce his 'sense of being daily more and more shut out and alienated' from his mother (4, p. 55). The process of alienation culminates in David's banishment; in his isolation, his only defence, and the only way in which he can maintain the self as hero, is through the alternative education of the imagination.

> . . . I can remember to have gone about my region of our house . . .
> the perfect realization of Captain Somebody, of the British Navy .
> . . The Captain never lost dignity, from having his ears boxed with
> the Latin grammar. I did; but the Captain was a Captain and a hero
> . . . (4, p. 56)

In Dr Strong's it is precisely this sense of significant selfhood that is encouraged. In the running of every aspect of the school there is 'an appeal . . . to the honour and good faith of the boys, and an avowed intention to rely on their possession of those qualities' (16, p. 237). With a shift in educational mode comes a shift in David's self-image and thus a change in the way in which he construes the real. The structures by means of which learning proceeds are not static, but dynamically related, and, therefore, time-dependent. Because *David Copperfield* is a novel about education, it is also a novel about time.

In the medium of time, the constructs David arrives at are not discrete – their inter-relation is less that between items in a series, and more that between the stages of a continuum. Thus the knowledge of his past contextualises and partly determines David's attitude towards Dr Strong's:

> . . . troubled as I was, by my want of boyish skill, and of book-learning
> too, I was made infinitely more uncomfortable by the consideration
> that, in what I did know, I was much farther removed from my
> companions than in what I did not. (16, p. 229)

Necessarily conditioned by his understanding of the past, David's understanding of the present is also the medium through which he reinterprets his own history. This kind of double process determines the mode of the novel, that of memory. Thus to the David who suffers under the loveless rule of Murdstone the time before his mother's second marriage assumes idyllic qualities. Happiness in the present can come only through recapturing the lost world of the past: 'I had never thought it possible that we three could be together undisturbed, once more; and I felt, for the time, as if the old days were come back' (8, p. 110). The past takes on new importances; qualities not apparent previously become clear in the light of later experience. But memory is never morally neutral: reinterpretation necessarily involves revaluation, and the moral impetus of the novel derives from the evaluative nature of retrospection. But retrospection is paradoxical. On the one hand, continuity is implied between past and present, enabling the remembering self to say, 'Such-and-such happened to *me*'; on the other hand, disjunction is implied, enabling the evaluating self to say, 'I believed so-and-so *then*, but I know differently *now*'. Moreover, learning from experience implies an ability to use one's experience to predicate action for the future: foresight is only possible because of hindsight. In the unfolding fabric of David's experience, learning, time, memory and evaluation are intricately interwoven. David's problem – and that of other characters – is how to find the proper relationship between past, present and future; from that, how to find a way of life – in every sense of a much-worn phrase – that provides, at once, an adequate interpretation of the experienced world, and an adequate protection for the self from the dangers inherent in that world.

The dangerous, indeed hostile, nature of the world outside the self is epitomised in David's flight from London to Dover. In *The Old Curiosity Shop*, despite constant retreat, Nell not only finds help on the road, but also retains her own identity unimpaired. Florence Dombey's hold on the informing reality of time is safeguarded, despite her father's rejection, by the availability of the Little Midshipman. In *David Copperfield*, for the first time, Dickens images, from the inside, the consequences to selfhood of a world that the self is forced to interpret as structureless. In such a world the very concept of self as a stable and stabilising centre of perception becomes untenable. Starting his journey to Dover, David, robbed of box and money, threatened by the obscure violence of ' "the pollis" ', is abandoned to a callously indifferent world in which he has no place and which he cannot control. The result has all the randomness and violence of nightmare.

> I ran after him as fast as I could, but I had not breath to call out with, and should not have dared to call out, now, if I had. I narrowly escaped being run over, twenty times at least, in half a mile. Now I lost him, now I saw him, now I lost him, now I was cut at with a whip, now shouted at, now down in the mud, now up again, now running into somebody's arms, now running headlong at a post. (12, p. 179)

The metaphysical fragmentation and the recurrent human isolation that characterise the image of the world Dickens creates in *The Old Curiosity Shop* are both concentrated in David's experience of the Dover Road. Contact between people is reduced to mere collision and David's journey takes on a hallucinatory intensity that suggests a distillation of Nell's pilgrimage.

> Sometimes in his rage he would . . . come at me, mouthing as if he were going to tear me to pieces.

> 'Come here, when you're called,' said the tinker, 'or I'll rip your young body open.'

... the tinker seized the handkerchief out of my hand with a roughness
that threw me away like a feather ... turned upon the woman with
an oath and knocked her down. (13, pp. 185–7)

Unsupported by family or social context, weak and alone, David stands
no chance in a world whose rationale is – to use a much misused word
– fascist, the world of *vae victis* and the rule of the bully-boy. Organised
in such terms, reality makes no sense, for it ceases to be an organisation
at all, becoming, rather, 'a world of isolated integers, terrifyingly alone and
unrelated'.[9]

The different strategies adopted by the novel's characters in their attempts
to cope with a world of such terrifying potential are not only ethical
structures but also – remembering the correlation between time and
learning – temporal structures. Mr Peggotty's boat in Yarmouth represents
an attempt to secure its inmates against the world outside by denying the
reality of change. Mr Peggotty imposes upon Emily an artificial innocence;
for him she remains 'little Em'ly', imaginatively and verbally held in the
limbo of a false childhood. Trapped in such a way, unreally isolated from
any potential threat – particularly that of adult sexuality – she cannot
recognise, any more than any of the Yarmouth people can, the danger
represented by Steerforth's combination of sex, cynicism and class
superiority. Mr Peggotty's refusal to acknowledge change is a species of
moral childishness. As Peggotty says to him just before the news of Emily's
elopement breaks, ' "You're a baby!" ' (31, p. 450). Her words echo those
of Betsey to David's mother: ' "Why bless my heart! . . . You are a very
Baby!" ' (1, p. 5). The verbal echoes point up a moral parallelism. Like
Mr Peggotty, Mrs Copperfield is a moral baby, and, like the Peggotty
boat, her world at Blunderstone is based in the myth of artificial innocence.
But, whereas he builds an affectionate but rigorously sealed environment,
she erects affection as the sole principle of moral action. By refusing to
countenance the possibility of evil, Mrs Copperfield maintains the self-
deception of innocence and attempts to opt out of a world that is
unmistakably fallen. Such a strategy is worse than useless against
Murdstone. David's mother can repeat assertions of kindhearted inten-
tions – ' "Whatever I am, I am affectionate" ' – but once Murdstone
dismisses such affection as ' "mere weakness" ' (4, p. 51) she is
helpless to defend either herself or David. By perversely arresting
moral development Mr Peggotty excludes, and David's mother ignores,
the possibility of an adult perception of the world as it really
is. Both Yarmouth and Blunderstone are trapped in the past, in
that imaginary past when human beings were innocent: Emily's false
childhood and Mrs Copperfield's ethical childishness both result from
what we might term the Edenic fallacy. To believe in the continuation
of Eden is, simultaneously, to ignore the reality of sin and the reality
of time and change. Learning, as a concomitant to growth, thus

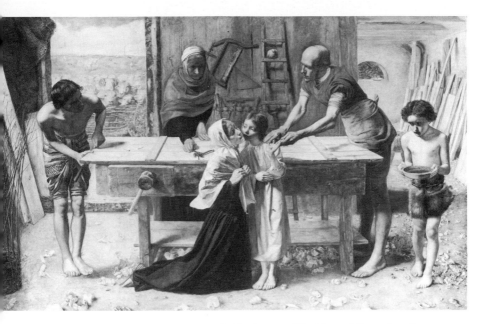

1 J. E. Millais, *Christ in the House of His Parents*. The Tate Gallery, London.

2 W. P. Frith, *Derby Day*. The Tate Gallery, London.

3 J. E. Millais, *Lorenzo and Isabella*. The Walker Art Gallery, Liverpool.

4 Holman Hunt, *The Hireling Shepherd*. City Art Gallery, Manchester.

5 Holman Hunt, *Valentine Rescuing Sylvia from Proteus*. City Museum and Art Gallery, Birmingham.

6 Arthur Hughes, *The Long Engagement*. City Museum and Art Gallery, Birmingham.

7 J. E. Millais, *Autumn Leaves*. City Art Gallery, Manchester.

8 Holman Hunt, *The Light of the World*.
City Art Gallery, Manchester.

9 Holman Hunt, *The Scapegoat*. The
Lady Lever Art Gallery, Port Sunlight.

10 William Dyce, *Pegwell Bay, Kent, a Recollection of October 5th 1858*, The Tate Gallery, London.

11 Ford Madox Brown, *Work*. City Art Gallery, Manchester.

12 Holman Hunt, *The Awakening Conscience*. The Tate Gallery, London.

becomes impossible, as also does, therefore, any proper moral understanding of experience.

Yet the Edenic fallacy, despite its moral inadequacy, is a permanently potent myth, and the need to believe in a lost world of innocent joy – whether that world is located in the past of the individual or the past of the race – is a perennial feature of the imagination. David's love for Dora is, in effect, an attempt to recapture the Eden of his childhood.[10] A fantasy, removed from the pressures of time and responsibility, their courtship takes place 'wandering in a garden of Eden' (26, p. 392), 'in Fairyland' (26, p. 396), and Dora's guitar provides the appropriate accompaniment. 'I heard the empress of my heart sing enchanted ballads in the French language, generally to the effect that, whatever was the matter, we ought always to dance, Ta ra la, Ta ra la!' (26, p. 393). Only after his marriage does David realise the inadequacies that, to the reader – and to the elder David – are evident from the start. The result is that Dora becomes a 'child-wife' and David suffers a double sense of loss, for he loses, simultaneously, both his chance for mature companionship in marriage and his dream of Eden. 'When I walked alone in the fine weather, and thought of the summer days when all the air had been filled with my boyish enchantment, I did miss something of the realization of my dreams' (44, p. 646). The loss of Edenic 'enchantment' matters, for the portrayal of David's courtship and first marriage is far more than an exposure of romantic delusions. David's feelings for Dora have an emotional and experiential immediacy that, despite the sentimental silliness that the older David can see, remains intensely real. The result is the complex nature of David's retrospection, which *simultaneously* acknowledges both the imaginative richness of the Edenic dream and the ethical necessity of an approach to the business of reality.

> At first we strayed to and fro among the trees: I with Dora's shy arm drawn through mine: and Heaven knows, folly as it all was, it would have been a happy fate to have been struck immortal with those foolish feelings, and have strayed among the trees forever. (33, p. 485)

It is precisely the tension between the restriction that comes from moral necessity and the liberation that comes from intense imaginative and emotional engagement that makes the whole account of Dora so moving. But this tension does not result simply from the conflict of Love and Duty: Love, Duty, the conflict itself, all proceed in the medium of time. As David's retrospective evaluation sets the past behind him, views it as over and done with, his retrospective imagination constantly remakes it as the experiential now.

> The scent of a geranium leaf, to this day, strikes me with a half comical, half serious wonder as to what change has come over me in a moment;

and then I see a straw hat and blue ribbons, and a quantity of curls, and a little black dog being held up, in bright leaves. (26, p. 396)

The power of memory to recreate the past gives to the Edenic dream the quality it cannot have in the everyday world – timelessness. In the everyday world Eden must be relinquished even as it is conceived, for an interpretative myth that postulates a permanent perfection is ironically inadequate for understanding a world that is imperfect and impermanent. Some other structure must be found. That David, through the process of memory, can give Eden and innocence their proper experiential weight – as his mother and Mr Peggotty cannot – is due to his recognition of Eden's inadequacy, and of the need for an alternative. That recognition is a result of what he learns from Betsey and from Agnes.

Betsey Trotwood's assertion of responsibility, for self and for others, as the fundamental principle of moral action is the ethical counterweight to the Edenic fallacy. By taking responsibility for David after his flight from London she succeeds exactly where Mr Peggotty fails. Her concept of responsibility, unlike his, is both flexible enough to allow David to grow through experience, and tough enough – as she so triumphantly shows in defeating the Murdstones – to defend him from the potential destructiveness of the big world. Moreover, Betsey's moral stance is also a way of organising linear time, for by taking responsibility for her own actions, and for others', Betsey asserts the moral logic of cause and effect. Responsibility postulates a morally significant pattern to the continuum of linear time. By perceiving such a pattern the individual has a chance to make sense of his own past and to exercise control over his own future, and thus ensure the continuity of his own identity. Betsey's affirmation of the causal relationship of past, present and future is central to both the events and technique of the narrative. Not only does she provide David with a structure through which he can survive as a character in his own life, she also provides the interpretative model through which, as retrospective narrator, he can understand his own life. Given the fiction that David is the author of the novel, Dickens validates Betsey's ethical structuring by the fact of the novel itself: without her world-view, *David Copperfield* could not have been written. Betsey's role in the moral organisation of the novel is inherited by Agnes Wickfield; David's marriage to her may thus be seen as the logical consequence of his attempt to make sense of the history of his own life. Once David has learnt the fundamental importance of responsibility, both as a moral strategy and as a means to self-understanding, marriage to Agnes becomes an imaginative necessity. The measure of its appropriateness as the final stage in David's moral education is the extent to which it also exemplifies a proper understanding of, and adjustment to, process and change. On his return to England, there is a real chance that David will lose the present in a fruitless regret for the past.

Whatever I might have been to [Agnes], or she to me, if I had been
more worthy of her long ago, I was not now, and she was not. The
time was past. I had let it go by, and had deservedly lost her. (58,
p. 818)

Imprisonment in the past similarly threatens Agnes; as she tells David, ' "I
have found a pleasure . . . while you have been absent, in keeping everything
as it used to be when we were children. For we were very happy then" '
(60, p. 840). Their marriage is a refusal to consign happiness to a nostalgic
past, a commitment to living in the present and to a common future.

The proper response to change demonstrated in David's marriage to
Agnes is a local example of a process that goes on throughout the novel.
As I have said, ethical strategies are necessarily also interpretations of the
nature of time. Inseparable from David's final moral consciousness is his
understanding of time and change as the world's dominant and determinant
realities. For all other characters time means personal time – memory and
anticipation. So also, of course, does it for David. But for him the personal
is increasingly registered in the context of the universal, which is understood
as an objective presence outside the individual consciousness.

. . . the bells, when they sounded, told me sorrowfully of change in
everything; told me of their own age, and my pretty Dora's youth;
and of the many, never told, who had lived and loved and died, while
the reverberations of the bells had hummed through the rusty armour
of the Black Prince hanging up within, and, motes upon the deep of
Time, had lost themselves in air, as circles do in water. (52, p. 743)

'The deep of time' keys this formal contemplation of transience into the
emblematic structure of the novel; the objective reality of time in *David
Copperfield* is expressed through the simultaneously realist and symbolic
treatment of the sea and its associates, the river and the wind. As in *Dombey
and Son, a priori* being and *a posteriori* meaning come together, and the
resultant semantic values are the same: the sea not only connotes impersonal
time and the river personal time, they both *are* what they *mean*. Similarly,
the wind is the actualisation of time as a destructive process. But whereas
Florence's knowledge of 'What the waves were always saying' remains
outside of, though ratified by, the narrative voice, in *David Copperfield* the
first-person narration enacts the dynamic process of understanding. Without
the distancing integral to third-person narration, and because no gap
separates signs and signified, *David Copperfield* renders the otherwise
abstract notion of time as a physical presence. The reader comes to
experience the emblematic nature of the real with an immediacy that is
analogous to David's experience of it. Because of the lacuna between the
reality of an event to the individual, and its reality as an event independent
of the individual, David, as a character, constantly misinterprets his

experience. As a narrator, however, he retrospectively contextualises events by symbolic systems within which meaning and being co-extend, and which, therefore, obviate the interpretative gap of subjectivity. In a world characterised by uncertainty and by the limitations of individual understanding, David alone has access to the semantic that inheres within external reality. Meaning comes to have a phenomenal existence: ideas, to quote George Eliot, are 'wrought back to the directness of sense, like the solidity of objects'.[11] Quite literally, for they are consciously imaged by David as having objective existence. That Dickens makes David conscious of this process is centrally important, and the reason behind making David a novelist rather than anything else: for David uses the co-extension of the symbol and the real both to unify his novel and to explicate the world that the novel is about. Dickens's identification with the hero is not simply autobiographical in the way that has, from Forster onwards, been so often suggested. David's novelistic and metaphoric technique is precisely that which Dickens developed in *The Old Curiosity Shop* and *Dombey and Son*. To say that is to state more than the banality that Dickens is the real author; by the stratagem of writing *David Copperfield* through the persona of David, Dickens is able to show his own symbolic technique in the act, as it were, of explicating the real. With the insertion of David between Dickens and his novel, the reader can be offered both the outcome of that technique – David's understanding of his life – and the complex experiences that made that technique available – David's life itself.

Contextualised by the symbolic realities of their world, individual characters are constantly set within the regimen of time, whether impersonal – the sea and the wind – or personal – the river. David loses the early Eden of his childhood: 'A great wind rises, and the summer is gone in a moment' (2, p. 16); when the Murdstones return to the Rookery after David's last happy afternoon with his mother, they bring 'a cold blast of air into the house' (8, p. 115). Steerforth remarks on his first visit to Yarmouth, ' "the sea roars as if it were hungry for us" ' (21, p. 311); moodily self-reproachful, he is in a ' "Devil's bark of a boat" ' (22, p. 322); later he describes himself as ' "a nautical phenomenon" ' (22, p. 323). For Barkis death is ' "going out with the tide" ' (30, p. 445). For Martha the Thames not only images her life, but also draws her to death, ' "it goes away, like my life, to a great sea, that is always troubled" ' (47, p. 681). Mr Peggotty, of course, lives in a boat, and David wonders if Ham is so called because the boat is ' "a sort of ark" ' (3, p. 32). Ham himself is a boat-builder with 'a natural ingenuity in that handicraft' (22, p. 325) – his trade ironically played off against Steerforth's leisure-class yachting. When Emily elopes the Yarmouth boat-house loses its *raison d'être*: ' "if ever a boat foundered" ', Mr Peggotty says, ' "that one's gone down" ' (32, p. 456). The whole complex of symbol and reality is also developed in a more straightforwardly metaphoric mode. David takes 'a last drowning look' (9, p. 53) at the lessons he recites before Murdstone; he has enough love for Dora 'to drown anybody in' (33, p. 474); Wickfield drowns his sorrows, a nice semantic revitalising of a stale phrase; Littimer speculates about Emily, ' "She may have drowned herself" ' (46, p. 670), a realist possibility that is a metaphoric truth. David in his chambers feels ' "like Robinson Crusoe" ' (24, p. 356); evidence in Doctors' Commons is 'just twice the length of Robinson Crusoe' (26, p. 387); Betsey sits amidst her baggage 'like a female Robinson Crusoe' (34, p. 497). Working for Heep, Mr Micawber — an indefatigable manufacturer of nautical images — is ' "the foundered Bark" ' (49, p. 701); after the 'explosion' of Heep he compares himself to ' "a gallant and eminent naval Hero" ' (52, p. 757), a role he turns into reality as the comically intrepid leader of his emigrant family. These are only a few examples out of many, for the actual sea that is the conceptual and realist core of it all is transposed through literally hundreds of variations. The fact that one can interpret these variations as the components of a semantic scheme — as figurative morphemes, so to speak — depends upon that conscious symbol-using that is central to Dickens's characterisation of David.

The conceptual organisation of the whole focuses upon David and the growth of what might be called his symbol consciousness. His first experience of the sea is at Yarmouth: 'I heard the wind howling out at sea and coming on across the flat so fiercely, that I had a lazy apprehension of the great deep rising in the night' (3, p. 34). The next morning, David's bravado before Emily has all the rash confidence of inexperience.

> 'You're quite a sailor, I suppose?' I said to Emily . . .
> 'No', replied Emily, shaking her head, 'I'm afraid of the sea.'
> 'Afraid!' I said, with a becoming air of boldness, and looking very big at the mighty ocean. 'I an't!' (3, p. 34)

One is reminded, irresistibly, of Yeats.

> Dance there upon the shore;
> What need have you to care
> For wind or water's roar?[12]

As David says, 'Time had not grown up himself yet' (3, p. 37); but it grows up very quickly, and after his mother's death David begins to understand the tragic significance of 'the mighty ocean': 'the wind came moaning on across the flat as it had done before. But I could not help fancying, now, that it moaned of those who were gone' (10, p. 143). After Emily's elopement, David recognises in the sea the almost inevitable analogue to the bereaved grief of Ham and Mr Peggotty.

> It was on the beach, close down by the sea, that I found them . . .
> they were both as grave and steady as the sea itself — then lying beneath
> a dark sky, waveless — yet with a heavy roll upon it, as if it breathed
> in its rest. (33, p. 456)

Reflective or not, the sea retains its separate life, breathing to a different rhythm than the men on shore. In his second 'Retrospect' David develops the relationship between the river and the sea – the same as that in *Dombey and Son* – though now seasonal imagery underpins the meaning.

> In a breath, the river that flows through our Sunday walk is sparkling in the summer sun, is ruffled by the winter wind, or thickened with drifting heaps of ice. Faster than river ever ran towards the sea, it flashes, darkens, and rolls away. (43, p. 627)

But, after all the changes of season, all the narrative developments – David's marriage, Emily's rescue – the constancy of change remains. Back at Yarmouth, David recognises that only the wind, the actualisation of transience itself, is continuous.

> In truth, the wind, though it was low, had a solemn sound and crept around the deserted house with a whispering wailing that was very mournful. Everything was gone . . . I thought of myself, lying here . . . I thought of the blue-eyed child who had enchanted me. I thought of Steerforth . . . (51, p. 739)

The climax of the process comes, of course, with the great storm scene in which Ham, Steerforth and the boat-house are all destroyed. The completion of a narrative pattern, the storm, simultaneously, completes a conceptual pattern, for all three are destroyed by time. The insistence upon the storm's being a real event is, at the same time, an insistence upon its emblematic significance. Not just *like* time the destroyer, the storm *is* time the destroyer. By this stage of the novel one has come to expect such a total identification of meaning and being; but the storm scene also carries the final movement in David's understanding of time, which is the final stage of his education in symbolic meaning.

> I was seriously affected, without knowing how much, by late events; and my long exposure to the fierce wind had confused me.

> Something within me, faintly answering to the storm without, tossed up the depths of my memory and made a tumult in them. (55, p. 789)

This is not a pathetic fallacy: David's mind does not merely reflect the storm, or the storm his mind. They become one; the storm lives equally and with equivalent effect in the perceiving consciousness and in the world it perceives. Steerforth's death realises David's memories.

> . . . he led me to the shore. And on that part of it where she and I had looked for shells, two children – on the part of it where some

lighter fragments of the old boat, blown down last night, had been
scattered by the wind – among the ruins of the home he had wronged
– I saw him lying with his head upon his arm, as I had often seen
him lie at school. (55, p. 795)

The long narrative, from Edenic childhood, through artificially prolonged
innocence, to betrayal and fall, is re-enacted, its successive stages become
simultaneous, concentrated into a single moment that is both actual and
emblematic. With this concurrence, the objective reality of time in the
physical presence of the tempest and David's individual awareness of
transience fuse. The process results in metaphysical therapy, teaching 'the
unhappy Present to recite the Past . . . where/long ago the accusations had
begun'.[13] In the storm David finds and understands the loss of Eden as,
simultaneously, an objective fact and a subjective reality. The Steerforth
who lies dead on the beach is also the Steerforth who has been 'tossed up'
from 'the depths' of David's memory. For David, at this point, there is
no separation between self and non-self or between self and others. By
reading his own consciousness in and through the tempest and its victims,
David identifies himself in man's tragic destiny in the lapsarian world, and
thus confronts the irreducible and ineluctable reality of death: 'never send
to know for whom the *bell* tolls; It tolls for *thee*.' By making such a
commitment David frees himself from the escapist delusions of the Edenic
fallacy. At the same time, he comes to an understanding of reality that,
metaphysical in its nature, goes beyond any solely ethical interpretation
of existence. Thematically, because the past has been confronted and
accepted, neither dwelt in nor forgotten, he can survive, rescue himself
from futile regret and Agnes from vain nostalgia, and remarry. David
becomes indeed the hero of learning, and what he learns, finally, is an
understanding of time and mortality.

Clearly, the function of emblematic realism in *David Copperfield* is a
development of *Dombey and Son*, more emphatic, more fully integrated with
the ethical concerns of the novel, more complex in orchestration. The
narrative movement that brings David, at last and inevitably, to the storm
at Yarmouth epitomises the conceptual movement of the novel. All attempts
to construe the real, all ethical structures, all responses to the need to survive
in the world resolve, at last and inevitably, in a confrontation with the nature
of time. Dickens conceives symbolism, realism, ethical inquiry and
conceptual patterning as parts of an imaginative whole, in which each and
every part is necessarily bound up in each and every other. This
interpenetration gives an extraordinary thickness, a multiple layering, to
the novel. The imaginative concentration of *David Copperfield* gives it a
unity unlike that of any earlier Dickens novel. But there is a further
development, not just of handling, but of concept and mood. In *Dombey
and Son* the meanings of symbolic reality are, essentially, positive. They
enable Florence to understand her world, and they translate easily into

action, thus becoming both the motivation for and the validation of her moral agency. In *David Copperfield*, however, the knowledge enforced by sea, wind and river is a knowledge of man's inevitable defeat by time. David can confront such knowledge and convert it into the basis for action and continuity, but the effort is prodigious. The more obvious strategy is retreat, a strategy David very nearly adopts in Switzerland. In *David Copperfield* the reality Dickens portrays is darker, more threatening, than in any of his previous novels, because its fundamental meanings imply negation. Retreat and defeat in the face of a world which seems insupportable and even nihilistic dominate the novels which follow.

5

'Bricked in on All Sides':
Symbolic Exemplification in *Bleak House* and *Hard Times*

As has been widely recognised, the fog and mud with which *Bleak House* opens are descriptive, simultaneously, of a physical and a metaphysical condition.[1] Fog is both a physical presence in the world the novel depicts and a symbol of spiritual blindness and of the suffocation of creative power. Immediately established as the epitome of such blindness and oppression, the Court of Chancery sits 'at the very heart of the fog' (1, p. 2). These are the semantic and expressive terms upon which the novel opens. In *Bleak House*, for the first time in Dickens's development, the coincidence of the symbolic and the real, and the meanings contained therein, are *données* and symbolic realism is the medium through which we must read the novel. Our acceptance of the fog as ' "a London particular" ' (4, p. 35), as a phenomenon in a real place at a real time, necessitates our acceptance of what it means, for meaning and being co-exist in the world described. But so also, in our response, there is no lacuna between experience and interpretation. Meaning and being are grasped in a single imaginative movement, their interpenetration recreated in the very process of reading. The world of the novel is read – as the novel itself is read – in terms of the fog, mud and water that are its pervasive realities.

In *Bleak House* the world 'possesses an immanent tendency toward decomposition'.[2]

> As much mud in the streets, as if the waters had but newly retired from the face of the earth . . . Smoke lowering down from chimney-pots, making a soft black drizzle . . . Fog everywhere. Fog up the river, where it flows among green aits and meadows; fog down the river, where it rolls defiled . . . (1, p. 1)

> The waters are out in Lincolnshire. An arch of the bridge in the park has been sapped and sapped away. The adjacent low-lying ground, for half a mile in breadth, is a stagnant river, with melancholy trees for islands in it, and a surface punctured all over, all day long, with falling rain. (2, p. 8)

Throughout the novel developments of and analogues to these basic emblematic realities stress the same process of deterioration and decay:

'the general smell and taste as of the ancient Dedlocks in their graves' (2, p. 9); the 'crowd of foul existence . . . in maggot numbers' (16, p. 220) in Tom-all-Alone's, and the 'nauseous air', 'infection and contagion', 'slime' and 'pestilential gas' (46, p. 626) the slum breeds. Chadband's 'oily exudations' (21, p. 357) and smoking forehead anticipate the 'thick, yellow liquor' and 'smouldering suffocating vapour' (32, pp. 454–5) that are the repulsive result of Krook's spontaneous combustion. The brickfields have 'miserable little gardens . . . growing nothing but stagnant pools' (8, p. 106); the burying-ground is 'pestiferous and obscene' (12, p. 151), Symond's Inn 'stale and close' with 'a loose outer surface of soot everywhere' (39, p. 547). Mr Tulkinghorn's chambers summarise the whole process and its universality: 'In his lowering magazine of dust, the universal article into which his papers and himself, and all his clients, and all things of earth, animate and inanimate are resolving, Mr Tulkinghorn sits' (32, p. 305). Natural decay towards death has accelerated; throughout the novel the world is actively running down, resolving itself into its primary elements of dust, slime and mist.

The symbolic realism through which the declining world of *Bleak House* is presented is, however, different in its nature from that of *Dombey and Son* and *David Copperfield*. In the earlier novels, the river, for example, symbolises personal time: the river is also, within the conventions of realism, real. Symbolic mediation – the sign standing between us and what is signified – and realist immediacy, forcefully held in the same entity, do not surrender their basic natures. They form, in effect, an amalgam. But in *Bleak House* fog cannot be said to symbolise opacity as the river symbolises personal time. It is precisely because the river is not, *in itself*, an instance of the operation of personal time that the mediatory nature of symbolism still obtains, whilst its presence in a realist medium gives its emblematic meaning immediacy. Fog, however, is, *in itself*, opaque: that is, connotation and denotation, metaphoric meaning and realist meaning are not amalgamated but synthesised. Such a synthesis is, more properly, labelled exemplification.

> An object [e.g. fog] that is literally or metaphorically denoted by a predicate [e.g. opacity], and refers to that predicate or the corresponding property, may be said to exemplify that predicate or property . . .[3]

Fog, literally and metaphorically, exemplifies opacity; similarly, details of physical disintegration exemplify a process of decay both actual and spiritual. It is precisely because the symbolism of *Bleak House* is exemplificatory that its meaning is a *donnée*: what the symbolism means is – in the most literal sense of the phrase – self-evident. *Bleak House* renders man's metaphysical condition tangible, exemplified in the very stuff of the world he inhabits. What is truly terrible about these self-evident meanings is that they seem inimical to life: confusion and decay are not just asserted as underlying truths, they are present in the very fact of the real.

As a defence against the intolerable prospect of such a world, people build their own worlds into which they can retreat. Society, as formulated in *Bleak House*, is, in effect, a kind of anti-society, a succession of private realities, each cut off from the other and sealed from the big world. The largest – and most intricately organised – private worlds are those of the Law and Chesney Wold. Law is self-perpetuating, maintaining itself on the endless reiteration of its own processes. Its systems expand to the proportions of what can only be called an alternative reality, epitomised by Jarndyce and Jarndyce: 'Innumerable children have been born into the cause; innumerable young people have married into it; innumerable old people have died out of it' (1, p. 4). Similarly self-perpetuating is the political world of the aristocracy, with its centre at Chesney Wold. National government becomes a choice 'between Lord Coodle and Sir Thomas Doodle – supposing it to be impossible for the Duke of Foodle to act with Goodle' (12, p. 160). The fatuous rhyming suggests meaningless yet perpetual repetition; in a system so tightly locked – verbally and actually – there can be no growth, only an illusion of change through the endless swapping over of the same aristocratic players. Both Chancery and Chesney Wold are solipsistic, concerned only with themselves: as such they are institutionalised analogues of the self-enclosure of the individual psyche. Characters live in mutual and self-imposed isolation, their cramped rooms and poky houses the physical realisation of their alienation: Krook's shop, the rooms of Nemo and Miss Flite, Mrs Jellyby's house, Tulkinghorn's chambers, the Snagsby drawing-room, Vholes's office in Symond's Inn, the Smallweeds' house, 'in a little narrow street, always solitary, shady, and sad, closely bricked in on all sides like a tomb' (21, p. 287). The kindly and well-meaning protect themselves by the same strategy: Charley locks up the other Neckett children for their own safety; Mrs Rouncewell sits in her housekeeper's room, speculating that ' "There may be a world beyond Chesney Wold that I don't understand" ' (7, p. 85). Absurdly, yet with an odd poignancy, the condition of the individual consciousness is epitomised by Prince Turveydrop's apprentice, who ' "waltzes by himself in the empty kitchen" ' (38, p. 537). The asylums that people build themselves are also prisons, and physical enclosure exemplifies man's spiritual imprisonment, just as the fog exemplifies his blindness. Characteristically, the prison/refuge generates its own, private, language, which results not in any communication which would alleviate the solitude of self, but in the perpetuation and aggravation of that solitude. Private language denies the whole basis of discourse because it establishes an esoteric relationship between symbol and referent. Words are denied their common currency – whatever reality they label is, ultimately, accessible only to the speaker. Consequently, the version of reality to which the speaker holds can never be scrutinised or – more important – criticised by anybody else. Thus the citadel of self-interest is protected by a wall of words. Turveydrop hides his selfishness by a solipsistic conversion of Deportment into an ethical – and conversational – *sine qua non*. Skimpole masks his callous indifference to anybody but himself in a calculatedly disingenuous arty patter that lacks moral or conceptual substance. Similarly exploitative, Chadband drains language of any specific meaning for the sake of a religiose aura.

> 'Now, my young friends, what is this Terewth, then? Firstly (in a spirit of love), what is the common sort of Terewth – the working clothes – the everyday wear, my young friends? Is it deception?' (25, p. 360)

The jargon of the Law and the self-interested Coodling and Doodling of the aristocracy are no different in kind. At the other end of the scale from these linguistic swindlers are those who cannot use language as a tool of social communication because they cannot construe themselves as part of any social context in which communication matters. Miss Flite chatters crazily in a language culled from Revelation; Jo, the victim of an exploitative and uncaring society, 'sums up his mental condition, when asked a question, by replying that he "don't know nothink" ' (16, p. 219).

The strategy of saving the self by the making of private worlds and languages tends always towards solipsism, which, by its very nature, makes even the idea of concerted action to stop the metaphysical rot impossible. The social – or, rather, anti-social – world of *Bleak House* derives directly from David Copperfield's experiences on the Dover Road. As Snagsby exclaims despairingly: ' "Why, this is a private asylum! Why, not to put too fine a point upon it, this is Bedlam, sir!" ' (47, p. 646). Without interpersonal contact, society ceases; people, mutually alienated and alienating, are reduced to the condition of objects randomly assembled without an informing organic pattern. *Bleak House* presents an exacerbation of the processes that characterise the world of *The Old Curiosity Shop*. With the radical fragmentation of human society objects break free, as it were, from their accustomed place in that society, and threaten to swamp it. Dickens's animism is expressive of a profound metaphysical disorder. When Esther and Caddy attempt 'to establish some order' in Mrs Jellyby's room, they are assailed by junk: 'bits of mouldy pie, sour bottles, Mrs Jellyby's caps, letters, tea, forks, odd boots and shoes of children . . .' (30, p. 420). The 'waste and ruin' that engulfs Mrs Jellyby's room is the physical expression of the incoherence of her moral view, for the ethical correlative to the disorder – social, linguistic and physical – that afflicts the *Bleak House* world is irresponsibility. As was discussed in the previous chapter, responsibility premises the significant relationship of cause and effect, a relationship that – if it obtains at all – cannot be perceived by so many of the novel's characters. Because complete irresponsibility negates any order between different social and/or metaphysical elements, junk is its perfect emblem, for junk is a collection of things which have no corporate meaning. Krook's shop, the brickfields, Tom-all-Alone's are all receptacles for the human and physical debris left from the collapse of social organisation. Jarndyce and Jarndyce resolves itself into the heap of rubbish it really is: 'great bundles of paper began to be carried out – bundles in bags, bundles too large to be got into any bags, immense masses of paper of all shapes and no shapes' (945, p. 865). Epitome and emblem of disorder, junk joins fog and slime in the novel's exemplificatory structure, presenting an image of a world in which irresponsibility, its analogues and consequences are universal.

Dickens's portrayal of a declining world comprising an implicitly infinite number of private realities, each one of which contributes to that decline, is, in effect, a portrayal of one time system within another. In the time system of the private world there is no temporal progression. Chancery proceedings and aristocratic politicking are entirely and endlessly circular, frustrating all attempts to move forward. Individual world-structures are similarly characterised by circularity or stagnation, by the constant repetition of the same patterns of thought and action. Such repetition must result in entrapment by the past. Because the exclusiveness of the closed world presupposes lack of responsibility towards others, the temporal structuring integral to responsibility becomes inaccessible. Cause and effect have no meaning to the solipsist to whom the self is both cause *and* effect. It becomes impossible to construe time as a linear progression: the present exists only as a dead enactment or recitation of the past and the future is literally unthinkable. Skimpole looks more like 'a damaged young man, than a well preserved elderly one' (6, p. 69); Mrs Bayham Badger obsessively catalogues the virtues of her dead husbands as Mrs Woodcourt obsessively recites the obscure mythology of her dead ancestor; for Turveydrop life ceased with Prinny and the Brighton Pavilion. This inability to escape the past – real or imagined – is, of course, the thematic spring of the novel's two main plots, Richard's involvement in Chancery and Lady Dedlock's secret history. Jarndyce and Jarndyce is ' "about a Will and the trusts under a Will" ' (8, p. 95); as such it suspends the present until the past is settled. By taking up the case Rick condemns himself to a kind of Limbo-on-earth: as he says to Esther, ' "There's no now for us suitors" ' (37, p. 524). Lady Dedlock's simultaneous obsession with, and rejection of, her past leaves her unreally suspended in time, condemned to a life that depends upon the constant reduplication of a self-image she knows to be false. The result is spiritual and emotional stasis. Her habitual enervation ('My Lady Dedlock says she has been "bored to death" ': 3, p. 9) and emotional sterility ('My Lady Dedlock . . . fell . . . into the freezing mood': 2, p. 10) are analogues to Richard's eternally postponed engagement with the present. But, if the private world is characterised by dead repetition and the absence of linear development, the time system of the big world offers little hope of release, for it is shown to be circular. The metaphysical deterioration exemplified

in fog, rain and mud does not form part of a linear progression, but part
of a temporal circle.

> As much mud in the streets, as if the waters had but newly retired
> from the face of the earth, and it would not be wonderful to meet a
> Megalosaurus, forty feet long or so, waddling like an elephantine lizard
> up Holborn Hill. Smoke lowering down from chimney-pots, making
> a soft black drizzle, with flakes of soot in it as big as full-grown
> snowflakes – gone into mourning, one might imagine, for the death
> of the sun. (1, p. 1)

At the commencement of the novel, the world appears to be returning to
its own beginnings, the retirement of the waters signalling the start of life
on earth. Just as surely, however, 'the death of the sun' signals its end.
Ending and beginning come together, the first chapter of Genesis occupies
the same space-time as the last chapter of Revelation.

If the self, in *Bleak House*, is a prison, the world outside the self – full
of people who cannot contact each other, lacking any apparent pattern,
with a time system that merely returns to its own beginning – is like a
maze. Just as the interiors in *Bleak House* exemplify the constriction of
self, exteriors and townscapes exemplify the labyrinthine nature of the world
at large. Krook's courtyard, Cook's Court, Lincoln's Inn all cluster together
in a mysterious urban network, where children play 'the game of hide and
seek' and lie 'in ambush about the byways of Chancery Lane' (32, p. 443)
in a comic parody of the adult world. George's shooting gallery is located
in 'that curious region lying about the Haymarket and Leicester Square',
'a large medley of shabbiness and shrinking out of sight' (21, p. 302). Tom-
all-Alone's, with its troglodyte population, is even more labyrinthine.

> Mr Snagsby passes along the middle of a villainous street . . . Branching
> from this street and its heaps of ruins, are other streets and courts
> . . . the crowd . . . fades away up alleys and into ruins, and behind
> walls . . . and flits about them up the alleys, and in the ruins, and
> behind the walls as before. (22, pp. 310–11)

The climactic maze image is that which dominates Bucket's and Esther's
pursuit of Lady Dedlock, whose doubling-back significantly suggests the
process of time itself. Through Esther's response, Dickens gives a
paradigmatic individual experience of the maze-world: 'I was far from sure
that I was not in a dream. We rattled with great rapidity through such a
labyrinth of streets, that I soon lost all idea where we were' (57, p. 770).
The effect of actually being *in* the maze – an effect that, as Esther
recognises, has analogies to dreaming – is realised directly in *Bleak House*
through Dickens's use of the historical present for the third-person
narration. Miller's account of this cannot, I think, be bettered:

'The actual manner of human existence in time is here represented in language in a way that it never can be in the past-tense form of narration. We are here in a world which has a non-determined future.'[4] Through its very linguistic nature, Dickens's narrative recreates a world in which everything is always in the process of becoming, in the process of being realised to the perceiver.

> On such an afternoon, if ever, the Lord High Chancellor ought to be sitting here – as here he is . . . some score of members of the High Court of Chancery out to be – as here they are – mistily engaged . . . in an endless cause . . . the various solicitors . . . ought to be – as are they not? – ranged in a line . . . (1, p. 2)

The movement from conditional 'ought' to definitive 'is' enacts the process of making real, the process of perception itself. At the beginning of the novel the reader occupies a position precisely similar to that of a character in it, unable to apprehend anything other than that which is immediately presented to him. Perceptually, this is like being in a fog; temporally, like being in a maze, unable to anticipate what lies around the next corner: the two exemplificatory symbol systems reinforce one another.

Within this historical-present narrative Dickens sets the first-person past-tense narration of Esther Summerson. The use of the past tense predicates finiteness, a future that is assured because already known, and Esther's narration becomes for the reader 'a point of rest in a flickering and bewildering world'.[5] But, although her narrative is a refuge, it only manages to be so by virtue of the drastic limitations it places on the world of experience so vividly and disturbingly enacted through the omniscient narration. The two narratives of *Bleak House* pull reader-response in opposite and potentially contradictory directions: the one towards imaginative safety, the other towards imaginative danger. Worked into this conflict, and a manifestation of it, is the presentation of Esther's moral agency. The world she organises in *Bleak House* has its basis in determinedly human values of love and mutual responsibility. But it is also a closed maze, and *Bleak House* itself has all the puzzlement typical of the labyrinth.

> . . . if . . . you came back into my room, and went out at the door by which you had entered it, and turned up a few crooked steps that branched off in an unexpected manner from the stairs, you lost yourself in passages . . . Or you might, if you came out at another door (every room had at least two doors) go straight down to the hall again by half-a-dozen steps and a low archway, wondering how you get back there, or had ever got out of it. (6, pp. 65–6)

The sinister parallels with Tom-all-Alone's and the London streets are to the reader, experienced in the omniscient narration, obvious; but for Esther the house is just 'delightfully irregular' (6, p. 65). She is, indeed, its perfect tenant, for the labyrinthine enclosure of Bleak House is the exemplification of her own obsessive, reiterative consciousness. Esther's constant need to record compliments, always with the same kind of disclaimer, her repeated apostrophes to the deity of Duty, the restrictive nature of the pet names she so gleefully rehearses – 'Old Woman, and Little Old Woman, and Cobweb, and Mrs Shipton, and Mother Hubbard, and Dame Durden' (8, p. 98) – all are diagnostic of the closed world. She binds together the different inmates of Bleak House in an inescapable and possessive emotionalism, for Bleak House is a prison as well as a refuge, and the emblem of Esther's wardership is, of course, her bunch of keys. Esther answers the threat of change by keeping Bleak House firmly locked, with herself and the others inside it. The keys are a constant reassurance, a constant restatement of her power.

> I thought, all at once, if my guardian had married some one else, how should I have felt, and what should I have done! That would have been a change indeed. It presented my life in such a new and blank form, that I rang my house-keeping keys and gave them a kiss before I laid them down in their basket again. (44, p. 612)

Whenever Esther leaves Bleak House, she does so with colonial intent, annexing other people's territory in a kind of philanthropic imperialism. She takes over the Jellyby household prior to Caddy's wedding, 'attempting to establish some order among all [the] waste and ruin' (30, p. 420). After Caddy's confinement, Esther tells us, 'I took the supreme direction of her apartment, trimmed it up, and pushed her, couch and all, into a lighter and more airy and cheerful corner' (50, p. 683). Caddy is, indeed, pushed into a corner, more cheerful perhaps, but a corner nevertheless. She exchanges the tyranny of her mother's anarchy for the dictatorship of Esther's ruthlessly efficient kindliness. Similarly, when Ada announces her marriage with a statement of her separateness, ' "I am not going home again" ' (51, p. 696), Esther's response is to take 'home' to Ada: ' "I am only going away to come back tomorrow . . . I shall be always coming backwards and forwards" ' (51, p. 698). Esther, in the end, rules a tiny benevolent empire: she is, as Skimpole recognises, the centre of ' "the whole orderly system" ' (37, p. 531). By consent of her subjects, her rule is absolute, and she maintains it with an unflagging zeal.

Outside Esther's empire, however, the big world remains, unamenable to her control: Jo and Lady Dedlock cannot be 'Bleak Housed' in the way others are. When Esther does leave home territory to try to help Jo, she half-recognises that, to do so, she would need a very different strategy towards the real.

. . . I had for a moment an undefinable impression of myself as being something different from what I then was . . . I have ever since connected the feeling with that spot and time, to the distant voices in the town, the barking of the dog, and the sound of wheels coming down the miry hill. (31, p. 429)

The next, and last, time she leaves Bleak House on a mission that is not colonial is to look for her mother, and Bucket points the parallel: 'As we ascended the hill, he . . . reminded me that I had come down it one night, as I had reason for remembering, with my little servant and poor Jo . . .' (57, p. 773). Esther could, indeed, have been 'something different', for her unacknowledged identity is that of a participant in the world that lies beyond the confines of Bleak House. The central tragedy of her story is that she cannot learn to live in that world; instead she builds a private world based upon retreat. After all the vicissitudes of the plot, Esther fetches up in a duplicate Bleak House, with Ada, Jarndyce and a new Richard, with Woodcourt safely drawn in as well. Everything merely repeats itself, with little hope for future vitality and, unlike David in *David Copperfield*, without any acknowledged engagement in the big world.

I have never lost my old names, nor has [Jarndyce] lost his; nor do I ever, when he is with us, sit in any other place than in my old chair at his side. Dame Trot, Dame Durden, Little Woman! all just the same as ever; and I answer, Yes, dear Guardian! just the same. (67, p. 879)

Esther's stability and the security of her benevolent rule are guaranteed by a self-perpetuating emotional clique; her potential for 'being something different', for active moral agency in the world, goes unrealised. The conclusion of *Bleak House* presents an ironic triumph of self-enclosure.

Only one character consistently eschews the safety of a private reality and survives – Inspector Bucket. In the context of symbolic exemplification, Bucket's knowledge of the London labyrinth – he guides both Snagsby and Esther through it – is expressive not only of professional expertise, but also of moral power. Bucket adopts none of the escapist strategies the novel presents. Instead he seeks a narrative logic that will link disparate realities and private worlds into a significantly related whole, a pattern of cause and effect that will explain the configuration of one part of the existential maze. Bucket has the clearest grasp of the implications of subjectivity. Discussing Tulkinghorn's murder, he explains, ' "When I depict it as a beautiful case . . . I mean from my point of view. As considered from other points of view, such cases will always involve more or less of unpleasantness" ' (53, p. 719). Bucket recognises both the authority of a reality beyond the self, and the limitations of the self's view of that reality. This understanding of the ambiguities in man's engagement with the real is combined with a willing acceptance of the unpredictability of the future,

the necessary condition of living in the present − ' "You don't know what
I'm going to say and do, five minutes from this present time" ' (54, p. 729).
Such insight gives Bucket a unique freedom of action: 'Time and place
cannot bind Mr Bucket. Like man in the abstract, he is here to-day and
gone to-morrow − but, very unlike man indeed, he is here again the next
day' (53, p. 713). Bucket's strength comes from his acknowledgement and
adoption of a *public* life in a world of private realities. His agency in that
public world is defined by his duty to detection; not, however, as a
professional exercise, but as a symbolic quest for truth, a quest that he knows
can be compromised by personal considerations. ' "Duty is duty, and
friendship is friendship. I never want the two to clash if I can help it" '
(49, p. 677). Bucket, in seeking truth, seeks to know an objective reality,
and his duty is towards that rather than towards a more or less private world
order. Bucket is the detective as quester and, as such, the moral hero of
Bleak House. His heroism is, however, qualified. Bucket can construe the
maze, he can even try to save people from it, but he has no power to change
it. Florence Dombey's knowledge of the meaning of the real converted easily
into positive and ameliorative action; David Copperfield's understanding
of time made possible a new and constructive alignment towards the past
and the present. The nature of the *Bleak House* world, however, means
that confrontation with the real is confrontation with negation exemplified.
Esther never risks such a confrontation; Bucket survives it because he is
not involved. His pursuit of abstract truth never threatens him, never
implicates him personally as a human being. His moral heroism − unlike
Florence's or David's − remains dissociated from life as it is lived and felt.

In *Bleak House* Dickens creates a world emphatically real in place, time
and social structure; but the components of this reality symbolically
exemplify circularity, frustration, fragmentation and imprisonment. No
human strategy depicted in the novel is, in the end, adequate to deal with
such a world. The unqualified positives the novel does offer are, for the
first time in Dickens's *œuvre*, not present in the world it pictures, for they
are the implicit positives of aesthetic coherence, the positives exemplified
by the complex organisation of an elaborate work of art. That reality as
presented in *Bleak House can* be construed and contained within an
intellectual, imaginative and emotional whole emerges self-evidently from
the fact of the novel itself. Nevertheless, the substance of that reality remains
inescapably negative. Esther, for all her virtues and her glimpses of a larger
spiritual life, never comes to terms with what the reality outside the walls
of Bleak House means. Bucket masters the maze, but only because he has
a final detachment from the human concerns of the people within it.
Characters who are exposed to the full inimical power of the real − Lady
Dedlock, Richard and Jo − lacking either Bucket's genius for detection
or Esther's for protection, are relentlessly destroyed.[6] As for the rest, Sir
Leicester, broken by grief, rides pathetically round the deserted Chesney
Wold with Trooper George as his nurse; Miss Flite stays locked in the

insane world of Chancery; Caddy's baby is deaf and dumb; Mrs Jellyby goes on with her futile schemes; the Smallweeds and Chadband carry on largely unmolested; Skimpole writes his autobiography and accuses John Jarndyce of ingratitude. The best one can say is that the Bagnets survive and that Woodcourt is probably a good doctor. It is pitifully little. Above all, nobody's survival or destruction affects Chancery, and nobody halts the progress of the world's decay. Forster, taking up Dickens's description of the novel as dwelling 'upon the romantic side of familiar things' (Preface, p. xiv), relabels it as 'the romance of discontent and misery'.[7] Esther might find comfort in her hope of another world 'that sets this right' (65, p. 871), but, meanwhile, the world of *Bleak House* is bleak indeed.

In *Hard Times* the reality that confronts man is phantasmagoric.[8]

> In the hardest working part of Coketown; in the innermost fortifications of that ugly citadel, where Nature was as strongly bricked out as killing airs and gases were bricked in; at the heart of the labyrinth of narrow courts upon courts, and close streets upon streets, which had come into existence piecemeal, every piece in a violent hurry for some one man's purpose, and the whole an unnatural family, shouldering, and trampling, and pressing one another to death; in the last close nook of this giant exhausted receiver, where the chimneys, for want of air to make a draught, were built in an immense variety of stunted and crooked shapes . . . lived a certain Stephen Blackpool. (I, 10, p. 63)

Coketown concentrates all those characteristics exemplified in the London of *Bleak House*: imprisonment, labyrinthine confusion, decay, fragmentation, a wilderness of junk invested with a weird and hostile animism. But there is a difference, which is more than one of compression. The condition of man in *Bleak House* results from and testifies to a colossal negligence, man's inability even to understand the necessity of putting his own world in order. Coketown, however, is the physical and metaphorical expression of a deliberate system, and Dickens clearly points us to a reading of the town as exemplificatory: 'Fact, fact, fact, everywhere in the material aspect of the town; fact, fact, fact, everywhere in the immaterial' (I, 5, p. 23). Coketown both means and is System. In *Hard Times* the existential characteristics exemplified by the world of *Bleak House* have become the *a priori* bases for a new and aggressively evangelical systematisation of industrial and urban man.

The system proper is an alliance of *laissez-faire* capitalism and the socio-political doctrines of utilitarianism, represented by Bounderby and Gradgrind respectively. The alienation of man from man is not the unforeseen consequence of their system, but its first cause. Bentham's greatest good of the greatest number is ironically reduced to the free play of market forces and the anti-ethics of a free-for-all. Bitzer sums up: ' "the whole social system is a question of self-interest. What you must always appeal to is a person's self-interest. It's your only hold. We are so constituted" ' (III, 8, p. 288). Antithetically generated by the combination of capitalism and utilitarianism is the equally systematised trade-union socialism of Slackbridge. A triumvirate of isms, the three systems carve up Coketown between them. Each system institutionalises the language of the closed world and turns it into jargon and cant. Gradgrind and the Commissioner chant their utilitarian magic word in a secular catechism: ' "Fact, fact, fact!" said the gentleman. And "Fact, fact, fact!" repeated Thomas Gradgrind' (I, 2, p. 7). Bounderby obsessively repeats self-aggrandising lies and self-justifying clichés; Slackbridge's mere 'froth and fume' (II, 4, p. 138) is a kind of automatic language, which, in its piling up of semantically void phrases and apostrophes, is directly reminiscent of Chadband. System-language is utterly irrelevant to human needs, for each system relies for its continuance upon the reduction of the individual to a manipulable object. A classroom full of children becomes an 'inclined plane of little vessels then and there arranged in order' (I, 1, p. 2) in which Sissy Jupe is ' "Girl number twenty" ' (I, 2, p. 3); capitalism, by a telling synecdoche, reduces the millworkers to ' "the Hands" ' and would have preferred them to have been born 'only hands, or, like the lower creatures of the seashore, only hands and stomachs' (I, 10, p. 63); Slackbridge's socialism in no way disputes such mass-labelling, merely turning it into the equally de-personalised jargon of ' "friends, and fellow-sufferers, and fellow-workmen, and fellow-men" ' (II, 4, p. 138). Despite the assertiveness – or, perhaps, because of it – the last thing such terms suggest is fellowship. Each system denies man any higher destiny than that of being an item in an ism, an economic object, one of many 'all very like one another' (I, 5, p. 22). Ironically, however, it is the champions of System who are the primary victims of their own programmes of de-humanisation. Gradgrind turns himself into a thing, his features surrealistically petrified into a 'square wall of a forehead, which had his eye-brows for its base, while his eyes found commodious cellarage in two dark caves, over-shadowed by the wall' (I, 1, p. 1). Bounderby's face has undergone a repulsive necrosis[9] that turns it into nothing but bloated flesh: 'a great puffed head and forehead, swelled veins in his temples, and such a strained skin . . . that it seemed to hold his eyes open, and lift his eyebrows up' (I, 4, p. 14).[10] As mechanical as his oratory, Slackbridge's gestures are those of a clockwork man, 'wiping his hot forehead – always from left to right, and never the reverse way' (II, 4, p. 141).

Although shown as their own victims, Bounderby, Slackbridge and – until the later stages of the novel – Gradgrind are presented without pathos. The pathetic and, to some extent, tragic dimensions of other victims of System – Stephen, Louisa, and even the despicable Tom – depend upon the characters' having some self-reflexive consciousness of their own fate.

The crusaders for System have no such self-awareness, for they are depicted as lacking any kind of inner life. It is precisely through this absence of inwardness that *Hard Times* makes its central statement, for it is not just a function of satiric characterisation, but of theme and thematic expression. Gradgrind, Bounderby and Slackbridge do not lose their inner life because Dickens, in his anger, has reduced them to the de-personalised representatives of world-views for which he has no sympathy. Imaginatively, it is not Dickens who de-humanises them: in their fixated pursuit of the systems they support, they de-humanise themselves. Just as Coketown exemplifies man's condition, so also do Gradgrind, Bounderby and Slackbridge exemplify their own systems – they *are* what System *means*. By the very nature of exemplification, the reader experiences their actual de-humanity, not just their endorsement of de-humanisation. The reader's more or less abstract understanding of thematic material is thus constantly registered as direct experience. With the synthesis of meaning and being in the characterisation of the trio of system-mongers, it becomes clear that Dickens is not primarily concerned with System as a socio-politico-economic – or whatever else – phenomenon, but with the ontology of System. Gradgrind, Bounderby and Slackbridge express, both verbally and in being, an alternative mode of existence. The 'life' they exemplify, and that they offer humanity, is nothing less than a conversion of man into machine, a hideous other-life in which limbs move and mouths talk in response, not to vitality, but to mechanical stimulation. The description of Gradgrind teaching the children makes this explicit:

> . . . he seemed a kind of cannon loaded to the muzzle with facts, and prepared to blow them clean out of the regions of childhood at one discharge. He seemed a galvanizing apparatus, too, charged with a grim mechanical substitute for the tender young imaginations that were to be stormed away. (I, 2, p. 3)

The children must first be killed and then, like so many products of Frankenstein, turned into galvanic creatures, socio-economic automata like Bitzer who 'looked as though, if he were cut, he would bleed white' (I, 2, p. 5). This metamorphosis is to be achieved not only by suppressing the imaginative and instinctive – epitomised by the injunction 'Never wonder' (I, 8, p. 48) – but also by proscribing all forms of understanding that have their basis in the world outside System. Thus Gradgrind refuses to allow Sissy even to mention the circus – ' "We don't want to know anything about that" ' (I, 2, p. 4) – and dismisses her actual experience of the horse-riding in preference for Bitzer's definition of a horse: ' "Quadruped. Gramnivorous. Forty teeth, namely twenty-four grinders, four eye-teeth, and twelve incisive . . . etc." ' (I, 2, p. 5). Such a process, in effect, de-contextualises the act of knowing, for Bitzer's horse does not inhabit any world that people really experience. It is an assembly-line product, made out of anatomical bits which once possessed the life the horse now simulates. Gradgrind is dangerously wrong to claim that Bitzer's equine machine is ' "what a horse is" ', for being can only be conceived holistically, never as an assemblage of attributes. Gradgrind mechanises the very process of experience and thus destroys the organic link between the perceiving consciousness and the world it perceives, very much the same process Wordsworth describes as leading to 'a universe of death'.[11] The phrase is apposite, for Gradgrind's system, in alienating the knower from the known, turns the world into a dead collection of dead fragments. It is System's effect upon man's sense of being that matters to Dickens. His engagement with the real in *Hard Times* is, as always, far more than 'social criticism'. To transpose terms from linguistics, the surface structure of social organisation stands, for Dickens, as the phenomenal evidence for a metaphysical deep structure. In this his debt to Carlyle, and in particular to the attack on the cash nexus in *Past and Present*, is obvious.[12] Dickens, like Carlyle, is concerned for the state man is in – the realm of the social critic – because his root concern is with the nature of man – the realm of the ontologist. The Coketown isms are wrong, not primarily because of their social inadequacy but, far more basically, because of their metaphysical inadequacy.

Man's metaphysical identity is conveyed, in *Hard Times* as in *Dombey and Son* and *David Copperfield*, through his existence in time, and it is upon the nature of man as a temporal creature that the systems founder, for they lack all concept of mankind 'walking against time towards the infinite world' (I, 8, p. 49). Time establishes the organisational principle of the novel through the traditional agrarian pattern of the three books, 'Sowing', 'Reaping' and 'Garnering'; 'the industrial period of the novel is thus set within the wider context of man's history'.[13] Time is also imaged as 'The Great Manufacturer', 'always with an immense variety of work on hand, in every stage of development' (I, 14, p. 90), both subsuming and parodying Bounderby's much vaunted industrial manufacture. But the universality of time, figuratively embracing both rural and urban man, is never actualised in the sense of becoming part of the realist fabric of the novel. The agrarian divisions, time as a manufacturer, remain as conventional symbolic structures. They form the parts of a specifically authorial technique for contextualising the events of the narrative. In contrast to *Dombey and Son* and *David Copperfield*, they have no presence in the real world in which those events take place, so to speak, that can be read as a key to man's role in a larger metaphysical pattern. The meanings exemplified in and by Coketown are wholly reductive and, indeed, nihilistic; they cannot even be countered by the partial strategies adopted by Bucket and Esther in *Bleak House*, since only those strategies prescribed by System are available. System turns temporal process into a bleakly mechanical pilgrimage to the grave, measured by Gradgrind's 'deadly statistical clock' (I, 15, p. 96), epitomised by the surreal image of the undertaker's black ladder, kept so that people 'who had done their daily groping up and down the narrow stairs might slide out of this working world by the windows' (I, 10, p. 66). Such a world is without hope, for there is not even the hope of man's being able to understand his own position. Louisa's despair is utterly logical: ' "my dismal resource has been to think that life would soon go by, and that nothing in it could be worth the pain and trouble of a contest" ' (II, 12, p. 217).

What is needed for the defeat of the nihilism exemplified by the Coketown world is an imaginative militancy consistently directed against the rule of System and towards a creative apprehension of man's relationship to time. The spiritual renaissance necessary to defeat the metaphysics of the machine never arrives. Although the circus, as Leavis has pointed out, does represent 'a humane, anti-Utilitarian positive',[14] by its very nature it is disengaged from the society the novel portrays. The circus is simply not central enough to become the agent of human regeneration. Rather, as Sleary recognises, it is a social placebo, the source of temporary relief from the inhumanities of Coketown. ' "People mutht be amuthed. They can't be alwayth a learning, nor yet they can't be alwayth a working, they an't made for it. You *mutht* have uth, Thquire" ' (III, 8, p. 293). System and circus exist in an uneasy truce, and the Sleary 'philosophy' is pragmatically reduced to ' "make the betht of uth: not the wortht" ' (I, 6, p. 41). The different forces of the novel are stalemated. Nevertheless, Dickens explores two new strategies of consciousness that attempt to resolve − or, at least, escape − the deadlock, strategies that are important in the development of Dickens's symbolic realism: Stephen's access to a transcendental vision, and Louisa's conscious use of interpretative metaphor. Dying in Old Hell Pit, Stephen perceives the real in two distinct ways. First, a social and political vision of urban man's condition, threatened by his own industrial creation, which has taken on a hostile life of its own.

> 'I ha' fell into th' pit, my dear, as have cost wi'in the knowledge o' old folk now livin', hundreds and hundreds o' men's lives . . . When it were in work it killed wi'out need; when 'tis let alone, it kills wi'out need. See how we die an' no need, one way an' another − in a muddle − every day!' (III, 6, p. 272)

Set against this, and significantly distinct from it, is the vision of the star, a specifically Christian vision of transcendence, derived directly from Esther Summerson's hope for 'the world that sets this right'.

> 'It ha' shined upon me . . . in my pain and trouble down below. It ha' shined into my mind . . . wi' it shinin' on me − I ha' seen more clear, and ha' made it my dyin' prayer that aw th' world may on'y coom toogether more . . .' (III, 6, p. 273)

The two world-views, taken together, are reminiscent of the 'dead mankind' figure in *The Old Curiosity Shop*. But, there, man's mortal condition and his immortal nature were imaged as the inter-related components of a single symbolic structure, as the two halves of a metaphysical whole. In *Hard Times*, the two halves have split apart. Man as defined by the muddle, and man as defined by the star are imaginatively discrete, their separation announced through the prose organisation itself in the clear demarcation between Stephen's two speeches. The meaning of the star, moreover, has none of the immanence of the symbolic reality of, for example, the sea and the river in *Dombey and Son* or *David Copperfield*. The meanings Stephen ascribes to it have, thus, no realist guarantee, for the semantic of time and eternity has been withdrawn from the world of direct experience. The symbol and the real have been divorced and, although Stephen's understanding is endorsed by Dickens – 'The star had shown him where to find the God of the poor' (III, 6, p. 274) – its justification is shown to rest in an act of faith, not in an act of perception. Unlike Florence, unlike David, Stephen must seek the metaphysical meaning of his own life beyond the empiric fact of the real.

Louisa Gradgrind consciously uses the metaphor of fire in a similar way, to provide an interpretative context within which she can seek to understand her own life – a strategy reminiscent of the furnace-man in, again, *The Old Curiosity Shop*. Fire, in *Hard Times*, is a binary image, simultaneously figuring energy and transience.

> 'Are you consulting the chimneys of the Coketown works, Louisa?'
> 'There seems to be nothing but languid and monotonous smoke. Yet when the night comes, Fire bursts out, father!' (I, 15, p. 100)

> 'I was . . . looking at the red sparks dropping out of the fire, and whitening, and dying. It made me think, after all, how short my life would be, and how little I could hope to do in it.' (I, 8, p. 54)

Fire exemplifies processes both vital and wasting; Louisa interprets such processes in the terms of a personal metaphor. She uses fire emblematically as a tool with which to interpret the determinant forces of her consciousness and her life. The night before Gradgrind announces Bounderby's proposal of marriage, Louisa, having spent the evening fire-gazing, stands outside Stone Lodge watching the Coketown chimneys.

> It seems as if, first in her own fire within the house, and then in the fiery haze without, she tried to discover what kind of woof Old Time, that greatest and longest-established Spinner of all, would weave from the threads he had already spun into a woman. But his factory is a secret place, his work is noiseless, and his Hands are mutes. (I, 14, pp. 94–5)

In *Dombey and Son* or *David Copperfield* the meanings Louisa seeks would have been *there*, built into the fabric of the empiric world. But in *Hard Times* all exemplified meanings – the semantic of Coketown – are negative, and, in complement, all transcendent meanings – the semantic of the star – are withdrawn. Without the support of the real, the quest for understanding is forced back into the self, and Louisa becomes a metaphor-maker. It is important to realise the way in which such metaphor-making works. Unlike the waves, for example, in *Dombey and Son*, the fire is *conventionally* symbolic in nature. Although fire exists objectively in the everyday reality of the novel, its specific meaning does not, for it is subjectively imposed by Louisa in the attempt to construe the self. Because meaning resides, not in the fire's being, but in Louisa's interpretation, its symbolism retains its mediatory nature. Thus, by thinking her life into the terms of a metaphor, Louisa can both identify the realities of living in the System world – the suppression of creativity, the exhaustion of energy, the transience of the individual – and protect herself, via symbolic mediation, from direct confrontation with the nihilistic force of those realities. Metaphor-making allows Louisa to face the truth without being destroyed by it.

Neither Louisa nor Stephen defeats System. Williams is right, I think, to say that Dickens provides 'no social alternatives to Bounderby and Gradgrind' and that, consequently, *Hard Times* has nowhere 'any active Hero'.[15] Nevertheless, Stephen's and Louisa's struggle towards a true apprehension of their state and, beyond that, towards some kind of hope, is heroic. The imaginative and spiritual alternatives to a world of repression and negation that they discover are, for Dickens, of crucial importance, and they recur as central elements in *Little Dorrit* and *A Tale of Two Cities*.

6

'The Prison of This Lower World':
Reality and the Transcendental in *Little Dorrit*

Lionel Trilling's seminal essay[1] on *Little Dorrit*[2] first identified the image of the prison and the theme of imprisonment as the imaginative core of the novel. In the context of Dickens's symbolic realism, however, his statement that the 'symbol, or emblem of the book . . . is the prison' needs closer definition.[3] Because a symbolic relationship is by its nature mediatory, the Marshalsea – to take the novel's major prison – cannot be said to *symbolise* imprisonment. The Marshalsea quite simply *is* an actual prison. The relationship between prison and imprisonment is exemplificatory rather than symbolic. The technique of exemplification is as central to *Little Dorrit* as it is to *Bleak House* with the fog and the London maze, and *Hard Times* with Coketown. Thus the prison – with its counterparts – is the novel's central realist property. The opening chapters present prison after prison: the Marseilles gaol, the quarantine quarters, London locked and barred for the Sabbath, Mrs Clennam's room, the Marshalsea itself. Come full circle, the novel ends with Amy and Clennam being married from the Marshalsea. Because of the nature of exemplification, however, the physical prison predicates the mental prison. Clennam cannot rid himself of a pervasive sense of family guilt; his mother locks herself away within the life-defeating austerity of religious mania; even with wealth and physical freedom William Dorrit cannot escape his own past; despite any and all kindness, Miss Wade paranoiacally reads reality as a conspiracy against herself. Indeed, her 'History of a Self-Tormentor' (II, 21) was expressly designed by Dickens as an epitome of the novel's imprisonment theme: 'In Miss Wade I had an idea . . . of making the introduced story so fit into surroundings impossible of separation from the main story, as to make the blood of the book circulate through both.'[4] As so often in Dickens, imprisonment both protects the self and alienates the individual from his fellows, that alienation being expressed in and through private languages. Flora's conversation, despite its inventiveness and energy, constantly becomes self-communion; both Plornish and Mrs Chivery lose all sense in a plethora of qualifying clauses; Edmund Sparkler drawls through the aristocratic slang that is his substitute for discourse; Casby supports his phoney reputation upon hollow phrases and empty repetitions; Mr F.'s Aunt reduces conversation to random outbursts of meaningless verbal aggression.

Conceptually, the social world of *Little Dorrit* is a series of self-enclosing and self-structuring realities. As in *Bleak House*, the nature of this social complex is labyrinthine, a maze of small prisons. The London streets are 'gloomy, close and stale' (I, 3, p. 28); the Clennam house is buried amidst 'the crooked and descending streets which lie (and lay more crookedly and closely then) between the river and Cheapside' (I, 3, p. 31). The Marshalsea, 'Itself a close and confined prison for debtors', contains within it 'a much closer and more confined jail for smugglers' (I, 6, p. 57). The theatre where Fanny works is 'a maze of dust, where a quantity of people were tumbling over one another' (I, 20, p. 234); Miss Wade's lodgings in London lie in 'a labyrinth near Park Lane' (I, 28, p. 324). Presiding over the labyrinth and epitomising it is the Circumlocution Office, a fusion of *Bleak House*'s Chancery and *Hard Times*'s System, apotheosised into the *primum mobile* of this 'right little, tight little, island' (I, 6, p. 57). Chancery and industrio-urban System at least premissed some kind of end-product; the Circumlocution Office is thought of as 'a heaven-born institution, that had an absolute right to do whatever it liked' (I, 10, pp. 106–7), accountable to nobody and nothing, committed only to self-perpetuation. Exemplifying its own system, and the national system it runs, the Circumlocution Office – like the world outside – is imaged as a physical maze of enclosing, gaol-like interiors.

> For Mr Tite Barnacle, Mr Arthur Clennam made his fifth inquiry one day at the Circumlocution Office; having on previous occasions awaited that gentleman successively in a hall, a glass case, a waiting room, and a fire-proof passage where the department seemed to keep its wind. (I, 10, p. 107)

The operating principle of the labyrinth, the 'Whole Science of Government' is 'HOW NOT TO DO IT' (I, 10, p. 104). In this context of paradoxically active irresponsibility, society re-forms on the basis of human fragmentation, the condition of the maze-world. Only the relationships of the cash nexus prevail – relationships, that is, between things not people; the only debts that can be understood are those of the account-book. Such a system precludes kindness, let alone *caritas*. Mrs Clennam's harshly retributive morality – 'Smite thou my debtors, Lord, wither them, crush them' (I, 5, p. 47) – has the same concept of debt and the same lack of charity as lie behind Pancks's ironic defence of Casby's *rentier* morality: ' "You're not going to keep open house for all the poor of London . . . You're not going to lodge 'em for nothing. You're not going to open your gates wide and let 'em come in free" ' (I, 13, p. 156). The 'them' of Casby's financial debtors and the 'them' of Mrs Clennam's moral debtors are similarly cast beyond the pale, reduced to an alien species.

Financial exaction, and the religious analogy to it, suborn and replace human connectedness in order to establish an anti-society that both epitomises and institutionalises human alienation. Because, in *Little Dorrit*, money maketh man, it also maketh the maze that ensnares him.

In a world that has dumped human inter-relation in preference for the ties bought by hard cash, the dynamic of a human moral order is replaced by the dead machine of propriety. By espousing propriety, Mrs General can make spurious sense of the labyrinth world.

> . . . it occurred to Mrs General . . . that she might harness the
> proprieties to the carriage of some rich young heiress or widow, and
> become at once the driver and guard of such vehicle through the social
> mazes. (II, 2, p. 447)

In providing a chimera of moral structure – her famous cultivation of 'surface' – for the indifference of the Circumlocution Office and the economic system it supports, she does the groundwork for Mrs Merdle's 'Society'. Thus, when Dorrit joins ' "wealthy and distinguished society" ' (II, 5, p. 480), he abandons the human context provided by Amy's love and substitutes the machinery of Mrs General's proprieties. As a consequence, Fanny must be educated out of consciousness, she ' "forms too many opinions. Perfect breeding forms none" ' (II, 5, p. 473). Amy, like Louisa Gradgrind before her, must learn that ' "it is better not to wonder" ' (ibid.), forget that language can be used as a means of expression, and learn an empty jingle in its place: ' "You will find it serviceable, in the formation of a demeanour, if you sometimes say to yourself in company . . . Papa, potatoes, poultry, prunes and prism, prunes and prism" ' (II, 5, p. 476). Proprieties are the shine on the socio-economic machine, a gloss of mannered decency upon the shoddy realities of exploitation. As the verbal relationships suggest, 'proprieties' depend upon the 'proprietor', and Mrs Gowan's morally evasive ' "it never does" ' (II, 8, p. 524) upon 'How not to do it'. Just as Gradgrind, Bounderby and Slackbridge exemplify the de-humanity of System, so also Mrs General exemplifies her own obsession with shiny exteriors in being 'an article of that lustrous surface which suggests that it is worth any money' (II, 2, p. 450). Casby has the same mechanistic attributes – ' "a screwer by deputy, a wringer, and squeezer" ' (II, 32, p. 800). Underlying it all are the same materialist values: *radix malorum est cupiditas*. In *Hard Times*, however, Gradgrind's values are more than superficial; they are honestly mistaken in their construction of the real. No such saving grace attaches to Mrs General. Her surface values, with their thin niceties – ' "Nothing disagreeable should ever be looked at" ' (II, 5, p. 477) – are hypocritically removed from their economic basis in Casby's sort of squalid money-grubbing. Such a disjunction between surface and actuality breeds characters like Rigaud, who can justifiably lay claim to the title of gentleman, since, in the world he inhabits, the word has no more than surface significance. Similarly, Dorrit indulges in a pompous make-believe, in both the Marshalsea and Italy, until he cannot distinguish between that and the truth. Casby hides rapaciousness beneath a mask of benevolence. Pancks's questions, ' "What do you pretend to be? . . . What's your moral game?" ' (II, 32, p. 800), need asking throughout the novel, for pretence, the separation of appearance and reality, is more than an adjunct to *Little Dorrit*'s social world; it is its fundamental *modus vivendi*.

The leading actor in this world of pretence is, of course, Merdle. As Dorrit says, with unconscious irony, ' "Mr Merdle is the man of this time. The name of Merdle is the name of the age" ' (I, 5, p. 484). That Merdle is a financial phoney becomes clear enough; that this phoney becomes an Emersonian Representative Man is, similarly, a clear enough indictment of contemporary society. But his significance is even greater than this, for Merdle and the material success he seems to epitomise take on the characteristics of a religious faith. Talking to his wife, Merdle defines their respective roles in the world they have created: ' "You supply manner, I supply money" ' (I, 33, p. 396). The 'manner', created by his money, dispensed by his wife, is, via a grim pun, the grotesque materialist version of manna. Mrs Merdle's manner/manna is a parody of spiritual sustenance; the world it feeds aspires to a parody of Christian salvation, with Merdle as the materialist Christ in triumph: 'Merdle: O ye sun, moon, and stars, the great man! The rich man, who had *in a manner* revised the New Testament, and already entered into the Kingdom of Heaven' (II, 16, p. 614; my italics). Materialism in *Little Dorrit* is far more than the moral aspect of commercial capitalism: it is an alternative religion. As Pancks says – in answer to his own question, ' "What's a man made for?" ' – ' "business" ', ' "grinding, drudging, toiling" ', which form ' "the Whole Duty of Man in a commercial country" ' (I, 13, p. 160).[5] Materialism elevates Merdle to the status of Messiah, his riches, 'the new constellation to be followed by the wise men bringing gifts' (II, 25, p. 710). But Merdle, of course, is a false Messiah, and the capitalist Magi arrive, not at a divine birth, but at a materialist death, 'certain carrion at the bottom of a bath'. The final irony is that Merdle's money does not even exist: the whole social, moral and metaphysical fabric he builds and represents is founded upon a lie. The falseness of commercial materialism, however, is not merely a matter of Merdle's being a cheat and a thief. It is guaranteed by the novel's representation of time: as so often for Dickens, time is the touchstone of reality.

In the representation of time in *Little Dorrit*, Dickens returns to the symbolic realism of *Dombey and Son* and *David Copperfield*. Beyond the condition of man exemplified in the maze and the prison, the natural world – wind and clouds, the river and the sea – enforces a message of transience.

The wind blew roughly, the wet squalls came rattling past them, skimming the pools on the road and pavement, and raining them down into the river. The clouds raced on furiously in the lead coloured sky,

the smoke and mist raced after them, the dark tide ran fierce and strong
in the same direction. (I, 9, p. 96)

The river that flows past the Meagles' house, the Thames at Twickenham
– specifically a real river at a real place – has a semantic dimension of
equal reality.

Within view was the peaceful river and the ferry-boat, to moralise to
all the inmates, saying: Young or old, passionate or tranquil, chafing
or content, you, thus runs the current always. Let the heart swell into
what discord it will, thus plays the rippling water on the prow of the
ferry-boat ever the same tune. (I, 16, p. 191)

Appropriately, the river receives the flowers that symbolise for Arthur his
unconsummated love for Pet Meagles: 'the flowers, pale and unreal in the
moonlight, floated away upon the river; and thus do greater things that
once were in our breasts, and near our hearts, flow from us to the eternal
seas' (I, 28, p. 338). The sea not only receives and annihilates all personal
time, as in *Dombey and Son*; it is, as in *David Copperfield*, actively
destructive. The description of Calais emphasises the littleness of human
enterprise under the regimen of transience and eternity.

Every wave-dashed, storm-beaten object, was so low and so little, under
the broad grey sky, in the noise of the wind and sea, and before the
curling lines of surf, making at it ferociously, that the wonder was
there was any Calais left. (II, 20, p. 653)

The symbolic reality of river and sea is, as in the earlier novels, extended
through metaphors of sea-voyage and shipwreck to set the narrative of the
individual within the context of impersonal temporal process. Dorrit is 'like
a passenger aboard ship in a long voyage, who has recovered from sea-
sickness' (I, 19, p. 223); in her spiritual pride, Mrs Clennam claims
immunity from time's depredations: ' "I shape my course by pilots, strictly
by proved and tried pilots, under whom I cannot be shipwrecked" ' (I, 30,
p. 356). Young John, comic though not absurd, sits lovelorn amidst his
mother's washing, 'like the last mariner left alive on the deck of a damp
ship without the power of furling the sails' (I, 21, p. 257). Casby, 'an
unwieldy ship in the Thames river', is constantly taken in tow by 'a little
coaly steam-tug', 'the snorting Pancks' (I, 13, pp. 149–50). The voyage motif
is also applicable to the state: the Barnacles, parasitic as their name suggests,
'stick on to the national ship' and 'if the ship went down with them yet
sticking to it, that was the ship's look out, and not theirs' (I, 10, p. 121);
even Gowan recognises that ' "the Circumlocution Office may ultimately
shipwreck everybody and everything" ' (I, 26, p. 310). When that darling
of Circumlocution, Merdle, does wreck, Dickens's figurative language
takes on a force of registration that expressively conflates the

voyage metaphor with the ships in London Pool and the sea at Calais. Symbolic enactment and realist description merge.

> . . . on the deep was nothing but ruin: nothing but burning hulls, bursting magazines, great guns self-exploded tearing friends and neighbours to pieces, drowning men clinging to unseaworthy spars and going down every minute, spent swimmers floating dead, and sharks. (II, 26, p. 711)

Dickens deliberately sets the semantic of wind and clouds, sea and river, against the human confinement exemplified by the gaol and the maze. Clennam experiences the resultant conflict after his accidental detention in the Marshalsea. 'The walls were so near to one another, and the wild clouds hurried over them so fast, that it have him a sensation like the beginning of sea-sickness to look up at the gusty sky' (I, 9, p. 90). Change is the semantic core, the irreducible meaning in the very substance of the moving world. Prisons create a stability that is illusory, because unrelated to the universal fact of transience: by building a world of prisons, man renders his own existence unreal. Clennam's sickness – with perfect metaphoric appositeness, sea-sickness – is the nausea that comes with the sudden apprehension of the instability beyond the illusion, an illusion that Amy perceives so clearly. She rightly thinks of her father's imprisonment as a separation from time's unceasing process, and, therefore, from reality itself: ' "To see the river, and so much sky, and so many objects, and such change and motion. Then to go back, you know, and find him in the same cramped place" ' (I, 22, p. 260). Release from the physical prison brings no access to the real, but only a compounding of illusion, 'this crowning unreality' of Venice (II, 3, p. 466). The Society of Merdle and materialism severs man from a life that is fully real just as surely as does the Marshalsea: in Italy, stone walls may not a prison make, but Prunes and Prism do. As Amy realises, Society is only 'a superior sort of Marshalsea' (II, 7, p. 511) incapable of recognising its own entrapment. The disjunction between appearance and reality, the core of the propriety cult, fundamental to Merdle's world and the false materialist heaven, is epitomised – like so many other existential characteristics in the novel – by the Circumlocution Office. Behind the apparent activity – 'half a score of boards, half a bushel of minutes, several sacks of official memoranda' (I, 10, p. 104) – lies the reality of total irresponsibility, 'How not to do it'. In *Little Dorrit*, as in *David Copperfield*, responsibility establishes temporal as well as moral order; irresponsibility destroys causal logic and thus negates any sense of meaningful continuity. In a world based upon the premises of Circumlocution, people, unable to perceive any connection between their own past and their own future, or between one another, either drift hopelessly or are turned into objects as the price of some stability. Thus Frederick Dorrit abdicates any responsibility for making sense of his own life – he survives through an indiscriminate acceptance of 'every incident of the labyrinthian world in which he had got lost' (I, 19, p. 221). Affery and Old Nandy adopt the same strategy of unnatural passivity, resulting in the same negation of self. At the other pole of behavioural strategy, but equally unnatural, Mrs Merdle turns herself into an object, the immaculate bosom, and undergoes a precisely equivalent loss of humanity: 'It was not a bosom to repose upon, but it was a capital bosom to hang jewels upon. Mr Merdle wanted something to hang jewels upon, and he bought it for the purpose' (I, 21, p. 247). The dispenser of manner, the queen of materialism, Mrs Merdle is also – with that inevitable Dickensian ironic justice – its victim. Social defeat and social triumph are both registered in terms of the impoverishment of human identity. Frederick's condition as the de-vitalised non-self and Mrs Merdle's identity as the de-humanised thing-self are both traceable to the same source – a society that has lost all human structure because it lacks any social or interpersonal responsibility. Because of the Circumlocution Office, a negative principle seems to determine not merely the operation of government, but the very identity and existence of human beings. An important focus for this negative principle is Arthur Clennam.

Clennam's personal morality – 'Duty on earth, restitution on earth, action on earth' (I, 27, p. 319) – is diametrically opposed to the irresponsibility of Circumlocution, but Clennam's moral potency is strangely neutered. His response to Pancks's embittered scepticism, ' "I like business . . . What's a man made for?" ', is central.

> 'For nothing else?' said Clennam.
> Pancks put the counter question, 'What else?' It packed up, in the smallest compass, a weight that had rested on Clennam's life; and he made no answer. (I, 13, p. 160)

Clennam, in fact, has no answer to make. Although he has a keen sense of the human disablement behind the surfaces of materialism and the commercial rat-race, he has no positive alternatives to offer. Unable to shake off the memory of his repressed childhood, his sense of responsibility is distorted into either patronage, in the case of Amy, or non-specific guilt. When he loses Doyce & Clennam money by speculation, his immediate thought is 'atonement', to be undertaken 'publicly and unreservedly' (II, 26, p. 715), a neurotic desire for a grand expiation that is out of proportion to the sin involved. His wish, 'at as small a salary as he could live upon . . . to be allowed to serve the business as a faithful clerk' (II, 26, p. 716), has the unmistakable ring of indulgence, the masochist's longing for abasement and martyrdom. Clennam is himself disabled, ironically, by the very virtue he possesses. In the face of the labyrinthine world of irresponsibility and indifference he almost wants to be beaten. His concept of responsibility lacks Florence Dombey's spiritual insight, Betsey's energy, and even Esther's power of self-preservation. Clennam's failure is one of self-construing which negates his own potential for active moral assertion. As he says to Meagles, ' "I have no will. That is to say . . . next to none that I can put in action now" ' (I, 2, p. 20). Clennam fails to believe in himself as a full human being, actually becoming, in his abortive courtship of Pet, a nobody. It is this process, the slide towards self-annulment, that epitomises the negative principle at the thematic and imaginative core of the novel.

In *Little Dorrit* the verbal patterning around the word 'nobody' concentrates the novel's debate about negation and the nature of personal identity.[6] 'Nobody', 'nothing' and 'nowhere' are the nodal items in a collocation of associated words and meanings: 'somebody', 'anybody', 'everybody'; 'something', 'anything', 'everything'; 'somewhere', 'anywhere', 'everywhere'. Certain chapter titles suggest the nuclear significance of these verbal clusters: 'Nobody's Weakness' (I, 16), 'Nobody's Rival' (I, 17), 'Nobody's State of Mind' (I, 26), 'Nobody's Disappearance' (I, 28), 'Something Wrong Somewhere' (II, 5), 'Something Right Somewhere' (II, 6). In its constant activity of perceiving the non-self – the 'something' that is the focus of perception – the self – the 'somebody' that is the core of identity – continually constructs the context for its own existence – the 'somewhere' that is the locus for experience. It is the specificness of knower and known that establishes existential stability; that, in many ways, actually creates our sense of the real. In *Little Dorrit* these very specifics are subject to a relentless attrition; ontological instability is expressed through a contant loss of definition, a constant replacement of the determinate by the indeterminate and, eventually, by the negative. Instead of construction, there is de-construction. The sequence of dissolution is, perhaps, most succinctly stated in Pancks's account of Miss Wade.

> 'She is somebody's child – anybody's – nobody's. Put her in a room in London here with any six people old enough to be her parents, and her parents may be there for anything she knows . . . She knows nothing about 'em. She knows nothing about any relatives whatever.' (II, 10, p. 540)

Because Miss Wade knows nothing specific about her parentage, ' "for anything she knows" ', the sense of a definite personal milieu, of being ' "somebody's child" ', slackens into indeterminateness, (' "anybody's" ') and eventually collapses into negation (' "nobody's" '). Such processes underpin the whole novel. By refusing to confront his own feelings about Pet, by desiring 'nothing uncertain or unquiet' (I, 16, p. 200), Clennam condemns himself to an emotional impasse in which self-acknowledgement is denied: 'It was not his weakness he had imagined, it was nobody's, nobody's' (ibid.); 'such a state of mind was nobody's – nobody's' (I, 26, p. 309). Trapped by the unreality of her life in Italy, paupers and beggars seem to Amy 'the only realities of the day', because they have specific reference to her own identity, 'to something in the days that were gone'.

Without the definition of 'something' there is only the negation that comes from the breakdown of the relationship of the self to the non-self: 'there seemed to be nothing to support life, nothing to eat, nothing to make, nothing to grow, nothing to hope, nothing to do but die' (II, 4, p. 465). Affery, faced by Flintwinch and Mrs Clennam, renounces any kind of self-determination, even in the matter of her own marriage: ' "If them two clever ones have made up their minds to it, what's left for *me* to do? Nothing" ' (I, 3, p. 38). The processes of negation, verbal and actual, are institutionalised in the Circumlocution Office and Merdle's materialism, and socialised in the doctrines of manner and surface. Omnipotent and omnipresent, the Office ' "is there with the express intention that everything shall be left alone" ' (II, 28, p. 736). Merdle eases the imbecile Sparkler into the bureaucratic racket because 'It was just as well that he should have something to do, and it was just as well that he should have something for doing it'; although in reality, naturally, 'There was nothing to do' (II, 14, pp. 586–7). Any public disquiet about such jobbing can be stilled by the convenient fiction that it is 'the business of some other Britons unknown, somewhere, or nowhere' (ibid.). Something is nothing, somewhere is nowhere: in a world of Circumlocution, negative and positive are synonymous. The linguistic procedures of Society operate in precisely similar terms.

> 'I don't expect you,' said Mrs Merdle . . . 'to captivate people
> . . . I simply request you to care about nothing − or seem to care
> about nothing − as everybody else does.'
> 'Do I ever say I care about anything?' asked Mr Merdle.
> 'Say? No! Nobody would attend to you if you did.' (I, 33, p. 397)

The depiction of Merdle, as Kincaid has remarked, demonstrates how 'the insidious social machine elevates those most capable of being nothing', so that Merdle becomes 'a funny and terrifying God of Nobodies'.[7]

The techniques of verbal negation used in *Little Dorrit* have a further effect. 'Nobody', 'nothing' and 'nowhere' reveal in Dickens's usage an indeterminateness in the relationship between their syntactic function and their semantic identity. Syntactic substantiveness is at odds with the negativeness of the referent. 'Nobody', in particular, is paradoxical: by giving it nominal, or pronominal, weight − as in 'Nobody's heart beat quickly' (I, 27, p. 321), 'Nobody knew that . . . Merdle . . . had ever done any good to any one' (II, 12, p. 556) − 'nobody' is made to label a substantive somebody, a relationship that, in terms of meaning, is clearly contradictory. The force of this usage accumulates throughout the novel. Its pressure is, perhaps, best appreciated when concentrated in the essay − parallel in many ways to *Little Dorrit* − 'Nobody, Somebody, and Everybody'.

> The government . . . is invariably beaten and outstripped by private
> enterprise; which we all know to be Nobody's fault. Something will

be the national death of us, some day; and who can doubt that Nobody will be brought in Guilty?[8]

The semantic paradox in this passage and in *Little Dorrit* is irresolvable. It is that implied in 'being nobody' or 'being nothing', where 'nobody' and 'nothing' preclude being altogether: ' "Little Dorrit? *She's* nothing" ' (I, 3, p. 40); 'Maggy counted as nobody, and she was by' (I, 31, p. 378). The novel's play between being and non-being is caught perfectly in a syntactico-semantic organisation which simultaneously asserts and denies the existence of an active subject. The effect is to imbue the verbal stuff of the novel with an analogue to the frustration and entrapment that are the novel's theme. The construction 'being nothing' is a linguistic snare which catches the reader between two mutually exclusive, but simultaneous, propositions – to be *and* not to be. Positive and negative chase each other round a verbal and semantic maze that is founded in ambiguity. The negative principle that informs the *Little Dorrit* world determines the very language in which the novel exists, just as it determined the novel's original title, 'Nobody's Fault'.[9]

Hopes for deliverance from the Circumlocution world focus, of course, upon Amy Dorrit. Yet, despite her extraordinary capacity for love, her sense of responsibility and the care she expends on an uncaring family, the narrative of her moral agency is a narrative of defeat. She cannot rescue her father from his own illusions; although she becomes a mother to 'Fanny's neglected children' and 'a tender nurse and friend to Tip' (II, 34, p. 826), she cannot save the one from Society nor the other from the Marshalsea. Her marriage has no effect on the world at large; after all, as Ferdinand Barnacle says, ' "the Genius of the country . . . tends to being left alone" ' (II, 28, p. 737).[10] Amy's centrality to the novel, however, is not primarily a function of her ethical efficacy, but rather of her understanding, of a comprehension of the real more profound than that of any other character. Amy can both recognise and confront the fact of imprisonment, seeing the spikes and shadow of the Marshalsea not only as the dominant reality of her own life, but also as the metaphoric dominant in the lives of the people around her.

As she gently opened the window, and looked eastward down the prisonyard, the spikes upon the wall were tipped with red, then made a sullen purple pattern on the sun as it came flaming up into the heavens. The spikes had never looked so sharp and cruel, nor the bars so heavy, nor the prison space so gloomy and contracted. (I, 20, p. 231)

The shadow of the wall was on every object. Not least upon the figure in the old grey gown and the black velvet cap, as it turned towards her when she opened the door of the dim room.
'Why not upon me too!' thought Little Dorrit . . . (I, 21, p. 245)

. . . the poor child Little Dorrit thought of him [Clennam] . . . in the shadow of the Marshalsea wall. (I, 23, p. 263)

Many combinations did those spikes upon the wall assume . . . while Little Dorrit sat there musing . . . but beautiful or hardened still, always over it and under it and through it, she was fain to look in her solitude, seeing everything with that ineffaceable brand. (I, 24, p. 291)

She felt that, in what he [Mr Dorrit] had just said to her, and in his whole bearing towards her, there was the well-known shadow of the Marshalsea wall. It took a new shape, but it was the old sad shadow. (II, 5, p. 478)

Imprisonment is construed as the fundamental condition of social man, and it is Amy who not only perceives it as such, but construes herself as being necessarily implicated in that condition. But imprisonment in *Little Dorrit* is more than the product of the society the novel depicts: it is also an inalienable element of man's metaphysical identity.

The last day of the appointed week touched the bars of the Marshalsea gate. Bleak, all night, since the gate had clashed upon Little Dorrit, its iron stripes were turned by the early glowing sun into stripes of gold. For aslant across the city, over its jumbled roofs, and through the open tracery of its church towers, struck the long bright rays, bars of the prison of this lower world. (II, 30, p. 763)

Captivity is the specific existential condition of the lapsarian world, the defining characteristic of man's separation from God, and in *Little Dorrit* it sets the frame within which the novel is to be read.

. . . the sun went down in a red, green, golden glory; the stars came out in the heavens, and the fire-flies mimicked them in the lower air, as men may feebly imitate the goodness of a better order of beings; the long dusty roads and the interminable plains were in repose – and so deep a hush was on the sea, that it scarcely whispered of the time when it shall give up its dead. (I, 1, p. 14)

The passage recombines central thematic elements from earlier novels: Nell's vision of the stars and 'dead mankind', the sea as temporal metaphor in *Dombey and Son* and *David Copperfield*, Esther's hope for 'the world that sets this right', Stephen Blackpool's vision of the star from Old Hell Pit. In this passage, what starts as a realist landscape takes on, through an ordered process of widening perspective, a cosmic significance. The primary elements of air, earth, fire and water contextualise man's ontological position, separated from the stars and 'a better order of beings', confined to and by 'the lower air' – the phrase clearly anticipating 'this lower world' in the passage already quoted. Human temporality and its associated firefly life of moral imitation are focused within an interpretation of time that, in its concentration upon 'last things', is eschatological, both predicting and asserting the apocalyptic cessation of time, when the sea 'shall give up its dead'. The ontological viewpoint of the passage is, as the quotation from the Book of Common Prayer indicates, definitively Christian. The land- and sea-scape described is macrocosmic: as such, moreover, it is not a metaphor for man's metaphysical state, but a metaphoric enactment of it, a physical and phenomenal representation in the real world of the novel. In *Little Dorrit* the base components of Christian metaphysics are infused with the actual, imbued with a real presence. The referential frame they provide precisely determines the connotative values of the different elements of symbolic realism within the novel. Thus, the imprisonment exemplified by the labyrinth-gaol carries throughout those Christian overtones of man's alienation from spiritual life made explicit in the 'prison of this lower world' passage. The message of earthly transience in wind and clouds, river and sea similarly takes a component place in a Christian semantic. The shadow that Amy perceives is necessarily evocative of the shadow of death. In terms of such schemata, the full meaning of 'Little Dorrit's Party' can be understood: 'And thus she sat at the gate, as it were alone; looking up at the stars and seeing the clouds pass over them in their wild flight − which was the dance at Little Dorrit's party' (I, 14, p. 174). The dance is metaphysical, the flux of mutability around the existential prison in which man is a captive; but, though obscured, beyond both captivity and change is the hope of heaven, of 'a better order' represented by the stars. In the social and moral dimension of the novel − the dimension of the mundane − this hope of transcendence is expressed through Amy's espousal of explicitly New Testament doctrine in direct antithesis to Mrs Clennam's Old Testament vengefulness.

'My life has been passed in this poor prison, and my teaching has been very defective; but let me implore you to remember later and better days. Be guided only by the healer of the sick, the raiser of the dead, the friend of all who are afflicted and forlorn . . .' (II, 31, p. 792)

Directly following Amy's rebuttal of the Old Testament dispensation is the famous transcendental sunset over London.

From a radiant centre over the whole length and breadth of the tranquil firmament, great shoots of light streamed among the early stars, like signs of the blessed later covenant of peace and hope that changed the crown of thorns into a glory. (II, 31, p. 793)

Although the similetic 'like' is retained, the resolution of the description upon 'glory' refers back to the 'red, green, golden glory' of the sunset in the novel's very first chapter. The meaning is now fully explicated: the mystery of Christian salvation is enacted in the world of direct experience. By a process that can only be described as transubstantiation, Amy's faith is triumphantly vindicated by and through the real. The London sunset is a realist manifestation of man's redemption. Implicitly, it is her belief in 'the blessed later covenant' that Amy gives to Clennam, a belief that enables him to secure the imaginative hope he lacks.

> Blossom what would [the Marshalsea's] bricks and bars bore uniformly the same dead crop. Yet Clennam, listening to [Amy's] voice as it read to him, heard in it all that great Nature was doing, heard in it all the soothing songs she sings to man. (II, 34, p. 814)

As 'great Nature' in *Little Dorrit* is the repository of a mystical semantic, 'the soothing songs she sings' are divine in their import. And this is Amy's function in the novel, for her agency is not primarily ethical but mystical, and the hope she announces, not moral or social, but transcendental.

The infusion of transcendental meaning into the novel's mimetic realism is complemented by a new expressiveness in the novel's actual fabric. I have already shown how, through the linguistic patterns built up around 'nobody', the existential character of the novel's world is rendered an integral part of the novel's verbal technique. Narrative structure functions similarly, as can be seen in the Rigaud–Blandois–Lagnier subplot. Rigaud's changes of name serve relatively little purpose; we know very little about him; he reveals a total lack of inner life – he is, in the novel's prevalent terminology, a nobody. Similarly, despite the black cape and mustachio attributes of the stage villain, he does nothing. Despite his journeyings across Europe, his mysterious exits and entrances, he arrives nowhere; his theme-song, announced in the opening chapter, ' "Who passes by this road so late?" ' (I, 1, p. 6), parodies the whole notion of peregrination. The complicated plot he sets in train merely collapses into a jumble of irrelevancies about wills and birthrights, just as the Clennam house collapses upon the impotent villain himself. It is all deliberately and pointedly absurd. Stylistically, Rigaud belongs in melodrama, in a world of sharply contrasted values: his whole presentation in the novel – ' "there are people whom it is necessary to detest without compromise" ' (I, 11, p. 127) – holds out a taunting invitation to hiss the baddie. Rigaud is indeed set up as a limelight Lucifer, complete with his own parody evangelist in John Baptist Cavalletto. But his evil deeds have all taken place before the novel opens; within the novel his Satanic output totals a dead dog and a spot of inept blackmail. The uncertainty of the maze, the defining absence of moral definition in *Little Dorrit*, utterly frustrates the conventional operation of evil. The negative principle renders overt evil as impotent as overt good, and the apparently Satanic Rigaud turns out to be little more than Mr Mantalini with a nasty streak. If the intricacy of the Rigaud plot exemplifies the labyrinthine nature of the *Little Dorrit* world, its lack of direction exemplifies the labyrinth's nullity and frustration. Almost all the novel's subplots typify this defeat of narrative expectation, this thwarting of the reader's desire for conclusiveness. Endings are deliberately engineered — like the arbitrary collapse of the Clennam house — or deliberately avoided, since within the maze, by definition, there is no point at which one can naturally come to a stop. Young John is left sentimentally lovelorn;[11] Miss Wade remains psychically locked into the role of self-tormentor; Tattycoram returns to the Meagles' patronage with the apparent intention of counting five and twenty for ever more; Meagles himself is left with the hollow consolation of the Gowan family tree. Profoundly and deliberately unsatisfactory, the narrative mood at the end of the novel is best summed up in Dickens's valedictory comment about Mr F.'s Aunt: 'who the person was, who, for the satisfaction of Mr F.'s Aunt's mind, ought to have been brought forward and never was brought forward, will never be positively known' (II, 34, p. 821). Rather than the narrative impulse of the novel being brought to a conclusion, it merely stops, to the facetious accompaniment of the final chapter titles, 'Going . . . Going . . . Gone'. Because Circumlocution dominates the world the novel depicts, it also dominates the way that novel is made. Imaginatively, *Little Dorrit* is the only kind of novel that could be written in the labyrinth, and its plot, like its world, ends not with a bang, but a whimper.

What Dickens has created, of course, is a symbolic narrative which enacts processes of entrapment and frustration in the reader's consciousness through the very act of reading. In terms of both linguistic texture and narrative structure, *Little Dorrit* exemplifies imprisonment and impasse. The novel thus offers two different sets — and two different sorts — of fusion between meaning and reality: the one set is transcendental, the meanings actualised in the physical reality the novel describes; the other set is mundane, the meanings actualised in the structural fabric of the novel itself. The two semantic sets are mutually opposed — the one positive, the other negative — and are only reconciled in Little Dorrit herself, the Child of the Marshalsea who is also the Child of God. In the reader's consciousness, however, the two sets remain separate, though complementary, for they are based upon existential premises and empirical data that are different in kind. It could well be argued that, through this separation, this final lack of resolution, Dickens expresses the central Christian tragedy of man's alienation from God, the dichotomy between the mortal and the transcendental.

7

'Recalled to Life':
The Christian Myth of
A Tale of Two Cities

The source for *A Tale of Two Cities* is, as Dickens's preface acknowledges, Carlyle's *The French Revolution*, and the indebtedness goes deeper than narrative incident or historical detail.[1] Carlyle's transcendental reading of history and his subsequent typological method jointly lie behind the imaginative strategies employed in Dickens's novel. In *A Tale of Two Cities*, as in most historical novels, actual past events are integrated with a fictional plot, but, unlike most historical novels, the resultant narrative is presented as a semantic structure, symbolic in nature and divine in content. The parallel with Carlyle's interpretation of the French Revolution is striking. Far more than simply adventitious, however, Dickens's adoption – and, as will become evident, adaption – of a Carlylean method is a logical outcome of his whole imaginative evolution. With the development I have traced through the novels – from symbolic realism, through exemplification, to the Christian transcendentalism and symbolism of fabric in *Little Dorrit* – it seems inevitable that *A Tale of Two Cities* should depict the world in terms of two distinct though interpenetrating levels of reality. The one level is mundane, man as the creature of society and history; the other is transcendental, man under the regimen of the divine. The historically real and fictionally realist episodes of the novel are set within an eschatological frame: human time, 'these days when it is mostly winter in fallen latitudes' (II, 10, p. 123), is bracketed between 'the days when it was always summer in Eden' (ibid.) and the day when 'the ocean is . . . to give up its dead' (II, 2, p. 59). Just as, for the Christian, the central fact of history is Christ, so also the narrative of *A Tale of Two Cities* is governed by a Christological myth: Dickens's historico-realist novel about the French Revolution is also, and co-extensively, a symbolic novel about resurrection.[2]

At the outset of the novel there is little to distinguish England and London under the Georges from France and Paris under the *ancien régime*. 'There were a king with a large jaw and a queen with a plain face, on the throne of England, there were a king with a large jaw and a queen with a fair face, on the throne of France' (I, 1, p. 1). The two localities of the novel together form the Augustinian City of Man, the biblical Babylon, Bunyan's City of Destruction.[3] The irresponsibility of Circumlocution in *Little Dorrit*, with its associated false Society and the pseudo-morality of surface, reappears as the governing force of the French system.

Monseigneur had one truly noble idea of general public business, which
was, to let everything go on in its own way. (II, 7, p. 98)

Dress was the one unfailing talisman and charm used for keeping all
things in their places. Everybody was dressed for a Fancy Ball that
was never to leave off. (II, 7, p. 101)

In London, Merdle's commercial materialism reappears in Tellson's Bank,
which also epitomises the stagnation of the English system.[4] After the
outbreak of revolution it is 'natural' for Tellson's to become 'the head-
quarters and great gathering-place of Monseigneur' (II, 24, p. 224). The
status quo is maintained by violent repression, its barbarity defended by
Tellson's 'ancient clerk' with the obscurantist – and Kafkaesque – slogan,
' "It is the law . . . It is the law" ' (II, 2, p. 55). France runs upon 'a system
rooted in a frizzled hangman' (II, 8, p. 102); in England, 'the hangman,
ever busy and ever worse than useless', is 'in constant requisition' (I, 1,
p. 3): 'Death is Nature's remedy for all things, and why not legislation's?'
(II, 1, p. 50). Babylon exists upon the wholesale slaughter of its inhabitants:
its identity as the City of Destruction is quite literal. Just as the shadow
of the Marshalsea dominates the world of *Little Dorrit*, so in *A Tale of Two
Cities* the shadow of the gallows lies across the whole of human society:
' "When I left the village . . . the shadow struck across the church, across
the mill, across the prison – seemed to strike across the earth, messieurs,
to where the sky rests upon it!" ' (II, 15, pp. 163–4). The shadow of the
gallows is the realist translation of the shadow of death, within which
'church', 'mill' and 'prison', religion, labour and the law – the fundamental
elements of the social fabric in the City of Man – all function. The
maintenance of the social fabric by force leads to moral chaos, to an
indiscriminate and institutionalised destructiveness; the London hangman
'to-day [takes] the life of an atrocious murderer, and to-morrow of a
wretched pilferer who had robbed a farmer's boy of sixpence' (I, 1, p. 3).

As in earlier novels, such socio-moral confusion is given physical
expression, is exemplified, in the images of the prison and the maze, with
both of which is associated darkness. As real as the Marshalsea in *Little
Dorrit*, and carrying the same emblematic weight, Newgate, Tyburn and
the Old Bailey lour over London as the Bastille lours over Paris. The people
of Saint Antoine inhabit a slum-maze that directly recalls Tom-all-Alone's.
The narrative proper starts with the fog-bound confusion and darkness of
the night coach journey to Dover; Lorry's first meeting with Lucie takes
place in 'a large, dark room, furnished in a funereal manner' (I, 4, p. 18);
the house where Defarge keeps Manette has a 'gloomy tile-paved entry to
the gloomy tile-paved staircase' (I, 5, p. 33), whilst the staircase itself is
'a steep dark shaft of dirt and poison' (I, 5, p. 34) and Manette's room is
'dim and dark' (I, 5, p. 37). The darkness centres on the life-in-death rookery
of Saint Antoine: 'And now that the cloud settles on Saint Antoine . . .

the darkness of it was heavy' (I, 5, p. 28). The inhabitants watch the lighting of the lamps that are slung across the street and 'conceive the idea of . . . hauling up men by those ropes and pulleys, to flare upon the darkness of their condition' (I, 5, p. 30). The concentrated images of moral chaos and physical confusion, of the scaffold and the shadow of the gallows, of spiritual and actual darkness form a figurative and conceptual cluster in which abstract propositions about the state of man are consistently expressed through physical realities. The cluster of characteristics that defines the world of *A Tale of Two Cities* derives from Job 10: 22: 'A land of darkness, as darkness itself; and of the shadow of death, without any order, and where the light is as darkness.' Each of the biblical terms is realised in the London and Paris of the novel. Human growth is stunted and suppressed. The inhabitants of Saint Antoine have 'undergone a terrible grinding and re-grinding in the mill . . . that grinds young people old' (I, 5, p. 28); having taken on a new clerk Tellson's 'hid him somewhere till he was old' (II, 1, p. 51). In the *beau monde*, contrastingly, but equally unnaturally, 'grandmammas of sixty dressed and supped as at twenty' (11, 7, p. 100). Sydney Carton, more conscious than any of the spiritual malaise that afflicts them all, sums up the existential position: ' "I am like one who died young" ' (II, 13, p. 143). The universal tendency is towards reversal, Sweeney's bleak and simple inversion: 'That's what life is. Just is . . . Life is death'.[5] Unnaturally young, unnaturally old, unreally suspended in time, the half-life of *A Tale of Two Cities* flickers in a landscape that 'the rulers of the darkness of this world'[6] – and the biblical phrase seems entirely apposite – have reduced to a wilderness. 'On inanimate nature, as on the men and women who cultivated it, a prevalent tendency towards an appearance of vegetating unwillingly – a dejected disposition to give up, and wither away' (II, 8, p. 107). In a moment of hallucinatory intensity, Carton sees this same sterility and desolation as the spiritual reality of the whole city.

> When he got out of the house, the air was cold and sad, the dull sky overcast, the river dark and dim, the whole scene like a lifeless desert. And wreaths of dust were spinning round and round before the morning blast, as if the desert-sand had risen far away, and the first spray of it in its advance had begun to overwhelm the city. (II, 5, pp. 84–5)

Physically and metaphysically, the City of Man seems without hope, and the denial of hope is a denial of the future. Repudiating any responsibility of the present for the past, rejecting any hopes for the future, coercing all things into the maintenance of the *status quo*, the world is smitten by 'the leprosy of unreality' (II, 7, p. 100), for time goes on regardless.

> The water of the fountain ran, the swift river ran, the day ran into evening, so much life in the city ran into death according to rule, time and tide waited for no man, the rats were sleeping close together in

their dark holes again, the Fancy Ball was lighted up at supper, all things ran their course. (II, 7, p. 106)

From opposed standpoints, Lucie and the Soho household, and Madame Defarge and the Saint Antoine revolutionaries, both try to remake the present by altering the prevalent 'unreality' of its relationship to time and change.

Lucie gives her father a new life; similarly, her marriage to Darnay sets the seal upon his new life. The society the three of them share seems not only safe, but also assured of continuity. As Manette says, ' "my future is far brighter, Lucie, seen through your marriage" ' (II, 17, p. 178). Lucie's primary quality of compassion creates a small social group, flexible enough to admit Lorry and Carton, resilient enough to withstand the death of one of the children. Living on the edge of the City of Man, she maintains an enclave of hope, keeping alive the chance for the present to grow towards a positive future. But Lucie's remaking of the present depends upon retreat from the past. Manette holds to his new life by suppressing all memories of his years in the Bastille and by having, in consequence, ' "that suppression always shut up within him" ' (II, 6, p. 91). Darnay overtly renounces his past, and the new life he finds with Lucie enables him to defer any genuine moral confrontation with it.

> . . . to the force of . . . circumstance he had yielded: − not without disquiet, but still without continuous and accumulating resistance . . . he had watched the times for a time of action, and . . . they had shifted and struggled until the time had gone by. (II, 24, p. 230)

Dickens's presentation of both men is sympathetic: after all, facing up to the past is for Manette a psychological and for Darnay a political impossibility. As events show, however, it is precisely the fact that Lucie's enclave of hope rests upon an inability − however innocent − to confront one's own history that renders the new life she offers so fragile. When Gabelle's letter arrives, Darnay is hopelessly compromised and, accepting the realities and responsibilities of being Evrémonde too late, is drawn, without hope of resistance, towards the 'lodestone Rock' of Revolutionary Paris and his own unacknowledged past. Manette's Bastille testimonial, which dooms Darnay, effectually condemns himself as well; the past he had so long fought off returns with a vengeance: 'As if all that had happened since the garret time were a momentary fancy, or a dream, Mr Lorry saw him shrink into the exact figure that Defarge had had in keeping' (III, 12, p. 325). As Darnay rightly recognises, ' "All things have worked together as they have fallen out" ' (III, 11, p. 318), and Lucie has no power to prevent them, to save her husband or, implicitly, her father. She can only respond with the limp platitudes of despair: ' "We shall not be separated long. I feel that this will break my heart by-and-by" ' (III, 11, p. 316). Despite its apparent potential and, for a time, its success, the hope that Lucie offers proves an illusion. The denial of the past destroys the future: only Carton's intervention gives any of them a genuine chance of new life.

When the spy, Barsad, asks Madame Defarge what her knitting is for, her punning reply, " 'Pastime" ' (II, 16, p. 172), defines the role of the revolutionaries. They are the agents of 'the Woodman Fate' and 'the Farmer Death' (I, 1, p. 2) in exacting reparation for the centuries of oppression inflicted upon them by the *ancien régime*. Thus, for Dickens as for Carlyle, the Revolution, both exemplifying the process of cause and effect and taking that process as its warrant for moral action, imposes a meaningful pattern upon time and change: the present is the direct product of, and must answer for, the past. Unlike Lucie's society, the Revolution is founded upon undeniable moral and temporal realities. Literally and symbolically, Madame Defarge knits the past to the present, but what she makes are ' "shrouds" ' (II, 15, p. 166). Just as Lucie's moral agency is defined by her compassion, Madame Defarge's is defined by her total lack of pity. Retribution personified, she envisages the future only as an endless expiation for the sins of the past. Beyond a certain point, the Revolution can make no progress, for it constructs nothing; with hopeless inevitability the stress of the 'Republic One and Indivisible, of Liberty, Equality, Fraternity, or Death' (III, 1, p. 234), falls, aurally and existentially, upon 'Death'. In a society in which retribution, absolute and unqualified, is the sole moral imperative, death and execution become the objects of an elaborate and perverted worship. When, in the first book of the novel, the wine-cask splits open in Saint Antoine, 'one tall joker . . . scrawled upon a wall with his finger dipped in muddy wine-lees – BLOOD' (I, 5, p. 28). On one level this is a realist gesture of insurrectionary defiance – Defarge, ever careful in a world of spies, makes sure he obliterates the message. On a conceptual and symbolic level, however, the act synthesises the Old Testament writing on the wall – the sign of inevitable retribution – with the eucharistic blood and wine of the New Testament – the sign of potential redemption.[7] Vengeance comes, but, as in *The French Revolution*, without mercy: in a perversion of the Eucharist, the sacrificial blood of the Revolution's victims becomes 'red wine for La Guillotine' (III, 5, p. 261). The new religion has its Old Testament champion in Samson the executioner and its New Testament 'missionary' (II, 16, p. 177) in Madame Defarge. Ultimately the executions that are its focal point have all the trappings of the Mass – 'The ministers of Sainte Guillotine are robed and ready' (III, 15, p. 355). Death was the dominant reality in the City of Man in its *ancien régime* guise: ironically the revolutionary overthrow of the rulers of that city turns death into the climax – indeed, the purpose – of existence, and the guillotine into 'the sign of the regeneration of the human race' (III, 5, p. 260). A direct and parodic inversion of Christianity, the revolutionaries' religion is the worship of Thanatos itself, a faith not in salvation, but in extinction. 'La Guillotine . . . superseded the Cross. Models of it were worn on breasts from which the Cross was discarded, and it was bowed down to and believed in where the Cross was denied' (III, 5, p. 260).

Condemned to physical and spiritual death in the City of Man, man cannot forge his own salvation. The hope represented by Lucie can only exist as long as the past can be ignored; the Revolution is bound to the past and destroys all hope of the future. In the eschatological frame of the novel, outlined at the beginning of this chapter, the past event as a result of which man is condemned, and the consequences of which he cannot escape, is the Fall. Lapsarian man is alienated from his fellow: that 'every human creature is constituted to be that profound secret and mystery to every other' is 'his natural and not to be alienated inheritance' (I, 3, p. 10). Paralleling this, and inherent in it, man's separation from God, as so often in the novels I have discussed, is announced through the physical, phenomenal world.

> And so, under a short grove of feebler and feebler over-swinging lamps, out under the great grove of stars.
> Beneath that arch of unmoved and eternal lights . . . the shadows of the night were broad and black. (I, 6, p. 48)

The semantics of the passage become clear in the context both of the rest of the novel and of earlier novels. As the fireflies mimic the stars and man imitates a 'better order of beings' in *Little Dorrit*, so here the 'unmoved and eternal' lights of heaven find echo in the 'feebler and feebler' lamps of the City of Man, contending inadequately with the 'broad and black' shadows of 'the darkness of this world'. Trapped in the City of Destruction, man's separation from the stars is fixed and, for anything he can do to help himself, final. When Darnay as Evrémonde is finally condemned, Carton's statement, ' "He will perish: there is no real hope" ' (III, 11, p. 320), has a suggestiveness far greater than its immediate function as part of the machinery of dramatic tension. Carton is right: the 'real' world of the novel is, quite literally, hopeless. The conclusion towards which so much of Dickens's imaginative development had been leading is, in Carton's statement, reached. In the 'real' world, man is inescapably doomed. That he is so is the logical consequence of his being, for Dickens, the creature not of one reality, but of two. Man as a socio-historical animal cannot save himself precisely because his identity is not determined *a posteriori*, by society and history, but *a priori*, by the premises of Christian metaphysics. The lapsarian City of Man cannot be redeemed by man because he himself has fallen: 'It is the blight man was born for'.[8] That blight can only be lifted, a future for man can only be guaranteed, by the advent of a saviour. Thus the theme of resurrection in *A Tale of Two Cities* results not from a religiose desire on Dickens's part 'to lead his readers in public worship',[9] but, profoundly and inevitably, from the imaginative premises upon which the novel is written. Consistent always within the defining terms of symbolic realism, Dickens has the realist manifestations of man's spiritual darkness, 'The shadows of the night', ask Jarvis Lorry the central question of the novel, ' "I hope you care to be recalled to life?" ' (I, 6, p. 48).

Dickens prepares for the narrative and thematic climax of Carton's rescue of Darnay through a technique akin to Carlyle's typological method.

Incidents in the historically and socially real world image and anticipate transcendental process: metaphysically, coming events cast their shadows before. Book the First, 'Recalled to Life', sets the typological pattern for the rest of the novel. Having been, effectively, buried alive in the Bastille, Manette must be unearthed – Jarvis Lorry travels to Paris 'to dig someone out of a grave' (I, 3, p. 12); once raised from the grave, Manette is emotionally reborn through Lucie's love. A physical and psychical prefiguration of resurrection, Manette's rescue is thematically linked to Darnay's first two trials, both types – though significantly distinct ones – of judgement and salvation. At the Old Bailey, Darnay's acquittal as a result of Carton's intervention clearly prepares for the final substitution that saves him from the guillotine. Significantly, Carton's intervention has nothing to do with any merit of Darnay's. In contrast, his acquittal by the Revolutionary Tribunal results from Manette's 'high personal popularity' and 'the straightforward force of truth and earnestness' (III, 6, pp. 270–1) with which the Doctor gives evidence of his son-in-law's innocence. Darnay is saved by the virtuousness of his own actions and the good deeds of his pleader, Manette. But Darnay's acquittal this time is only a stay of execution, his triumphal entry into freedom 'dreamlike' (III, 6, p. 272) in its unreality, the Doctor's repeated boast, ' "I have saved him" ' (III, 6, p. 273), a trenchant irony of spiritual pride, for man cannot forge his salvation through his own efforts. Darnay's sin is the legacy of his past, inherited, quite literally, from the history of his race, from being Evrémonde, and thus cannot be cancelled by his personal guiltlessness: man cannot be justified by works. The sudden knock on the door that summons Darnay back to the Tribunal is the knocking of Death itself (III, 7, p. 277), the summons to the inevitable condemnation for which good works have no answer. Prefiguration in the novel also works through parody: both Cly and Foulon arrange mock-funerals for themselves, their disappearance and subsequent return thus becoming travestied forms of resurrection. As Carton says – with a nicely weighted use of the word 'mystery' – Cly ' "has the mystery about him of having feigned death and come to life again" ' (III, 8, p. 289); with similar irony, the tidings of Foulon's return to life are announced as ' "News from the other world" ' (II, 22, p. 212). Most obvious of the parodic prefigurations, Jerry Cruncher, the resurrection-man, is a parody saviour. As Gold has pointed out, 'his initials are those of Jesus Christ' and through him 'the metaphysical mysteries are reduced to blasphemous literalities'.[10] A grim burlesque, body-snatching is the nearest the City of Man, in its fallen state, can come to resurrection. Through all these anticipatory images and episodes, the stage is set for Sydney Carton.

Carton understands the City of Man, its brutal indifference, its negation, its spiritual desolation, better than any other character, because he has taken it into himself: 'Waste forces within him, and a desert all around' (II, 5, p. 85). Yet he carries the despair of the world he lives in without, oddly, being part of that world. Throughout the novel – and, indeed, in Hablôt

Browne's illustrations[11] – Carton's separateness is stressed: thus, in reply to Lorry's bourgeois enthusiasm for the virtues of commerce, ' "bless you, *I* have no business," said Mr Carton' (II, 4, pp. 76–7). Carton seems always peripheral to events, constantly coming into the action, as it were, from outside. After the Old Bailey trial, he stands apart from the congratulatory group surrounding Darnay: '[He] . . . had not joined the group, or interchanged a word with any one of them, but . . . had been leaning against the wall where its shadow was darkest' (II, 4, p.76). He holds himself outside the cosily safe world of the Soho house: 'Some half-dozen times a year, at most, he claimed his privilege of coming in uninvited' (II, 21, p. 201). Just before Darnay's first trial in Paris, Carton arrives, but – without explanation – he 'must not be seen' (III, 5, p. 206). Mysteriously, he appears 'at Mr Cruncher's elbow as negligently as he might have stood at the Old Bailey itself' (III, 8, p. 382) to recognise Barsad. When Lucie faints after Darnay's sentence, it is Sydney who comes out 'from the obscure corner from which he had never moved' (III, 11, p. 318) to pick her up. Writing his final letter in his cell, Darnay, we are told, 'never thought of Carton. His mind was so full of the others, that he never once thought of him' (III, 13, p. 331). Sydney Carton, peculiarly, is in the world of the novel, but, habitually, not of it. His separateness is very different in kind from Lucie's, his spiritual 'otherness' nicely contrasted with her conventional domestic piety. Carton is a man whose real self is in hiding, in disguise.

> If Sydney Carton ever shone anywhere, he certainly never shone in the house of Doctor Manette. He had been there often, during a whole year, and had always been the same moody and morose lounger there. When he cared to talk, he talked well; but the cloud of caring for nothing, which over-shadowed him with such a fatal darkness, was very rarely pierced by the light within him. (II, 13, p. 142)

Carton carries the full weight of man's 'fatal darkness' as the disguise hiding 'the light within him'. In a figurative context that constantly refers the darkness of man's condition to the shadow of death, Sydney's 'inner light' is much more than a cliché. In Carton, man's two identities, mortal and immortal, meet and conflict. Conscious of the clash, Sydney evinces a clarity of spiritual awareness and insight unique in the novel. Although Lucie retrieves him from despair and gives him a human perspective whereby he can see some hope for the future, when she asks ' "can I not save you, Mr Carton? Can I not recall you . . . ?" ' he dismisses the idea of a new start as ' "a dream, that ends in nothing, and leaves the sleeper where he lay down" ' (II, 13, p. 144). Lucie's questions both echo the title of the first book and anticipate Manette's ' "I have saved him" ': Carton's rejection is an act of extraordinary spiritual wisdom. He knows, as Lucie does not, that the recall she offers is illusory because it ignores the past; he knows, as Manette does not, that no man can save another. Carton cannot fit the

moral and emotional neatness of Lucie's world because, quite simply, he
knows too much. He carries the spiritual burden of the City of Man, the
knowledge, *de profundis*, of man's inescapable condemnation, and of man's
inability to secure salvation by his own exertions. He knows, in the passage
referred to earlier, that ' "there is no real hope" '. The knowledge of human
mortality that disguises and obscures Carton's real self also imprisons him,
as Lorry, for one fleeting moment, recognises: 'Taking note of the wasted
air which clouded the naturally handsome features, and having the
expression of prisoners' faces fresh in his mind, he was strongly reminded
of that expression' (III, 9, p. 294). It is as if Lorry has seen him for the
first time. Sydney can only shed his disguise and attain freedom by fulfilling
his metaphysical destiny; the account of his walk around Paris the night
before Darnay's trial makes that destiny clear.

Hemmed in by the darkness of the City of Man, the final stage of Carton's
journey towards his spiritual identity, the journey 'of a tired man, who
had wandered and struggled and got lost, but who at length struck into
his road and saw its end' (II, 9, p. 297), begins with the formal
announcement of the Christian doctrine of resurrection.

> These solemn words, which had been read at his father's grave, arose
> in his mind as he went down the dark streets, among the heavy
> shadows, with the moon and the clouds sailing on high above him.
> 'I am the resurrection and the life, saith the Lord: he that believeth
> in me, though he were dead, yet shall he live: and whosoever liveth
> and believeth in me, shall never die.' (III, 9, p. 298)

During the night, with the words of the covenant of resurrection 'in the
echoes of his feet, and . . . in the air', Carton walks contemplating 'the
whole life and death of the city' which, 'dominated by the axe', has 'travelled
that length of self-destruction' to the denial of Christian hope. The
procession of victims is endless and futile; the graveyards promise only
'Eternal Sleep'. Finally, Carton arrives at the river, temporally and
spiritually at the point of Eliot's 'uncertain hour before the morning/Near
the ending of interminable night'.[12] What follows is so important to the
novel's imaginative and semantic pattern, so important to the whole
development of Dickens's symbolic realism, and, indeed, so extraordinary,
that it needs quotation at length.

> . . . the day came coldly, looking like a dead face out of the sky. Then,
> the night, with the moon and the stars, turned pale and died, and for
> a little while it seemed as if Creation were delivered over to Death's
> dominion.
> But, the glorious sun, rising, seemed to strike those words, that
> burden of the night, straight and warm to his heart in its long bright
> rays. And looking along them, with reverently shaded eyes, a bridge
> of light appeared to span the air between him and the sun, while the

river sparkled under it.

The strong tide, so swift, so deep, and certain, was like a congenial friend, in the morning stillness . . . he lingered there yet a little longer, watching an eddy that turned and turned purposeless, until the stream absorbed it, and carried it to the sea. – 'Like me!'

A trading boat, with a sail of the softened colour of a dead leaf, then glided into his view, floated by him, and died away. As its silent track in the water disappeared, the prayer that had broken up out of his heart for a merciful consideration of all his poor blindnesses and errors, ended in the words, 'I am the resurrection and the life.' (III, 9, p. 299)

The passage builds through two parallel semantic movements, from death to rebirth that simultaneously figure shifts of existential level from the mundane to the transcendental. The first of these movements is cosmic, universal. The day of Thanatos comes, 'looking like a dead face out of the sky'; Sydney watches the created world die, the City of Man become a City of the Dead. But the triumph of Thanatos lasts only 'for a little while'. The brevity of 'Death's dominion' has specific biblical reference and authority: 'Christ being raised from the dead dieth no more; death hath no more dominion over him.'[13] The rising of 'the glorious sun' is, via traditional religious punning, the rising of the Son, in glory, over the kingdom of Death. As in *Little Dorrit*, the mystery of the Christian resurrection is enacted through the physically real world. But, whereas the connection between the sunset manifestation of the 'blessed later covenant' and Amy was imputed, Dickens makes the connection between the sunrise of the risen Christ and Carton quite explicit. The 'long bright rays' not only realise the resurrection for Carton, but also bridge the gulf between the inner self and the sun/Son, between man and the Godhead. Nor is the bridge only a seeming reality: verbally and semantically bi-valent, the 'bridge of light' both appears in the sense of 'seems', and appears in the sense of 'is made manifest'. The bridge exists both subjectively, in Sydney's perception, and objectively, a fact of the phonemal world. In a single movement at once actual and symbolic, Carton's spiritual self, 'the light within him', disguised by mortality, imprisoned by the mundane world, is liberated through direct mystical communion with the transcendental non-self, the light of the risen sun, and becomes one with it. With the sudden immanence of the transcendental, Sydney Carton is ready to assume his spiritual identity.

The second half of the passage must be read in the context of the death and resurrection pattern of the first half, a pattern which it echoes and completes. Carton considers his mortal condition as it is imaged in the external world through the habitual Dickensian emblem of transience, the flowing river, 'so swift, so deep, and certain'. But 'the strong tide' that carries the assurance of mortality is 'like a congenial friend', for, in the Christian paradox of man's two states, death is the precondition to life. Carton's reading of the meaning of the river is not only an acceptance of inevitable mortality, but also, through the image of the eddy, a nihilistic renunciation of his life as 'purposeless'. In the parallelism set up by the paragraph divisions, and in the transcendental context of the preceding part of the passage, Carton's renunciation, the dismissal of his own life, may be seen as a symbolic death, a resignation of the ' "me" ' that is the mortal self to 'Death's dominion'. As before, that dominion does not last long. Straightforwardly, but with potent effect, the figurative meaning of the eddy is, at the beginning of the next paragraph, imaginatively transferred to the trading-boat, with its sail, evocatively, 'the softened colour of a dead leaf'. With the passing of the boat, Sydney prays for forgiveness, his prayers ending coincidentally with the disappearance of the boat's 'silent track'. This juxtaposition of processes effects a symbolic transmission: the dying-away of the boat and the fading of its wash signal the relinquishing of mortal life and its attendant 'blindnesses and errors'. 'For he that is dead is freed from sin.'[14] What is left is the statement of resurrection. The movement through death to rebirth in the first half of the passage is re-enacted in the personal microcosm of the second half. The liberation of Carton's spiritual inner self that concludes the first two paragraphs is completed by the relinquishment of the mortal and its attributes in the second two paragraphs. Overall, a cumulative process releases the transcendental from the mundane and climaxes in a final prayer that is also an affirmation: ' "I am the resurrection and the life." ' The speaker is Carton and, with the shock that comes from a suddenly apparent switch of focus, one realises that the supplicant has become the author of the prayer. Carey has complained that the quotations from the burial service occur with 'no explanation of who in the novel [the resurrection is] supposed to be occurring to';[15] yet the attribution here is perfectly clear, but so daring that Carey has missed it. In the final prayer, the full significance of the 'bridge of light' spanning the air and the mortal river between Carton and the sun/Son becomes clear. 'Saith the Lord' is omitted from the end of the phrase because it would now be tautological. The transubstantiation that in *Little Dorrit* turns an empirically real sunset into an affirmation of immortal grace in *A Tale of Two Cities* produces the literal apotheosis of the hero. Carton's secret self, hidden, disguised, imprisoned by mortality throughout the novel, is shown to be, again quite literally, immortal. In a mystical fusion of identity(-ies) that amounts to a confirmation of identity, Sydney Carton takes on the divinity of Christ. What this passage describes is nothing less than a Christophany. Going to their mortal deaths, Carton and the seamstress are indeed 'two children of the Universal Mother'; but when she says to him, ' "I think you were sent to me by Heaven" ' (III, 15, p. 356) we must take her statement at its face value.

Carton's death saves Darnay, and allows the construction of a positive future. The account of this future is not to be taken simply on a historico-realist level, any more than is the rest of the novel. In contrast to Lucie's enclave of hope earlier, the future envisaged by the end of the novel is firmly rooted in a recognition of the reality of the past. The rescue of Darnay and his family leads to Carton's memory holding 'a sanctuary in their hearts, and in the hearts of their descendants, generations hence' (III, 15, p. 358). Paralleling this rescue, moreover, the City of Man is redeemed by Carton's sacrifice: he sees 'a beautiful city and a brilliant people rising from this abyss'. Similarly again, the future city is grounded in a proper adjustment to the past: Carton, 'sublime and prophetic', foresees 'the evil of this time and the previous time . . . gradually making expiation for itself and wearing out' (III, 15, p. 357). Sydney Carton's sacrifice saves Darnay: but Carton does not die for *Darnay*, for Darnay himself is disguised throughout the novel, using a name that will not tie him to his past.

> 'I heard that you were released, Citizen Evrémonde. I hoped it was true?'
> 'It was. But, I was again taken and condemned.'
> 'If I may ride with you, Citizen Evrémonde, will you let me hold your hand?' . . .
> As the patient eyes were lifted to his face, he saw a sudden doubt in them, and then astonishment . . .
> 'Are you dying for him?' she whispered.
> 'And his wife and child. Hush! Yes.' (III, 13, p. 337)

Carton's reply to the seamstress's final question makes it clear that the preposition 'for' is to be understood not only in the sense of 'in the place of' but also 'because of' or 'on account of'. Carton dies not 'for' Darnay, but 'for' Evrémonde. Carton takes the name of Evrémonde, dies in his place and on his account and that of his family. As even Barsad recognises, Carton pays ' "the forfeit" ' (III, 15, p. 354) for being Evrémonde. Unable to save himself despite his own good works, ' "taken and condemned" ' by the law for the past sins of his race, rescued by a divine saviour who takes his name and dies for him, who else is Evrémonde but – as the half-pun reveals – Everyman? The whole novel is a fable in which a secret Christ, burdened by the knowledge of the mortality he has taken on,[16] in hiding in the City of Man, eventually pays the forfeit for Citizen Everyman and, redeeming him from the consequences of the Original Sin of his race, offers him resurrection and the chance of future life. Written throughout upon two levels, the one realist, the other symbolic, narratively built around a typological method, *A Tale of Two Cities* is a Christological myth about salvation; the end term of Dickens's symbolic realism, it is also the nearest he ever came to writing allegory.

8

'Our Feverish Contact Fly':
Arnold and the Symbol in Retreat

For both Dickens and Carlyle, symbolic realism was not only a way of representing the world but, simultaneously, also a way of guaranteeing the imaginative authority of such a representation. By asserting the presence of a semantic scheme in the very stuff of experienced reality Carlyle and Dickens sought to obviate the subjective basis of their interpretative models. Meaning was not, as it was for the Romantics, an interpretative structure generated from the self's engagement with the non-self, but a structure that had objective existence in, and on the same terms as, material reality. The quest for an authority beyond the self, for the healing magic of certitude, was a constant element in the development of Victorian thought. The most obvious form in which it expressed itself was religious: Newman's progress from the liberal theology of Oriel under Whately, to the High Anglicanism of the Oxford Movement, to the *principium et fons* of authority, Rome itself, is paradigmatic. Precisely the same quest could find the Grail totally elsewhere, in the narrow fundamentalism of Protestant dissent, in the no less dogmatic atheism of a man like Charles Bradlaugh. The need for spiritual authority has secular parallels, in the doctrinaire formulations of Utilitarianism and political economists: Coketown is all 'fact'; how reassuringly final is the Iron Law of Wages! The quest for authority finds aesthetic expression, as subsequent chapters will show, in the work of Ruskin and in the architectural theories of Pugin and the Ecclesiologists. Ironically – and inevitably – the proliferation of final solutions rendered the quest simultaneously more urgent and more impossible of resolution. 'The age was learning, but it had not mastered, the lesson that truth lies not in the statement but in the process: it had a childlike craving for certitude, as if the natural end of every refuted dogma was to be replaced by another dogma.'[1] The symbolic realism of Carlyle and, even more, of Dickens retains its currency for us where other Victorian solutions to doubt do not precisely because it relies upon the experiential process of art rather than upon statement; its strategy is primarily imaginative, remaking the very world that it also seeks to explain. As conscious as his contemporaries of the need for answers to doubt and confusion, Matthew Arnold adopted a different strategy, but one that gives an important perspective upon symbolic realism and – because of the terms upon which, it seems to me, it fails – serves to highlight the particular achievement of Carlyle's and Dickens's fusion of the real and the symbolic.

Like Master Humphrey's vision of London at the beginning of *The Old Curiosity Shop*, the contemporary world in Arnold's 'The Scholar Gipsy'[2] is characterised by feverishness and lack of purposeful direction, a society infected by 'this strange disease of modern life,/With its sick hurry, its divided aims,/Its heads o'ertaxed, its palsied hearts' (11. 203–5). Against such a world Arnold sets the Scholar Gipsy and his search after arcane knowledge. The Scholar, 'tired of knocking at preferment's door', quits Oxford and sets out to learn from the gipsies how 'to rule . . . The workings of men's brains': ' "And I," he said, "the secret of their art,/When fully learned, will to the world impart" ' (11. 46–9). The Svengalian secret is, of course, never learnt or imparted; but it is not in its possession or otherwise that the Scholar Gipsy's importance for Arnold lies. Rather, he represents the quester whose unworldly dedication to his unlikely quest can be counterpoised against the modern world's loss of direction: 'Thou hadst *one* aim, *one* business, *one* desire' (1. 152). As such, he takes on, for Arnold, a symbolic quality that transcends the historical identity he has in Glanvil's *Vanity of Dogmatizing*, the source of the story.

> But thou possessest an immortal lot
>   And we imagine thee exempt from age
>   And living as thou liv'st on Glanvil's page,
>   Because thou hadst − what we, alas, have not! (11. 157–60)

Yet the Scholar Gipsy's spiritual agency remains oddly undefined and its application to the 'strange disease of modern life' uncertain. The 'immortal lot' to which Arnold consigns − one is tempted to say condemns − his Gipsy is not one of engagement in human life, but of estrangement from it. Indeed, Arnold specifically enjoins him to run away from the contemporary world: 'fly our paths, our feverish contact fly!' (1. 221). But, if the role of the poem's central character, and indeed the character himself, is indistinct, the reality from which he is in apparently permanent retreat is registered with conviction. Arnold's depiction of the natural world is both sensuously evocative and physically precise.

> Through the thick corn the scarlet poppies peep,
> And round green roots and yellowing stalks I see
>   Pale pink convulvulus in tendrils creep;
>   And air-swept lindens yield
> Their scent, and rustle down their perfumed showers
>   Of bloom on the bent grass where I am laid,
>   And bower me from the August sun with shade . . . (11. 23–9)

The countryside through which the Scholar Gipsy drifts so uncertainly is mid-century Oxfordshire, with its seasonal pattern of agricultural labour and country custom, its particular work and particular places.

> Shepherds had met him on the Hurst in spring . . . (1. 57)

> And boys who in lone wheatfields scare the rooks . . . (1. 64)

> Maidens who from the distant hamlets come
> To dance around the Fyfield elm in May ... (11. 82–3)

> And, above Godstow Bridge, when hay-time's here
> In June, and many a scythe in sunshine flames,
> Men who through those wide fields of breezy grass
> Where black-winged swallows haunt the glittering Thames,
> To bathe in the abandoned lasher pass ... (11. 91–5)

Both immediate and timeless, specific and associative, the descriptions carry a powerful emotional and imaginative charge. In no other poem is Arnold's deep attachment to the Oxfordshire countryside so evident, or so persuasively conveyed. Yet the Scholar Gipsy has only a peripheral relationship to it. 'Seen by rare glimpses' (1. 54), his existence in the poem of which he is the central creation remains lacking in context. The values to which Arnold seems to be committed, and which the Scholar Gipsy represents, are not only undefined, they are too frail and perhaps – remembering 'the lone alehouse on the Berkshire moors' (1. 58) – too priggish to survive the very world that the poetry realises for us. For the good of his health, as it were, the Gipsy is dispatched instead to the never-never land of the Arnoldian pastoral.

> Still nursing the unconquerable hope,
> Still clutching the inviolable shade,
>   With a free onward impulse brushing through,
> By night, the silvered branches of the glade –
>   Far on the forest skirts, where none pursue,
>   On some mild pastoral slope
> Emerge, and resting on the moonlit pales,
> Freshen thy flowers, as in former years,
> With dew, or listen with enchanted ears,
>   From the dark dingles, to the nightingales. (11. 211–20)

Weakly denotative though vaguely uplifting – 'the unconquerable hope', 'the inviolable shade' – and over-reliant upon a stock assemblage of Romantic props – moonlight, dewy flowers and nightingales – the whole stanza is tired and imaginatively second-hand, particularly in contrast to the earlier discriptions. The language that characterises Arnold's pastoral asylum precludes vitality as surely as the way in which he conceives the Gipsy's quest precludes significant engagement with human society. Verbally and narratively divorced from the imaginative life of the poem, the Scholar Gipsy becomes an abstraction. The contrast with the creative strategies of Carlyle and Dickens is striking. For Carlyle, human history is to be read typologically through the archetypal patterns of biblical narrative: the meaning of the Invisible world becomes knowable in and through the Visible. For Dickens, material and phenomenal reality forms an articulated semantic structure: the meaning of man's life is to be found in the fabric of the world he actually inhabits. 'The Scholar Gipsy', by converting the central symbolic character in whom the poem's apparent values are invested into an abstraction, divorces the symbol from the physically real. I say 'apparent' values, not only because of their relative lack of definition, but also because the imaginative values of the poem are invested elsewhere, in Arnold's compelling realisation of the Oxfordshire countryside. It is these latter values that command our assent because they are actualised through our experience of the poem; they are, moreover, indissolubly wedded to the representation of a world that we can recognise as belonging to the empirical reality of time and space. In consequence, the values represented by the Gipsy have none of the realist authority that we find in Carlylean history or Dickensian fiction. Arnold finds his quester after truth in a mythical vagrant from seventeenth-century Oxford; Dickens finds his quester in Bucket of the Detective threading the labyrinth of Victorian London. As both character and symbol the Scholar Gipsy never sheds a limitingly bookish identity; despite all claims for the permanent significance of his quest he remains the creature of Glanvil's page or of Arnold's enervated pastoralism. Similarly, the authority for Arnold's diagnosis of contemporary malaise derives not from the poem's imaginative values but from generalisation and abstraction.

> . . . repeated shocks, again, again,
> Exhaust the energy of strongest souls,
> And numb the elastic powers. (11. 144–6)

> O Life unlike to ours!
> Who fluctuate idly without term or scope,
> Of whom each strives, nor knows for what he strives . . . (11. 166–8)

> . . . strong the infection of our mental strife,
> Which, though it gives no bliss, yet spoils for rest . . . (11. 222–3)

In its overall strategy and argument 'The Scholar Gipsy' not only rejects the specific, the physical and the imaginatively immediate in favour of the self-consciously literary and the abstract, but also implicitly asserts that the latter have superior authority. It is impossible to assent to that authority because its moral thrust is divergent from, and even counter to, the direction of the poem's creative vitality. In the argument of 'The Scholar Gipsy', Arnold effectively reneges on his own imagination.

The rejection of the specific and the physically actual in favour of the abstract and the non-specific is a major tendency of Arnold's prose writings. In *Culture and Anarchy*[3] the objects of Arnold's satiric criticism – the Liberal Free Traders, the Non-Conformist churches, 'the young lions of *The Daily Telegraph*'[4] – are realised with a creative vigour and immediacy that gives them an authentic imaginative presence. When he advocates the superior values of culture, however, Arnold's language loses focus and, instead of definition, 'we are offered a succession of suggestive imprecisions'.[5] Culture means 'getting to know, on all the matters which most concern us, the best which has been thought and said in the world'; 'it is *a study of perfection*', proposing ' "To render an intelligent being yet more intelligent" ' and thus, somehow, ' "To make reason and the will of God prevail" '. Culture is, in the most famous and most vapid of Arnold's definitions – or, rather, non-definitions – 'Sweetness and Light'.[6] Apparently having little clear idea of what he means by his central concept, Arnold conveys even less idea of how culture might function in society. It is seemingly invested, or to be invested, in 'a certain number of *aliens* . . . who are mainly led . . . by the love of human perfection'.[7] Theirs is to be the responsibility for the dissemination of culture, although this is not to be undertaken by direct political action, which Arnold associates with Hebraism and with his society's anti-Hellenic 'preference of doing to thinking'.[8] It is true that Arnold does propose that the state should take a far more central role in public education but, in *Culture and Anarchy* at least, he fails to suggest how this could realistically come about – particularly when the cultured are to keep their hands clean of politics.[9] The whole argument of *Culture and Anarchy* exemplifies a classic impasse of liberal thought: the very terms on which the critic's dislike for social abuse or deprivation is founded, and in which it is formulated, necessarily disable him from suggesting specific remedies. The consequences, in Arnold's case, are well summarised by Raymond Williams.

> Culture was a process, but he could not find the material of that process, either, with any confidence, in the society of his own day, or, fully, in a recognition of an order that transcended human society. The result seems to be that, more and more, and against his formal intention, the process becomes an abstraction.[10]

It is, however, in his religious writings – in *St Paul and Protestantism, Literature and Dogma* and *God and the Bible*[11] – that Arnold's tendency to replace the material and immediate by the abstract becomes most apparent. Indeed, rather than being the product of his mode of argument – as it seems to be in *Culture and Anarchy* – it becomes a primary element in his religious thesis. That thesis has its basis in Neoplatonism, in the view that God is only fully actual in the realm of the ideal, which is thus understood as having superordinate existence: 'it is as an ideal that the divine has its best worth and reality'.[12] Arnold's stated purpose in entering the mêlée of Victorian religious debate was to assert the permanent value and necessity of Christianity whilst accepting that biblical criticism and scientific rationalism had rendered traditional faith untenable: 'at the present moment two things about the Christian religion must surely be clear to anybody with eyes in his head. One is, that men cannot do without it; the other, that they cannot do with it as it is.'[13] In particular, empirical science had, for once and for all, discredited the miraculous element in Christianity: 'our popular religion at present conceives the birth, ministry, and death of Christ, as altogether steeped in prodigy, brimful of miracle; – *and miracles do not happen*'.[14] What was needed, according to Arnold, was another Reformation. 'Miracles have to go the same way as clericalism and tradition.'[15] Along with miracles must go the whole materialising tendency of Christianity: the belief in a personal God, the concept of the Trinity as defined by the Athanasian Creed, the idea of a physical New Jerusalem, ultimately the Incarnation and the Resurrection itself. 'The immortality propounded by Jesus must be looked for elsewhere than in the materialistic aspirations of our popular religion.'[16] All such notions were the product of man's addiction to anthropomorphic modes of thinking and of the historical conditions governing the writing of both Old and New Testaments. What they obscured was, for Arnold, the real core of both Hebraism and Christianity: moral teaching. Conduct, as *Literature and Dogma* so tirelessly and tiresomely reiterates, is 'three-fourths of life'[17] and the future, as Arnold saw it, lay not with the mysteries of traditional faith – inescapably involved in the substance of the material world – but with a religion of spiritual conduct, with, in short, ethical idealism. The reformulation of Christianity he envisages has important linguistic, and therefore imaginative, consequences. The language of ethical idealism necessarily resolves itself in the direction of the non-physical: Christianity follows cultural process and the Scholar Gipsy down the road to abstraction. The Old Testament terms for God are replaced by 'The Eternal',[18] thereby obviating the discredited personal deity of traditional religion. 'The Eternal' operates in the mundane world not through physical agency but as 'the not ourselves which makes for righteousness',[19] a definition which manages to keep God in the world but ensures that he is hardly miraculous at all. The same process is dominant in Arnold's account of the New Testament. 'To the mind of Jesus, his own resurrection after a short sojourn in the grave was the victory of his cause after his death, and at the price of his death. His disciples materialised his resurrection . . .'[20] Taking Arnold's religious writings as a whole, it is difficult to see how such processes of idealisation and abstraction fulfil his intention of giving to religion 'a basis in something that can be verified'.[21] It is even more difficult to understand how Arnold could believe that by replacing the physical Incarnation and the bodily Resurrection with an ethical scheme founded in Neoplatonic idealism he was somehow saving Christianity. As Gladstone sardonically remarked: 'He combined a fervent zeal for the Christian religion with a not less boldly avowed determination to transform it beyond the possibility of recognition by friend or foe.'[22]

Whatever one's response to Arnold's religious thesis, however, what it is important to recognise here is that behind the whole argument is the attempt to arrive at a viable relationship between what Arnold construes as two different sorts of reality: between, on the one hand, the numinous and, on the other, the materially actual. It is precisely in the area of this relationship that the processes of symbolic realism employed by Carlyle and Dickens operate. But, by virtue of his whole argument, symbolic realism is the very strategy that is unavailable to Arnold. In rejecting what he sees as the reliance of traditional Christianity upon material phenomena, Arnold necessarily rejects the traditional language of Christianity; in particular, biblical language, because it is there that he finds a habitual fusion of the

physical and immediate with the figurative and emblematic. In his preface to
God and the Bible, Arnold tackles the issue head-on. Religious language

> is approximative merely while men imagine it to be adequate; it is *thrown
> out* at certain realities which they very imperfectly comprehend. It is
> materialised poetry, which they give as science; and there can be no worse
> science than materialised poetry. But poetry is essentially concrete; and
> the moment one perceives that the religious language of the human race
> is in truth poetry, which it mistakes for science, one cannot make it an
> objection to this language that it is concrete.[23]

Much of this is well said: the valency of poetic discourse *is* different from that
of scientific, even given the broad definition of 'science' that is evidently
intended here. But Arnold's development of these ideas is unexpected, not to
say downright odd. As a consequence of the 'essentially concrete' nature of
religious language

> the religious consciousness of humanity has produced in Christianity not
> ideas, but imaginations; and it is ideas, not imaginations, which endure.
> The religious consciousness of humanity produced the doctrines of the
> Incarnation and of the Real Presence, – beautiful imaginations, but if
> Christianity depended upon them it would dissolve.[24]

Arnold's argument is based upon a false dichotomy between imaginations and
ideas; quite simply, the Incarnation is both idea and imagination – as a mental
construct it is holistic. This dichotomy is productive of more, however, than
a false analysis. Arnold objects to 'imaginations' becoming objects of worship
and items of doctrine because, as he says earlier, it is 'at realities that this
worship and its language are aimed'.[25] The clear inference is that, whereas
'ideas' for Arnold are real, 'imaginations' produced by the 'materialised poetry'
of 'the religious consciousness of humanity' are unreal: 'it is ideas, not
imaginations, which endure'. Because he has abstracted the conceptual from
mental process and located what is enduringly real in that abstraction, Arnold
is left asserting that the poetic imagination produces unrealities. It is a peculiar
position to find a poet adopting. It is even more peculiar when set against
another of Arnold's accounts of the relationship between religion and poetry.

> Our religion has materialized itself in the fact, in the supposed fact;
> it has attached its emotion to the fact, and now the fact is failing it.
> But for poetry the idea is everything; the rest is a world of illusion,
> of divine illusion. Poetry attaches its emotion to the idea; the idea *is*
> the fact. The strongest part of our religion today is its unconscious
> poetry.[26]

The passage reveals false dichotomies similar to those in the passage from

God and the Bible, but the conclusions are quite different. Poetry here is committed to the ideal not the concrete; as such it cannot be held responsible for the 'materialism' of religion, but becomes, rather, its 'strongest part' – albeit apparently unconsciously. The obvious contradictions between this and the argument in *God and the Bible* are suggestive of the utmost indecision on Arnold's part; nevertheless, the evident differences obscure an identity of purpose. In both is the attempt – central, as I have argued, to all Arnold's religious writings – to determine the relationship between the numinous and the physically actual, and, in these particular passages, to locate the role of the creative imagination in that relationship. Arnold comes nearest to success in his assertion that, in poetry, 'the idea *is* the fact'; he fails overall because he can only partly accept the implications of this, that our sense of what is real is continually generated from our imaginative apprehension of the world and that, in Basil Willey's succinct phrase, 'Faith, like Imagination, is alive and creative, ever *realizing* its own objects'.[27] It is here that the potency of symbolic realism, both as a mode of perception and as a creative technique, is so apparent. Not only are the abstract and the material fused within a single percept, but the essential creativity of imagination actualises that percept in the consciousness of the perceiver. The authority for what is believed, whether it be Carlyle's view of history or Dickens's presentation of the nature of time, comes from a double process of actualisation, from the fusion of symbol and reality in the external world and from the realisation of the fusion through the agency of the individual imagination: the self is dynamically united with the non-self, the knower with the known. Arnold never achieves such a creative and authoritative sense of reality. What must be seen as his retreat from the imagination, evident as early as 'The Scholar Gipsy', results in a false dichotomy between the ideal and the material and a false location of reality in abstraction. It is both significant and unsurprising that he stopped writing poetry in the 1860s. Despite the sincerity of his quest for authority, for verification, the abstracts at which Arnold eventually arrived have little validity and have proved to have less endurance. A narrower but more rigorous science than that to which he trusted for what was verifiable has replaced Arnold's God of moral conduct with genetic heredity and social conditioning. The poetic imagination, its 'reality' impugned, has lost its context in the everyday world. A century after Arnold's death, the great majority of people in Britain have little concern for either poetry or religion, for either Literature or Dogma.

Throughout his prose writings Arnold constantly enjoins the necessity of 'seeing things as they really are':[28] this is the function he assigns to criticism, to Hellenism, to culture. Yet, in Arnold's usage, and in the context of the whole tendency of his work, the metaphor of seeing has lost its physical basis. Arnoldian 'seeing' is a process of abstract understanding. In contrast, the process of seeing generated from the symbolic realism of Carlyle and, even more, of Dickens is simultaneously cognitive and

physically actual: David Copperfield 'sees' the nature of time because he
sees the storm that lays waste to Yarmouth beach. Seeing things as they
really are in this latter sense is fundamental to Ruskinian aesthetics and
Pre-Raphaelite painting.

PART TWO

9

'Bona Fide Imitation':
Pictorial Realism and
Modern Painters

According to J. G. Millais, the original aim of the artists who comprised the Pre-Raphaelite Brotherhood was 'to take Nature as their only guide'.[1] In the quotation with which he prefaced his pamphlet, *Pre-Raphaelitism*, Ruskin amplified the prescription: '[Young painters] . . . should go to nature . . . having no other thought but how best to penetrate her meaning; rejecting nothing, selecting nothing, and scorning nothing' (3, p. 623).[2] The result of this demand for the scrupulously exact registration of the external world was a concentration upon the closest physical detail, a concentration Ruskin applauded in the Pre-Raphaelite precursor, John Lewis: 'a refinement of drawing almost miraculous, and appreciable only, as the minutiae of nature itself are appreciable, by the help of the microscope' (12, pp. 363–4). The recurrence of precisely similar terms in Bagehot's essay on Dickens is suggestive. 'His works . . . well exemplify the telling power of minute circumstantiality . . . a detective ingenuity in microscopic detail.'[3] Taine made the comparison I have implied explicit: '[Dickens] . . . will be lost, like the painters of his country, in the minute and impassioned observation of small things.'[4] Certainly, sheer physical presence – both as individual details and as massive accumulations – loom large in Dickens's imagination. Parallels to Dickens's awareness that, physically and metaphysically, ' "aw's a muddle" ' have been drawn with Carlyle and with Arnold, although in this latter case that awareness is abstracted into a sense of moral disarray. If a parallel also holds – and, according to Taine, holds more directly – with Pre-Raphaelite painting, in what way can a work of visual art be compared with a work of literature? The grounds of such comparison being found, more specific questions can be asked. Does the concentration upon physical detail in any particular Pre-Raphaelite picture show the kind of integrity with the painting's overall statement that we find in a Dickens novel? How far does the Pre-Raphaelite registration of the real take on that emblematic character that we have seen in Dickens and Carlyle? How far, indeed, are the paintings of the Pre-Raphaelites an expression of symbolic realism?

In order to answer such questions, it is necessary to clear some preliminary theoretical ground, to analyse, in the first place, quite how it is possible to describe a painting as a representation of reality. The attempt 'to bring reality back alive',[5] to capture a three-dimensional world through the two-dimensional means of paint and canvas, has been a recurrent feature of Western art. But is such a transcription even feasible? Wollheim sets out the 'commonsense' argument with clarity: 'the fundamental explanation of why one thing is a representation of something else lies in the simple fact of resemblance: a picture or drawing is a representation of Napoleon because it resembles Napoleon'. As Wollheim goes on to say, 'the concept of resemblance is notoriously elliptical',[6] but even if one ignores this tendency towards mere tautology it must be asked quite *what* in the infinite complexities of the external world is picked out for representation, and in what way a static stroke of paint can be said, quite categorically to resemble the elusive and fluctuating quality of the world as we see it. The whole process of seeing involves the operation of techniques of selection and discrimination. 'It is the essence of attention that it is selective. We can focus on *something* in our field of vision, but never on *everything*. All attention must take place against a background of inattention.'[7] These techniques of concentration may be paralleled in painting for effects of emphasis or dramatisation, but they cannot be simply duplicated. In looking at a painting of realist intent, we will always see more than we would in looking at the real thing, or less than we would. Art can thus become, as Gombrich suggests, a means of visual discovery, a means of restructuring and realigning the conventions of vision; but it cannot simply reproduce what is seen. Indeed, the very notion of an unequivocal reality, identical for all who experience it, is suspect. Vision is dynamic, acts of perception and response, 'far from being mere acts of passive registration, are creative acts of grasping structure'.[8] We 'make' the outside world through the act of looking at it, as surely as we 'make' it by labelling it: 'Nature is a product of art and discourse.'[9] However, this does not suggest a kind of perceptual solipsism; many conventions of visual organisation are the products of cultural and historical expectation. The mythology of *trompe l'œil* realism – Parrhasios' grapes, Giotto's fly – is well established, but tends to show the power of cultural conditioning, rather than to record moments at which artists have broken into a world of pure illusion. Indeed, what may seem to us to be a perfectly acceptable image of external reality may be visually incomprehensible to an observer outside the Western European tradition.

Artistic structures, then, simply cannot provide a duplication of the visual world: there are too many variables both in what is seen and in the way it is seen. And yet we all know what is meant by a realistic painting and direct comparison beween a pictorial image and a visual image of reality is possibly the commonest aesthetic act in response to a painting. It is common, moreover, to responses at both high and low levels of aesthetic complexity. Once we have accepted that there can be no simple one-for-one relationship between image and reality, how are such correlations and parallels possible? The answer lies, I believe, in the essentially symbolic nature of all image-making. The pictorial image is, *in some way*, a symbol for the external world. I stress 'in some way' because any semiotic theory of aesthetics runs up against an initial problem. In order for a pictorial image to be a symbol, it must signify something outside itself: the sign must have a denotatum. But, as several critics have pointed out, this seems to contradict the sense of direct experience, of confronting the thing in itself, that we feel in our experience of art.[10] Put at its simplest, the argument against the semiotic theory is that an experience cannot be described as simultaneously direct and symbolic, for to experience symbolism is necessarily to experience a process of mediation. Such an argument assumes a substantial distinction between direct perception, the characteristic of which in 'the aesthetic experience' is immediacy, and indirect perception, the feature of any experience of symbolism. Underlying this view is an atomist model of the consciousness, a model disputed, most tellingly perhaps, by Arnheim.

> Academic psychology . . . is accustomed to distributing psychological phenomena into the three compartments of cognition, motivation, and emotion instead of realizing that every mental state has cognitive, motivational, and emotional dimensions and cannot be defined properly by any one of the three.[11]

The distinction between direct and indirect perception assumed by the anti-semiotic argument is artificial. How do we *know* when we perceive something directly or indirectly? When we receive the percept 'white bear', to take a Shandean example, do we *directly* perceive only shape, position, colour, and only *indirectly* identify the brute as a polar bear and recognise danger? Surely Arnheim's argument for the complex unity of every mental state corresponds far more closely to experience. At most, directness or indirectness are only aspects of a homogeneous state or act. To see a white bear is to experience an immediate interaction of perceptions of size and shape, ideas of savageness or ferocity, emotions of helplessness or terror, and the motivation, probably, to run away. The potentially endless discourse that attends Mr Shandy's white bear is a true reflection of the complexity of our actual experience. What is important for us is the specific pattern or order in which these multiple responses are arranged. Precisely the same applies in an aesthetic transaction. Rigidly to demarcate direct and indirect perception is to assume that artistic symbolisation works in the same way as that employed in formal logic. It does not. The symbols used are not classically mediatory; the values and equivalences assigned to them are complex, not simple; and they are determined by our experience of the work of art as a whole, not by any prior system of one-for-one relationships. But a painting is no more a purely symbolic vehicle than it is a straightforward assemblage of form and colour; its status, I would suggest, is always somewhere on the line between the pole of pure painterly values and the pole of purely symbolic values. Any response to a work of art is dichotomous, being drawn on the one hand towards seeing the painting as an organisation of colour-masses, and on the other hand towards 'reading' the painting as symbolic of 'real-life' objects, concerns, values and ideas. At one pole, Art for Art's sake; at the other, art as a wholly social phenomenon. The one response sees artistic structures as opaque, the other as transparent. Pure abstraction, as in some of the work of Nicholson and Mondrian, will tend to the pole of minimum denotation; other art forms, such as Soviet Social Realism, will tend towards the opposite extreme.

Given that a painting may stand in a symbolic relation to the real world, I have still offered no explanation as to *how* a formal configuration can be symbolic of some element of external reality. Gombrich has argued that we accept an image as representing external reality because of cultural conditioning, but this offers no suggestion as to why we accept certain images as adequate representations *in the first place*.[12] Why, for example, is Figure 9.1 an adequate symbol for 'man', but not Figure 9.2? It is here that one can see some point in the argument that Representation is Resemblance; the obvious reply to the question is simply that Figure 9.1 *looks* more like a man than does Figure 9.2. But such a reply really avoids the central issues of why

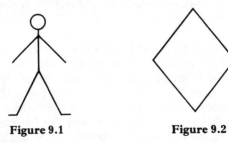

Figure 9.1   **Figure 9.2**

this is so. A possible answer is given by Arnheim in the aesthetic argument he derives from Gestalt psychology. Figure 9.1 offers a closer parallel — though not an equivalent — to the way we actually see than does Figure 9.2 for, as Arnheim insists, 'vision is not a mechanical recording of elements but the grasping of significant structural patterns'.[13] However crudely, Figure 9.1 immediately displays a seizing upon structural qualities that are felt to be visually essential, a process that is fundamental to all perceptual organisation, and fundamental to the perception of resemblance in a representational painting. Thus painting may be seen as being justified in terms of 'the real' without being realistic. An adequate symbol is rarely entirely dissociated from the visual appearance of the real-life object; the strategies of individual perception may be subjective but, as had already been remarked, they are not solipsistic. In finding a workable artistic symbol for external reality an artist objectivises individual perception; he makes a personal vision public property. Important as the 'structural map'[14] of such a symbol may be, however, structure is only one dimension of a painting's significance. In *Art and Visual Perception* Arnheim is noticeably less comfortable when dealing with the expressionist properties of light and colour, and Gestalt theory in general underplays the importance of stylistic and iconographic traditions. A picture means upon different levels and with different degrees of complexity, and the total experience of a painting is essentially an experience of the multiple interactions of those different levels. Figure 9.3 is a structural interpretation of a man running; the significance of that symbol in a painting would

Figure 9.3

be determined by its status in relationship to the other dimensions of meaning in the rest of the picture: by its relationship to the structural map of the painting as a whole; by how it relates to the major lights and shades; by the expressionist connotations of its colour, and the connection of that colour to the overall tonal scheme; by the style in which it is conceived and its relation to individual, period and national styles; by the iconographic traditions in which the figure is set. Each level offers a different technique for interpreting the real, and the individual symbol within a painting relates to each one of those levels: a pictorial sign, taken in relation to its context, offers a means of organising and formulating the components of reality.

Like all language-use, all use of pictorial symbols implies an interpretation of the real. We have no difficulty in labelling the central figures in *Our Lady of Vladimir*,[15] Hogarth's *The Shrimp Girl*[16] and Picasso's *Weeping Woman*[17] as 'woman'; the extreme differences in style do not prevent our recognising the correlations of painterly structure and everyday visual experience. But the question as to which of the three is the *most* realistic poses fundamental problems. Hogarth is probably closest to the reality of visual appearance, but it is obvious nonsense to claim that the other paintings are more or less incompetent attempts to achieve visual realism. The reality that concerned the anonymous icon-painter was spiritual, that which concerned Picasso emotional. The pictures are all 'realistic', but each in a different way, a way determined by the painter's organisation of the symbolic and expressive techniques at his disposal. In all three cases the artist has selected from his real-life context, establishing, by means of what he chooses from that context, a hierarchy of visual and referential values. Hogarth's celebration of earthy vitality, emphasised by the gusto of his coarse brush-strokes, is in direct contrast to the delicate rendering and static, calm and conventionalised forms in *Our Lady of Vladimir*. Because the painters understand the world in totally different terms, the value systems implied by their paintings are totally different. Precisely because every painting is interpretative, every painting is also a value judgement. No pictorial symbolisation can ever be entirely neutral. Nor does it matter if the painter's 'real-life context', the data that generated the painting, is inaccessible to us, for the pictures establish their own terms of reference, identifying the relevant data by means of the visual cues employed. These cues operate in at least two directions: towards symbolising the physical world beyond the painting – the hand and eyes in *Woman Weeping*, the contemporary, proletarian dress in *The Shrimp Girl* – and towards expressionist values. The rhythmic, etherialised forms of *Our Lady of Vladimir* direct response towards spiritual evaluation, just as surely as the harsh tonalities, the structural fragmentation and staccato repetition of jagged forms in *Woman Weeping* localise response in specifically human emotions. But this fragmentation pulls our attention towards the geometric forms in the centre of the picture, away from any symbolic function and towards the pictorial surface, existing in and for itself; a stuctural drama develops in the painting as abstracted forms usurp the place of symbolically rendered reality. Both the pictorial status of the symbol and the importance of the symbolisation as such are changed. The greater awareness we have of the interacting techniques of a painting, the more complex becomes the consequent aesthetic experience and the more involved the resulting semantic. Meaning develops, moreover, from the *way* in which pictorial elements are synthesised, as well as from the resultant synthesis. One reason we feel a work of art to be meaningful is because its semantics evolve dynamically from the pictorial structure: meaning and being are experienced simultaneously, as part of one another and as directly as one another.

Some conclusions can now be drawn. A painting relates to the real world by presenting series of visual parallels and affinities that are symbolic in nature; our ability to key pictorial images to the images of visual experience depends upon the types of parallel that exist between the structuring a picture imposes upon our perception and the structuring our perception imposes upon day-to-day reality. Much of the ease with which this symbolic translation is made is dependent upon the experience and visual education of the audience, and the extent to which the painting adopts or rejects the visual and symbolic theses of its stylistic and cultural context. Because an artist must always choose to stress particular aspects of his visual, intellectual and emotional milieu – his real-life context – the resulting picture will always be, explicitly or implicitly, interpretative. Artistic meaning is essentially dramatic, evolving from the interplay of symbolic techniques and interpretative patterns within the painting. The importance of the symbolisation of the actual in a picture is relative, not to the degree of any supposed resemblance to extra-pictorial realities, but to the way in which that symbolisation meshes with the other patterns and structures within the picture. Thus a picture may be described as visually realistic when the inter-relations of its figurative and formal systems direct attention to the symbolic rendering of the real world as a central feature, or as *the* central feature in the picture's make-up.

The figurative and symbolic systems adopted by the young men who comprised the original Pre-Raphaelite Brotherhood were incomprehensible – and positively insulting – to the mid-nineteenth-century critical and artistic establishment. After Rossetti's indiscreet – if not, perhaps, uncalculated – revelation of the meaning of the esoteric cypher, PRB, the highbrow press replied with all the fanatic zeal of a religious inquisition confronted by rank apostasy.[18] Hunt, Millais, Rossetti, even poor Charles Collins, ceased to be mere artists: they became violators of accepted good taste – 'Their trick is, to defy the principles of beauty and the recognized axioms of taste',[19] 'a marked affectation of indifference to everything we are accustomed to seek and to admire'.[20] Heretics against the gospel of progress, they were thought to imply that 'all art since the days of Masaccio is wrong';[21] they return to 'the infancy of their profession',[22] producing 'a mere servile imitation of the cramped style, false perspective, and crude colour of remote antiquity'.[23] One critical voice can stand for the many raised against them:

> What a wilful misapplication of powers is that which affects to treat the human form in the primitive and artless manner of the Middle Ages, while minor accessories are elaborated to a refinement which belongs to the latest days of executive art.[24]

Yet, despite such assertions, it is not to the early Renaissance or to the Middle Ages that one must look for the theoretical basis of Pre-Raphaelite realism. It is to the contemporary aesthetics of John Ruskin and to the critique of Romanticism contained in *Modern Painters*.

Romantic aesthetic theory tends towards the subjective and – in the end – the esoteric. The stress that Romanticism placed upon individual genius had, as its inevitable consequence, a demand that the writer or artist should evolve a distinct personal vocabulary to express his uniquely personal vision. In much late-Romantic work the search for new languages and new schemata led to an abandonment of the public nature of a work of art, to artistic self-communion rather than communication between artist and audience. For Carlyle, as we have seen, this process was directly responsible for the unreality that struck him as the prevalent characteristic of contemporary literature. Remedy could only be found if writers would 'Sweep away utterly all frothiness and falsehood from [the] heart' and commit themselves to 'the faithful study of Reality'.[25] It was this study that John Ruskin set himself to re-establish at the centre of artistic activity.

At the beginning of the section in the first volume of *Modern Painters* entitled 'Of Truth', Ruskin set out the proper object of landscape painting:

> . . . the landscape painter must always have two great and distinct ends: the first, to induce in the spectator's mind the faithful conception

of any natural objects whatsoever; the second, to guide the spectator's mind to those objects most worthy of its contemplation, and to inform him of the thoughts and feelings with which these were regarded by the artist himself. (3, p. 133)[26]

Ruskin conceives the second purpose as more important, 'yet it is altogether impossible to reach the second without having previously reached the first' (3, p. 136). Art's initial purpose, then, is the precise reproduction of the external world. This purpose is valid because Ruskin restates the relationship between man and his works and the reality of external nature. For the eighteenth-century artist, un-ideal realities were to be improved and refined; for the Romantic, reality was to be remade from the imaginative fusion of the self and the non-self. Ruskin's view was quite different.

> Nothing can atone for the want of truth, not the most brilliant imagination, the most playful fancy, the most pure feeling . . . not the most exalted conception, nor the most comprehensive grasp of intellect . . . first, because falsehood is in itself revolting and degrading: and secondly, because nature is so immeasurably superior to all that the human mind can conceive, that every departure from her is a fall beneath her. (3, p. 137)

The initial criterion for any aesthetic judgement, then, is a painting's fidelity to the appearances of the external world. The primacy of 'fact' is a dominant motif of Ruskin's criticism: 'The representation of facts . . . is the foundation of all art' (3, p. 136). The painters of the past are great in proportion to the degree of their mimetic accuracy: 'Orcagna disdains both poetry and taste; he wants the *facts* only' (12, p. 147).[27] The technical quality of 'finish' is translated into another aspect of mimesis: 'All true finish is *added fact*' (5, p. 164). Such an emphasis upon the primacy of fact necessitates what amounts to a fundamentalist theory of perception.

In *Modern Painters*, Ruskin virtually denies the variations in individual perception, or at least claims that there is a 'right' way of seeing an external object, and that any other way of seeing is erroneous, ignorant or – in the case of Salvator and Claude – just plain vicious. One positive consequence of this is Ruskin's demand for a reawakening of our visual sense. Each man has a positive duty 'to bring every sense into that state of cultivation in which it shall form the truest conclusions respecting all that is submitted to it' (4, p. 56). Much of the power of *Modern Painters* comes from the passion which Ruskin brings to simply looking at the world, and from the way in which the minute detail of imaginative observation communicates a sense of visual adventure and discovery.

> Every large wave of the sea is in ordinary circumstances divided into, or rather covered by, innumerable smaller waves, each of which, in all probability, from some of its edges or surfaces reflects the sunbeams;

and hence result a glitter, polish, and vigorous light over the whole
flank of the waves . . . (3, p. 505)

Yet the visual drama of *Modern Painters* is externalised; visual phenomena are
presented as being independent of individual perception. Thus Turner's
superiority springs from his ability to see things as — according to Ruskin —
they actually and objectively *are*: his paintings give 'an entire transcript of the
whole system of nature' (3, p. 616). The eye must innocently receive images
from a natural world that, *a priori*, is more perfect and more beautiful than any
of man's imaginings. Only thus can Ruskin justify his demand that 'from
young artists nothing ought to be tolerated but simple *bona fide imitation* of
nature' (3, p. 623). Ruskin's theory of perception attacks the whole basis of
Romanticism, for it demands a formal demarcation between the perceiver and
the perceived. If, as Ruskin argues, one hope for modern man lies in a love of
nature, it is nature conceived in a very special way, 'pure, separate, felicitous'
(3, p. 193). The key-word is 'separate'. Ruskinian aesthetics rests upon a radical
dualism, an absolute distinction between inner reality and outer reality, subject
and object, and an *a priori* assertion of the supremacy of the object. *Ex
hypothesi*, external nature is inviolable. *Ex hypothesi*, again, any alteration in
that nature initiated by the individual consciousness is not only mistaken, it
is immoral, an act of human presumption. *Modern Painters'* slighting
references to Claude, Poussin and Salvator follow logically from such a theory,
as also does the famous attack upon the pathetic fallacy, permanently invalid
as an artistic technique, according to Ruskin, because it suggests 'that it does
not matter much what things are in themselves, but only what they are to us'
(5, p. 202).[28] Ruskin's argument, here at its most succinct, is revealing. The
phrase 'what things are in themselves' prejudges the whole matter, for it
assumes not only that objects in the external world have an irreducible essence,
but also that, as perceivers, we have access to their quiddity. In fact, we do not
know things in this way; we know *about* things, and both knowing and
perceiving are processes of contextualisation. We can say, to take the Shandean
example again, that we know what a white bear *is* by virtue of the number of
conceptual and perceptual matrices within which we place it; by virtue, as Mr
Shandy knew, of the number of questions that can be asked and answered
about it. But 'by no manner of make-believe can we discover the *what* of
referents. We can only discover the how.'[29] The 'whatness' of a thing is
determined by its 'howness'; Ruskin assumes the opposite to be the case. In
discussing metaphor, he selects as perfect Dante's image of the rebel angels
falling ' "as dead leaves flutter from a bough" ' because 'the clear perception
that *these* are souls, and *those* are leaves' (5, p. 206), is never lost. Reality, by
implication, is composed of discrete entities, a series of 'what' elements that
can be known in themselves, and even metaphor is not allowed to forget the
fact.

In order to defend and to justify his theory of perception, and to safeguard
the separateness of external nature, Ruskin had also to evolve a theory that

would deny to imagination the power of recreating reality assigned to it by the Romantics. Thus, in Ruskin's theory, Imagination simply alters the pure impressions received by the innocent eye: 'the imaginative operations . . . are not creative . . . no new ideas are elicited by them . . . their whole function is only a certain dealing with, concentrating or mode of regarding the impressions received from external things' (4, p. 223). Despite subsequent elaboration in the tripartite division of imaginative functions – Imagination Associative, Imagination Penetrative, Imagination Contemplative – the focus of Ruskin's argument never shifts from 'the impressions received from external things'. Thus Imagination Associative unifies impressions to form a picture, not as a positive act of structuring but as a reassemblage of different images in an order as near as possible to that which Ruskin asserts as nature's own.

> For instance, the landscape above mentioned of Titian's St Jerome may, for aught I know, be a pure transcript of a rocky slope covered with chestnuts among his native mountains. It has all the look of a sketch from nature; if it be not, the imagination developed in it is of the highest order. (4, p. 247)

The Imagination Penetrative does not, as one might expect, seize upon thematic and visual matter and organise it into pictorial statement: it simply discovers more facts about a subject that is, implicitly, adequately structured already. Once again, the inviolability of the external is maintained. Even so, Ruskin feels he must add a final warning against the perilous seductions of the subjective: 'many painters of powerful mind have been lost to the world by their suffering the restless writhing of their imagination in its cave to take place of its healthy and exulting activity in the fields of nature' (4, p. 288). If 'healthy and exulting activity in the fields of nature' sounds like a manifesto for the Great Outdoors, an aesthetic variant upon *Scouting for Boys*, the banality is surely a measure of how far Ruskin is willing to go in his attempts to discredit the Romantic concept of imagination. Only in his description of the third division of the imagination does Ruskin allow any suggestion of creativity. The Imagination Contemplative depends upon regarding the object with a certain 'indistinctness of conception' (4, p. 291) – a mode of awareness already suspect, surely, as inconducive to a due registration of 'fact'. By allowing a play of concepts and images around an object this 'indistinctness' creates new images and image-clusters. This is Ruskin's theory of metaphor, and, despite some rather unconvincing attempts to relate it to abstraction in painting, he considers its proper ground to be literature, for 'it is not to be by lines or colours represented' (4, p. 299). The supreme sway of fact is maintained, in the visual arts at least, and subjective imagination, the monarch of Romantic aesthetics, effectively exiled.

Ruskin's perception of the external world as both endlessly diverse and ineluctably other has all the characteristics of a quantitatively and qualitatively heightened consciousness of physical reality. In this Ruskin is clearly close to Carlyle and Dickens, to the former's almost morbidly acute sensitivity and the latter's intense imaginative apprehension of physical detail – for, whatever its theory of the imagination, *Modern Painters* amply demonstrates, as I have already said, the extraordinary imaginative concentration which Ruskin brought to his observation of the natural world. It could well be argued that the particular type of heightened awareness evident in all three had a common basis in the sheer rate and scope of nineteenth-century expansion. Ever more industrial manufacture, more houses, more streets, whole new towns linked by a railway system that had grown from some thirty miles to nearly seven thousand miles in the twenty years after 1830; more books from the press, more journals and periodicals than ever before – 222 English provincial newspapers, 110 Scottish and 102 Irish in 1850; scientific advance discovering and reclassifying more and more of the natural world, from the new fossils unearthed by Charles Lyell to the new species found by Charles Darwin – an expansion, in fact, of man's whole consciousness of his world, aptly celebrated in all its variety by the Great Exhibition of 1851. Such multitudinousness had not only to be imaginatively encompassed but also to be organised on terms that carried some measure of authority. Carlyle and Dickens, in their different ways, found structure and control through a fusion of the symbolic and the real – essentially creative strategies that, as I have argued, still retain an imaginative validity that is particularly apparent when set against Arnold's alternative recourse to abstraction and ethical idealism. The need for order and authority confronted Ruskin as acutely as it did Carlyle, Dickens and Arnold. If the external world, with all its detailed complex of 'facts', was to be ordered, a hierarchy of value and significance had to be found in its diversity. That Ruskin found such value and significance in his own experience of both art and external nature is unquestionable. But how were such feelings to be validated when the Romantic subjective, in its imaginative fusion of self and non-self, was so suspect? Clearly, if the sense of spiritual significance in the external world is not a product of the creative action of the individual consciousness, then it must be a property of the external world itself.

The justification of Ruskin's aesthetic, and, at the same time, its consequence, is that significance belongs to the object, not to the subject's perception of it. Meaning is a phenomenon of outer reality, not inner. We are mistaken if we believe that our structurings of the real word are adequate: the structures and semantics are there already, outside of us, to be read aright by all those who can see them. What Ruskin wants are artists who, in a metaphor I used earlier, can read the surface syntax of the external world in such a way as to reveal the deep structure meanings it contains. Mere imitation is therefore insufficient. Aristotle's claim that people instinctively enjoy works of imitation would seem superficial to Ruskin, who demands far more: 'Ideas of imitation . . . act by producing . . . the mean and paltry surprise which is felt in jugglery' (3, p. 101). Purely mimetic art is unworthy, not because it fails to mobilise the potentialities of art, but because it is incapable of realising the potentialities of what it imitates: 'it is impossible to imitate anything really great, we can "paint a cat or a fiddle so that they look as if we could take them up"; but we cannot imitate the ocean, or the alps' (3, p. 102). It is not the art which determines the quality of its object, for beauty, sublimity, meaning, all exist in nature quite independently of man's awareness of them. It is a short step from here to a thoroughgoing anthropomorphism.

> It is a strange thing how little in general people know about the sky. It is the part of creation in which nature had done more for the sake of pleasing man, more for the sole and evident purpose of talking to him, and teaching him, than in any other of her works. (3, p. 343)

Ruskin is describing something far more precise than a vaguely spiritual communion with things natural. The impulse from a vernal wood is not, for Ruskin, a pantheist day-dream, but an articulated message. When he describes nature as 'teaching' man, he means precisely that, and it is beauty that carries the didactic purpose of nature. The precondition to being taught is our recognition of the 'otherness' and the other-life of plants and animals: 'sensations of beauty in the plant arrive from our unselfish sympathy with its happiness' (4, p. 152). This upsurge of floral felicity is not an empathetic consequence of our looking at the plant, nor a reflection of our own emotions. The flower is happy in the same way as human beings can be happy. But this is only a first stage.

> Let us observe how [Beauty] is concerned with the *moral functions* of animals, and therefore how it is dependent on the cultivation of every moral sense. There is not any organic creature but, in its history and habits, will exemplify or illustrate to us some moral excellence or deficiency, or some point of God's providential government, which it is necessary for us to know. (4, p. 156)

A divinely ordained structure of meaning, a moral order expressing itself through physical beauty, is the organisational principle of the natural world. This semantic order is not generated by the perceiving consciousness but is a property of the outer world it perceives, as palpably real as colour, form and mass. What we have, of course, is Ruskin's version of symbolic realism. The form which it takes in *Modern Painters* is closer to Dickens than to Carlyle. In order to read history in the way Carlyle does, biblical narratives and thematic patterns must be used as interpretative models. To this extent the meanings inherent in reality are coded and only to be reached through the correspondences established by a typological method. The symbolism of Ruskin's natural world, however, is not conventional in this way, not dependent upon a specific interpretative key. It is understood immediately in and through the act of perception – in the same way, that is, as symbolic meaning is grasped by characters in Dickens's fictional world. Just as the sky and the mountains in *Modern Painters* function semantically to instruct those who have the humility to understand, so also do the ocean and river in *Dombey and Son* and *David Copperfield* communicate the nature and meaning of time to Florence and David. Nor does the material world lose one jot of its physical reality: a geological hammer can be taken to Ruskin's Matterhorn just as certainly as Steerforth drowns in the Yarmouth storm. When Ruskin talks of 'heavenly light, holy and undefiled . . . glorious with the changeless passion of eternity' (3, p. 276), he is reading the same kind of transcendental meaning in sunlight as, in *Little Dorrit*, infuses the sunset over London, and which Sydney Carton reads in 'the glorious sun, rising' over Revolutionary Paris. Differences between Ruskin and Dickens are obvious. Principally, of course, *Modern Painters* is not concerned with the urban environment in which so much of Dickens's fiction is set and which, for Dickens, contains its own structure of symbolic meaning. Nevertheless, for both men – as also, in his different way, for Carlyle – symbolic realism is a central determinant of the imagination and of the very process of perception. The attempt of all three 'to see things as they really are' never becomes the cognitive abstraction it becomes for Arnold.[30] Instead, symbolic realism provides them with a strategy whereby the complexities of experience – the sheer quantity of things needing to be seen as they really are – may be set in significant order, given a structure of meaning inalienable from and ratified through the physical and phenomenal make-up of the material world itself. The same strategy underlies Pre-Raphaelite painting.

10

'The World without Eyelids':
Symbolic Realism
and Pre-Raphaelite Painting

When Holman Hunt wrote *Pre-Raphaelitism and the Pre-Raphaelite Brotherhood* he could look back upon a lifetime dominated by his commitment to the first principles of Pre-Raphaelitism.[1] The bitterness of the opening sentences seems essentially true to the feeling of the young man of the 1840s: 'Art is generally regarded as a light and irresponsible pursuit, entailing for its misuse no penalty to the artist or to the nation of which he is a citizen.'[2] Hunt's demand, in 1847 as in 1905, was for significance in art. It was a demand that, for him, could not be met by the established painters of his day: 'Much of the favourite art left the inner self untouched.'[3] As he argued to the young John Millais, such art was slick and hollow. 'When art has arrived at facile proficiency of execution, a spirit of easy satisfaction takes possession of its masters, encouraging them to regard it with the paralysing content of the lotus-eaters.'[4] The argument here is clearly derived from Ruskin's criticism of Raphael and his successors. In his autobiography Hunt was uncharitably vague about the significance of *Modern Painters* in his artistic development, tending to play down any but his own role in the Pre-Raphaelite movement. Writing in 1886, however, he was more liberal and, one suspects, more truthful: 'the echo of its [*Modern Painters*] words stayed with me and pealed a further meaning and value in their inspiration whenever my more solemn feelings were touched in any way'.[5] Ruskin's arguments and exhortations coincided with Hunt's sense of there being something lacking in the academic art of his day. It was a feeling echoed by John Millais and enthusiastically shared by a born rebel, Dante Gabriel Rossetti. Rossetti, as events turned out, was the odd man out of the trio. The establishment of a brotherhood gave a false coherence to Pre-Raphaelitism: the three central protagonists shared a sense of what art should not be, rather than a common commitment to what it should be. It should not be academically posed, should not be blotched by heavy chiaroscuro, it should not be cheaply sentimental or merely pretty. In their expressive, if somewhat imprecise, critical vocabulary all this was written off as 'slosh',[6] and it was 'slosh' that, for them, characterised the establishment art of David Scott, Landseer or Etty, the last of whom displayed 'the tawdry taste of a paper-hanger'.[7] Positive agreement among members of the Brotherhood was less coherent. They all agreed that art should concern itself with higher spiritual values: but how was this to be achieved? Pre-Raphaelitism, as conceived by Hunt and Millais, was fundamentally a realist movement, but realism with a decided Ruskinian slant: 'deeper devotion to Nature's teaching was the real point at which we were aiming'.[8] Millais, as quoted by his son, saw Rossetti's painting as having other objectives.

'His aims and ideals in art were ... widely different from ours, and it was not long before he drifted away from us to follow his own peculiar fancies ... his paintings ... were highly imaginative and original, and not without elements of beauty, but they were not Nature.'[9]

Hunt similarly rejected Rossetti from inclusion under the Pre-Raphaelite banner, attacking particularly the formulaic quality of his later work.

The manner he developed showed a settled aversion to the vertebrate principle of Pre-Raphaelitism in its original inception, for this was primarily the exercise of discrimination in the individuality of every character depicted, in order the better to make manifest how varied and beauteous Nature is in her gift of beauty to the world.[10]

Hunt's Nature has the same separate and inviolable quality as Ruskin's, and the same manifold particularity. By contrast, Rossetti's painting brings everything under the stamp of his own sensibility, so much so that his later work, in particular, now seems depressingly reiterative. His obsession with the same sort of woman, swan-necked, heavy-tressed, thick-lipped, 'sensual and voluptuous, mystical and inscrutable, but always humorless',[11] turns his model – whether it be Lizzy Siddall, Fanny Cornforth or Jane Morris – into a lifelessly fixated image posed in a setting that is conventional rather than natural, decorative rather than referential.

Despite his development away from the original aims of the Brotherhood, however, Rossetti's art cannot be dismissed as irrelevant to Pre-Raphaelitism. William Michael Rossetti, admittedly predisposed towards his brother but, as a man on the edge of the later controversies, with a rather wider view of Pre-Raphaelitism, accepted Hunt's version of who founded the Brotherhood, but denied that his brother's art was undeserving of the name Pre-Raphaelite.[12] This seems right; the three founders of Pre-Raphaelitism shared a demand for new spiritual values, for seriousness in art. Similarly, in both *The Art of England*[13] and the essay 'The Three Colours of Pre-Raphaelitism'[14] Ruskin argued that different developments of the movement should be seen as responses to different kinds of truth. As artistic means determine artistic ends, these variations may be seen as different uses of the symbolic languages employed by the three painters. The key to the split in Pre-Raphaelite art is in the way in which the different artists elected to synthesise the structures of meaning and expression in their paintings. The work of the early years of the Brotherhood reveals a consensus as to the nature of that synthesis. In 1850,

Hunt, Millais and Rossetti spoke a common language. There are obvious affinities between *A Converted British Family Sheltering a Christian Missionary from the Persecution of the Druids*[15] by Hunt, *Christ in the House of His Parents* (1)[16] by Millais, and Rossetti's *Ecce Ancilla Domini*.[17] All three reject academic composition; all three are brightly lit; all three use a combination of intense colour, sharp outline and shallow perspective to force an intricacy of detail forward from the picture to confront the audience. But, most important, all three are religious pictures that eschew conventional reverence and insist upon physical impact – upon a sense of physical 'thereness' – for their effect. Salvador Dali, fascinated by this aspect of Pre-Raphaelitism, saw in such paintings 'cette espèce de frénésie qui consiste à vouloir tout toucher avec les mains'.[18] This art insists that we think of its subjects as *real*. To quote from my earlier discussion of realism, 'a picture may be described as visually realistic when the inter-relations of its figurative and formal systems direct attention to the symbolic rendering of the real world as a central feature, or as *the* central feature in the picture's make-up'. Yet, even this early in Pre-Raphaelitism, Rossetti's picture betrays different emphases in its organisation. Despite the meticulous detail of the Virgin's hair, despite the realistic drapery and the awkward naturalism of her pose, there are far fewer insistent details than in the pictures by Hunt and Millais. The bits and pieces of mundane reality are far less important, and far less in evidence. Instead our attention is drawn to the purely formal chromatic rhythm of the painting, the horizontal movement from white to blue to white to red. Increasingly, after 1850, this is the direction of Rossetti's art; away from representation and the symbolisation of the real and towards formally decorative surfaces like those of *Dantis Amor*[19] and *Beata Beatrix*,[20] in which symbolism and reference have become occult, significant for the artist rather than for his audience. Figures are schematised and rhythmically repetitive, as in *The Bower Meadow*,[21] and colour stylised, as Ruskin pointed out, 'founded on missal painting, in exactly that degree conventional and unreal'.[22] The differences between the founders of the Brotherhood, differences of emphasis at first but becoming 'perfect and ineradicable distinctions',[23] led to a divergence of aesthetic aims and to the splitting of the movement. One Pre-Raphaelite tradition grew from the art of Hunt and the young Millais to influence Arthur Hughes, John Brett, Ford Madox Brown and William Dyce; the other developed from Rossetti to Burne-Jones, to the decorative art of Morris and the stylisations of stained-glass design.[24] Ruskin presided, often uncomfortably enough, over both lines, but it is in the first of these two developments – and particularly in the paintings of Hunt – that we find the clearest attempt to follow the prescriptions of *Modern Painters*. The result is a visual form of symbolic realism which not only goes far beyond the Brotherhood's original aspiration to 'follow nature', but also finds in nature and the physical world meanings very different from those found by Ruskin.

As the contemporary reviews quoted earlier so clearly show, the early paintings of the Brotherhood were attacked as reactionary, wilfully retreating to the past. John Ballantyne, in the first extended criticism of Pre-Raphaelitism, even pushed back its origins before the Renaissance: '[they] more properly might be called the Gothic school'.[25] In vain did Ruskin protest what now seems so obvious, that 'These Pre-Raphaelites . . . do *not* desire nor pretend in any way to imitate antique paintings as such'.[26] Much modern commentary has found Pre-Raphaelite painting symptomatic of a different sort of retreat, an escape from 'the drab monotony and ugliness of the industrial towns in which [Pre-Raphaelitism] found its chief admirers'.[27] But Hunt saw his art and that of his fellows neither as reactionary – 'Antiquarianism . . . as to manner of design and painting was quite foreign to our purpose'[28] – nor as escapist. His account of the relationship between inherited representational conventions, subject-matter and artistic contemporaneity is revealing: 'while artists must ever be beholden to examples from the past for their tuition, the theme that they treat must ever be new, or they must make it so by an infiltration of thoughts belonging to their own times'.[29] The particular sort of relevance to 'their own times' that the Pre-Raphaelites sought meant more than just reflecting the contemporary scene and more than simply obeying Ruskin's directives to copy faithfully the facts of external nature. The wanted a non-conventional visual language that would maintain the objectivity of realism but, simultaneously, would embody an interpretation of the reality depicted – a language, in other words, that would give to the 'infiltration of thoughts' the authoritative status of the real. The technique of Pre-Raphaelite painting is thus not only the means whereby the world is represented, but also the primary vehicle for carrying the meaning of the world so depicted.

The first formal characteristic of Pre-Raphaelite realism is the linear quality of its images. Linearity, according to Wölfflin, is a primary quality of Pre-Raphaelesque, classical Renaissance art.[30] Emphasis is placed upon the tangible, separable 'thereness' of the objects represented. Things are fixed by their clarity of outline, by 'the metallic distinctness of lines and surfaces'.[31] Ruskin wanted an art that emphasised the factuality of external realities, and linear art does precisely that: it is, fundamentally, 'representation of being'.[32] The stress upon line in early Pre-Raphaelite art may perhaps best be seen in Millais' drawing, *The Disentombment of Queen Matilda*.[33] Forms are rigorously demarcated, each existing in its own right, unrelated to values of mass and chiaroscuro. Reality is a succession of formally discrete elements. The impact of such a technique in a Pre-Raphaelite painting or drawing is more palpable than in the classic art that Wölfflin discusses. Remembering Ruskin's directive to paint the real in all its complexity, the Pre-Raphaelites always seem to have painted so much *more*, so many more *things*, than the classic linear artists. This, it will be remembered, was the ground of Taine's comparison between Dickens and contemporary painting, ironically so initially, for it was precisely this feature of Millais' *Christ in the House of His Parents* that so irritated Dickens: 'it is particularly gratifying', he wrote sarcastically, 'to observe that such objects as the shavings which are strewn on the carpenter's floor are admirably painted'.[34] Detail is, indeed, the most immediately striking quality of Pre-Raphaelitism. There is a consistent refusal to blur the hard edge of even the minutiae of external reality. The foreground of Hunt's *Valentine Rescuing Sylvia from Proteus*,[35] is a painstaking inventory of woodland flora – twigs, leaves, mushrooms and all; the same passion for accuracy animates Millais' *Ferdinand Lured by Ariel*[36] and *The Woodman's Daughter*.[37] The passion communicated itself to the movement's followers: the vegetables tied to the emigrant ship in Ford Madox Brown's *The Last of England*,[38] the ivy and lichen of Arthur Hughes's *The Long Engagement*,[39] the amazing accumulation of domestic bric-à-brac in R. B. Martineau's *The Last Day in the Old Home*.[40] This concern to register the every detail of external reality is found in the work of other mid-century artists, from the conventional realism of W. P. Frith to the fantasy painting of Richard Dadd. But the effect of the accumulated detail in a Pre-Raphaelite painting is quite different. In Frith's *Derby Day* (2),[41] for instance, the detailed, separate figures are strictly organised, the triangular structure of the foreground grouping focuses attention upon the central anecdotal incident, this central complex balanced by figure groups on either side. In Pre-Raphaelite painting this kind of formalism is missing; detail remains visually unrelated, the separable identity of each thing is undiluted. Frith imposes a hierarchy of interest – both visual and narrative – upon his picture, Pre-Raphaelitism rejects any such process. Everything in a painting like Millais' *Lorenzo and Isabella* (3)[42] is visually equal, rendered with the same scrupulous care. The mass of detail in Frith's canvas, by contrast, is organised in terms of our conventional pictorial expectations. The visual world, for all its complexity, is reassuringly manageable. But Ruskin claimed that the Pre-Raphaelites shared with painters like Orcagna the desire to paint things as they really are or were, that they always asked themselves the question 'How would this thing, or that, actually have occurred?'[43] The desire to record events 'as they really happened' initiated an attack upon the visual and structural conventions of Victorian painting. Hunt and Millais tried to arrange their canvases with all the casualness of real life, refusing to impose a hierarchy of structural or narrative values. Whatever happened in reality simply *happened*, without any predisposition towards order or arrangement. Thus in *Lorenzo and Isabella* there are few of the traditional cues to draw our attention towards the ominous exchange between the lovers; instead, the figures are crushed together in an awkward perspective across the canvas, the arrangement heavily weighted to the left, the whole interior evenly lighted with as much care taken over the precise delineation of the wall-hangings or the food upon the table as there is over the two figures at the centre of the narrative.

If such singularity was acceptable in the illustration of an as yet little-known poet, it was a different matter when the subject was the childhood of Christ. In *Christ in the House of His Parents* the implications were more obviously semantic rather than simply aesthetic. Christ was seen to be lost in a hotch-potch of meticulous detail: 'no portion gives way to another, but, like Milton's description of Pandemonium, each ingredient strives for mastery'.[44] The figure of Christ, rather than demanding our unequivocal attention, has to compete for visual centrality amidst objects which – no longer hidden in diplomatic chiaroscuro or arranged into conventional patterns – threaten to swamp him.[45] The importance of the picture's ostensible subject is qualified and diminished. Christ becomes a little boy surrounded by all the bric-à-brac of our physical world, and in Millais' accumulated detail it is not difficult to see an analogy to the material clutter of an emerging industrial and urban society, an analogy, in fact, to the lumber that covers Quilp's wharf and the rubbish that fills Krook's shop. The effect of Pre-Raphaelite detail has been constantly misunderstood, interpreted merely as evidence of a breakdown in artistic control. Ballantyne claimed that 'the subordinate parts, or what ought to be subordinate, are more highly finished . . . than the principal portions'.[46] A more recent critic has complained that 'Every object, every accessory, whether half-glimpsed or not, is felt to be of equal importance with the main subject'.[47] Both responses make the mistake of reading a Pre-Raphaelite picture upon terms other than those laid down by the structures of the picture itself. It is the pictorial complex itself that decides what the 'principal portions' or the 'main subject' should be. There are no *a priori* main subjects. The title *Christ in the House of His Parents* simply determines the subject-area of the painting, doing no more than generally indicating what the picture is about. The meaning of a picture is unique to that picture, determined by these particular forms in this particular configuration. It is invalid to talk about a main subject when the whole pictorial organisation refuses to employ any traditional hierarchy and contradicts any notion of centrality or subordination. In *Christ in the House of His Parents*, Pre-Raphaelite detail works, with subversive irony, to set the traditional religious significance of Christ amidst the new, mid-Victorian, significance of material objects.

The traditional techniques for establishing visual hierarchy in painting – the techniques Pre-Raphaelitism eschews – are analogous to the processes of concentration and attention in everyday perception. When I concentrate upon this paper I see it and the writing upon it with a clarity that is purchased at the expense of the other objects in the margin of my field of vision. Perception is selective. By a similar process, the artistic technique of central perspective is analogous to perspectival vision. The visual world is gradated by size, colour, clarity and so forth.[48] The further away an object, the smaller it is, the more indistinct, the less definable its colour. Both hierarchy and gradation affect the distinctness of physical objects. We have seen how, in Pre-Raphaelite painting, the uniformity of delineation and finish, and the refusal to employ traditional formal structuring cause a breakdown in hierarchy; the same processes destroy the illusion of three-dimensional space. The vegetation on the far bank of Millais' *Ophelia*[49] is as clearly delineated as that of the foreground. The distant cliffs in Hunt's *Our English Coasts*[50] have a fineness of detail that brings them jumping into the frontal plane. The visual impact of this kind of loss of perspective is nicely described by Allen Staley in his account of *Ferdinand Lured by Ariel*.

> The microscopic natural detail appears at the expense of space, atmosphere, or any feeling of light and shade. It fills a substantial part of the picture, but, allied to the fairy subject . . . it seems to belong to a world of dreams and enchantment rather than to the world as we normally know it. The hyper-real clarity of delineation does not contradict, but enhances the sense of fantasy.[51]

Pre-Raphaelite perspective seems to tilt upwards, forcing the massed detail of the pictures into the foreground, forcing the spectator to take account of the registration of every form and image. 'The Brotherhood looked at the world without eyelids', and it was a process of looking that transformed what it acted upon: 'the labour that went into the copying of each particle was sharpened by a kind of frenzy which goaded them into a burnishing and polishing of their handiwork to a point beyond representation, at which it shone with a feverish clarity'.[52] In a letter purporting to have been written from Cimabue Cottage, Camden Town, a *Punch* persona lamented: 'My husband *used* to see things as other people do – but he has lately become a Pre-Raphaelite.'[53] This is really the crucial point. Despite Hunt's and Millais' claim to be simple reproducers of external reality, despite Ruskin's defence of their rendering of the external world, the art of the Pre-Raphaelites constructs a unique visual reality. Theirs is a realism of parts, not of wholes. Their paintings seem to argue that reality can no longer be structured in any conventionally coherent manner: there are too many separate realities within it. Perspective, gradient, chiaroscuro are felt to be evasive techniques, encouraging a retreat from the insistent physicality of external things. In *The Hireling Shepherd* (4),[54] Hunt displays the world with an almost shocking clarity: the bark of the trees, the wing markings of the moth, the individual blades of grass, the hair of the rustics, crisp and clear as copper wire. Here is a realist technique that, by the demands it makes upon the spectator's visual grasp, disrupts realism, constantly restricting perception to a low level of integration, a level at which the component parts of a percept resist integration into a larger whole. With subversive effect, Pre-Raphaelitism represents the reality we *know*, empirically, to exist upon a high level of integration in such a way that we *see* it as existing upon a low level. *The Hireling Shepherd* remains hauntingly disturbing because it suggests – with an odd reminiscence of Bitzer – that the world is made up of parts, not living wholes.

Other techniques within the paintings press home this attack upon visual comprehensibility. The Pre-Raphaelite intention to paint events 'as they really were' led them to intricate compositional arrangements and to a complex overlapping of forms. Overlapping forces disparate objects into a homogeneity of proximity, but, at the same time, can render form incomprehensible by visually detaching the part from the whole. Thus, in *Lorenzo and Isabella*, the portrait head of Charles Collins seems to float free; the spectator cannot key it to any other form in the picture that would make it a part of an empirically acceptable whole. The left hand of the shepherd in *The Hireling Shepherd* has been visually amputated from the rest of his body, an effect even more pronounced in Millais' *The Order of Release 1746*.[55] Similarly, the deliberate awkwardness of gesture cultivated in early Pre-Raphaelite paintings in the cause of naturalism tends both to isolate the individual figure and to generate – in *The Disentombment of Queen Matilda*, for instance – a staccato rhythm of conflicting forms. Such techniques are not mannerist or merely idiosyncratic, they are part of a developed and coherent pictorial technique. Insistent linearity, isolation of the individual form, the forcing of random detail to the frontal plane, the de-structuring of the visual field, overlapping and awkwardness are all aspects of the same intention: to challenge our conventions of perceptual organisation and, by extension, the existential and metaphysical structuring we derive from that organisation. The visual world of Pre-Raphaelitism constantly escapes the spectator's control, for the demands upon visual comprehension have deliberately been pushed too far. Yet the pictures cannot be dismissed as cranky or fanciful, for each one parades the painstaking labour with which the visual identities of the external world are captured. The registration of the external is such that we are forced to recognise the objects represented as 'real'. Pre-Raphaelite painting seems to argue that visual hierarchy and organisation are only habits by means of which man ignores or dismisses so much of the real, and that what actually lies beyond the self is a visual field of vast complexity, a world of insistently individual things challenging for supremacy, and challenging – most importantly – the control of man himself.

The insistent formal dislocations of Pre-Raphaelitism are complemented by a strident discordancy of colour. Despite our present-day familiarity with Fauvism, Abstract Expressionism and the harsh primary colours of Pop Art, Pre-Raphaelite colour still has the power to shock. The Brotherhood's refusal to employ any heavy chiaroscuro and their habit of working pigment into a wet white ground gave their colour an enamelled intensity. It was an intensity, moreover, that was keyed directly to the linear realisation of individual forms. Thus in Hunt's *Valentine Rescuing Sylvia from Proteus* (5) colour and light are firmly localised into sharply differentiated areas: the highlights upon flesh, cloth and armour spring out from the picture; the bright primary colours of the costumes are startlingly vivid against the emerald grass; strong but relatively small areas of colour are not subordinated within an overall scheme. The attention of the spectator is constantly drawn to regard the colour in terms of its abstract interaction rather than to consider it as imitative of real-life colour. Rather than merging or blending, colours are resolved into a series of chromatic oppositions and conflicts. Like forms, colours are mutually isolated and isolating; but their impetus towards dissolution goes farther. The more attention is pulled towards colour in its abstract interactions – in its aspect as surface – the more its operation is dissociated from any mimetic dimension it might have, and the more it is visually divorced from the realist functions of Pre-Raphaelite forms. This is most obvious in the work of a minor but, in any study of Pre-Raphaelite vision, significant associate of the movement, Daniel Alexander Williamson. One of the Liverpool School headed by Windus, Williamson's two most important landscapes, *Morecombe Bay from Warton Crag*[56] and *Spring: Arnside Knot and Coniston Range of Hills from Warton Crag,*[57] display an extraordinary stridency of colour co-existing with meticulous detail: 'the colours are so heightened that the landscape seems to glow . . . the world is seen frozen for a moment, and with hyper-clarity'[58]. 'Frozen' is apposite, for Pre-Raphaelite colour generates little or no sense of movement, no sense of coming into being; it is simply *there*, a final chromatic statement. The tendency towards a divorce of form and colour forestalls any animation of form by colour that could suggest movement in the real world. The figures in *Valentine Rescuing Sylvia from Proteus* are totally static; one cannot believe that the kick aimed at the dog in *Lorenzo and Isabella* will ever land; in *The Hireling Shepherd* everything has been petrified at the moment of vision. In a Pre-Raphaelite painting everything is overwhelmingly *there*, for ever and ever, and 'everything' includes discord and fragmentation.

The complex visual unsettlement that characterises Pre-Raphaelite realist painting distinguishes it from other Victorian graphic art, including, most interestingly, a form to which it often bears affinity – narrative painting. Widely popularised through the availability of engravings, Victorian narrative painting covered an extraordinarily wide thematic range: historical subjects by Paul Delaroche, Frederick Goodall or W. F. Yeames – most famously in *'And When Did You Last See Your Father?'*;[59] the contemporary and dramatic from Arthur Elmore, Frank Holl and Abraham Solomon, the last most notably in *Waiting for the Verdict* and *The Acquittal*;[60] the domestic and sentimental in the work of Sir Edwin Landseer, who could also be savage, and Thomas Faed, who in a picture like *Baith Faither and Mither*[61] could be genuinely touching; costume drama in the romanticised images of the eighteenth century presented by Marcus Stone and W. D. Sadler. Turning his hand to all of these, the ubiquitous W. P. Frith, whose two series *The Road to Ruin*[62] and *The Race for Wealth*[63] convincingly reinterpret Hogarth through the eyes of bourgeois realism and give to the narrative genre the quality of minor epic. The sequential linking of Frith's paintings indicates one of the basic semantic characteristics of the genre. Because a painting exists primarily in space and a narrative primarily in time, narrative paintings can only tell their stories by encouraging the spectator to extend the represented action off-canvas. Frequently using a form of theatrical tableau — when the royal neck touches the block, when the sailor boy waves goodbye, when the fatal card is turned — narrative painting registers the moment as dramatic epitome and thus implies a complete causal chain leading up to that moment. Much of the meaning of a narrative painting, therefore, must be located extra-pictorially, in the willingness and ability of the spectator to fill in the rest of the story. In Pre-Raphaelite painting, by contrast, meaning is determined not by an imputed narrative but by the interacting structures of the painting itself. The disorder consequent upon irresponsibility that is the didactic theme of *The Hireling Shepherd* is conveyed not primarily by narrative, but by the pictorial technique — the fragmentation of forms, the disturbing perspective, the absence of visual hierarchy, the abstract disharmonies of colour. In precisely the same way as meaning in a Dickens novel is carried through the fictional technique and stuff of the prose itself — the double narrative in *Bleak House*, the linguistic negation of *Little Dorrit* — so also, in a painting like *The Hireling Shepherd*, meaning is conveyed immediately, for it is integral to the visual texture and organisation of the picture.

Nevertheless, specific features of a Pre-Raphaelite painting can invite a form of narrative extension. Thus in Brown's *The Last of England* narrative possibilities are opened up by certain details of the crowd packing the rail of the emigrant-ship: a roughneck shakes his fist at the White Cliffs, the young mother clasps the hand of a baby hidden in her shawl. Similarly, the names carved on the tree in Arthur Hughes's *The Long Engagement*(6) suggest the anecdotal background to the picture. Yet their function is more than anecdotal and different from that of similar details in more simply narrative paintings. The carved initials form a sign that demands interpretation rather than narrative elaboration. This symbolic role is amplified by other images in the picture. The names are covered with moss and ivy, signs of time's decay; the woodland is in blossom, nature regenerates herself, a squirrel and his mate sit in the branches, but a shadow is across the face of the man. The images must be 'read' as something more than straightforwardly realist, and something other than loosely narrative. They demand interpretation as cognitive symbols, as signs of more or less abstract concepts rather than pieces of a story. The physical world has a meaning that we must interpret, a semantic dimension to its reality. This interplay between narrative and conceptual dimensions is a central feature of Millais' work: the ominous blood-orange and the motiveless kick in *Lorenzo and Isabella*, the images of crucifixion and the anticipation of the stigmata in *Christ in the House of His Parents*. In both paintings a typological method is employed; in the latter its basis is traditional, in the former the method is transposed to a secular context.[64] Coming events cast their shadows before, and both paintings depict moments at which the meaning implicit in reality is revealed through the components of that reality itself. Millais' use of such a method in his early paintings suggests parallels with Carlyle's adaption of typology to explicate historical events. Indeed, the correct reading of Millais' symbols, as of events in Carlylean history, depends upon an independent interpretative key: in the case of these two paintings, the New Testament and — far more esoterically — Keats's 'Isabella'. In *Autumn Leaves* (7),[65] painted during his last Pre-Raphaelite phase, Millais comes closer to Dickensian symbolic realism. The pile of dead leaves, the autumnal woods, the dark landscape and setting sun, all exemplify transience, and the four children, clothes coloured to match the season, their faces flushed in the dusk, are implicated in the general movement towards death. Set in a garden touched with decay, the symbolic inference of the half-eaten apple held by the girl on the right of the canvas is unmistakable. At the same time, the picture also represents, according to Ruskin, 'the first instance existing of a perfectly painted twilight'.[66] Symbolic values are coupled with realist values and — as in Dickens's fictional world and Ruskin's natural world — the details of the real function symbolically, though the meaning that Millais reads in nature is nearer to that of *David Copperfield* than of *Modern Painters*. In the year after *Autumn Leaves*, Millais' main Academy picture was *A Dream of the Past: Sir Isumbras at the Ford.*[67] Like *Autumn Leaves*, its theme is death, but its symbolic character is more evident, tending to subordinate in importance the realist registration that the painting also exhibits. Ruskin's hostile review of the picture brushes aside what seems to me the main issue in its interpretation. 'It does not matter whether we take it as a fact or as a type.'[68] Ruskin is wrong; it *does* matter, for it is in the relationship between symbolic elements and realist elements that the picture's distinctive semantic lies. Such considerations are even more central in the work of Holman Hunt and when, a few years earlier, he exhibited *The Light of the World* (8)[69] it was precisely the question of fact or type that was seen as crucial to an understanding of the painting.

The Light of the World is probably the most familiar English religious image, and, as such, it is difficult to free oneself from the casual acceptance engendered by long acquaintance, and to see that the painting presents very real problems of interpretation. Its exhibition in 1854 drew forth a letter to *The Times* from the influential critic, Dr G. F. Waagen. Waagen found Hunt's Christ iconographically inconsistent.

> . . . the painter has voluntarily . . . sought to combine both those conceptions of the Saviour which the feeling of religious art, at the period of its widest prevalence and highest development, always kept strictly distinct. Our Lord . . . was either conceived as the man dying for all men — the *Ecce Homo* . . . or as the glorified Lord of the World.

Waagen goes on to be specific.

> . . . while the hardly painted golden glory belongs altogether to the idealistic and conventional tendency and time of art, the effect of light

from the lantern is rendered with all that skilful reality with which the knowledge of the present day represents such effects.[70]

The ideological motivation for the picture is clear enough; the dual humanity and divinity of Christ is a point of accepted doctrine. What Waagen complains of is Hunt's breaking the iconographic rules, his refusal to be bound to the conventions and expectations of religious art. Hunt recognises no distinction between idealisation and realisation, between images symbolic of a metaphysical reality and images representative of a physical reality. Nor is this synthesis restricted to the depiction of Christ; the door, the brambles, the apples on the grass, all demand to be read as bits of physical reality, 'the complex of space as a whole invites a naturalistic reading'.[71] All this does not result – as Waagen suggests it does – from ignorance or incapacity; Hunt knew very well what he was doing. In his autobiography, he describes his artistic purpose as the revelation of 'the truths of sublime meaning'.[72] It is a surprising phrase. A claim to reveal 'the meaning of sublime truth' would be more conventional, an exegetic impulse to justify the ways of God to man. But Hunt does not see himself as the interpreter of a divine message that is shrouded in oracular mystery; for Hunt, 'sublime meaning' is not withdrawn, but immanent. Meaning is *there*, on the face of experienced reality, and what needs demonstration, therefore, is not the self-evident existence of that meaning, but its truth. Hunt responds, more directly than any other Pre-Raphaelite, to Ruskin's call for artists who can see – quite literally – the semantic structure that resides within the facts of the external world. Such a call parallels Dickens's creation of the hero/heroine – Florence Dombey, David Copperfield, Amy Dorrit, Sydney Carton – who is defined in and by his or her perception of that semantic dimension. They all see – again quite literally – more than their fellow-characters. The aesthetic consequence of such demands for the amalgamation of semantic perception – so to speak – and actual perception are directly similar. Waagen's criticism of *The Light of the World* is precisely that levelled by John Carey against *Dombey and Son*: the 'symbolic sea collides curiously in the novel with the real sea of ships and tar and tackling'.[73] Both critics fail to grasp the imaginative principle underlying the works of art they criticise. There is no 'collision' in *Dombey and Son* because there are not two separate seas – the one 'symbolic', the other 'real' – to collide. There is one sea that is both wholly real and wholly symbolic. Similarly, in *The Light of the World*, Christ's symbolic significance is indivisible from his realist being. Because Hunt's pictures and Dickens's novels are full of the stuff of the empirically real, it does not follow that either of them is, simply or exclusively, a Realist. Neither does it follow that, because symbolic values attach to their work, either of them can adequately be discussed as a Symbolist. For both Hunt and Dickens – as, in their different ways, for Carlyle and Ruskin – the symbolic and the actual coincide. Reality is meaning as well as, and as a predicate of, being, and the constituents of the real are to be handled as the components of a semantic structure. The consequences of this are ontological, for the Pre-Raphaelite images of what the world looks like are simultaneously accounts of what the world means. To see precisely how this process works, a small number of paintings must be discussed in detail.

11

'Things as They Really Are':
Four Pre-Raphaelite Pictures

Holman Hunt painted *The Scapegoat* (9)[1] under conditions of the most appalling difficulty with the intention of creating something 'unlike anything ever portrayed'.[2] He succeeded: a unique and unforgettable image, *The Scapegoat* exhibits the qualities of nightmare. The Pre-Raphaelite sensitivity to physical detail is almost morbidly apparent: every hair on the goat is recorded, every salt crystal, every stone, every muddy encrustation. Consonant with this heightened sense of the physical is a discordantly garish intensity of colour that tends towards hard-edged abstraction. Assigned to specific areas of the canvas, colours clash along precisely drawn boundaries. But the violence of the chromatic discords generates no movement. Instead, there is the stasis that results from the collision of forces of equal weight and power. The colour, the tendency to abstraction, the absence of gradients flatten everything into the frontal plane: the background, with its intricate rock texture and cloud pattern, gives no sense of distance; middle-ground details of skeletons and brushwood seem indeterminately placed in the spatial organisation of the whole. The effect is both hallucinatory and frozen. The checking of all movement is reinforced by the emphatic horizontals of cloud, mountain and sea and by the placing of the goat at the visual centre of the canvas – an arrangement that Ruskin deplored.[3] Yet the central placing is essential, for the visual centre is the point at which the disparate and conflicting lines of visual concentration cancel one another out – it is the still centre of the pictorial world. Shapes or objects placed upon that point are visually static, and there is no drama or struggle about the scapegoat, but instead a pathetic – almost absurdist – acquiescence. The stasis of the central image reiterates the paradoxical stasis engendered from the violence of chromatic discord in the painting as a whole. Hunt's scapegoat is the alien epitomised, and the landscape he inhabits is infused with a correlative sense of alienation – not only realistically, in being a wasteland, but also visually.[4] Colours rebuff one another, forms – each one intensely distinct – are reciprocally alienated and alienating. Yet from this conflict there derives no hope for eventual reformation, for the dominant fragmentation has been paradoxically deprived of motive power. The world is locked in an unresolved discord, and its immobility – like that of the goat that is its focus – is the immobility of exhaustion. It is an exhaustion that, ironically, the intended atonement of the goat's sacrifice cannot remedy, for the pictorial organisation of the canvas implicitly refutes any connotations of redemption and thus any hope. Such an image of utter negation has been found repellent by many critics, evidence of 'a morbid spirituality which absorbs the laboriously literal matter of the paintings with a private world of religious fantasy'.[5] This is surely wrong, for it is precisely the laboured literalness of Hunt's work that makes it non-private: always, his art insists that the spectator takes the images it offers as ineluctably real. Nor, historically, is the negation expressed by *The Scapegoat* an isolated vision. Parallels to it may be found throughout Victorian literature in its recurrent nightmare of social and spiritual collapse, of alienation and hopelessness, most often imaged as physical desolation. The 'ignorant armies' of Arnold's 'Dover Beach' clash blindly on 'a darkling plain',[6] and the 'agony of lamentation' that accompanies Tennyson's Arthur on his last journey shrills like a wind 'in a wasteland, where no one comes,/Or hath come, since the making of the world'.[7] This is the landscape confronting Browning's Childe Roland, endless and sterile, 'Nothing but plain to the horizon's bound',[8] and the protagonist in *The City of Dreadful Night*, who can only repeat, hopelessly, in verse after verse, 'As I came through the desert thus it was,/As I came through the desert'.[9] Most precisely of all, perhaps, Hunt's hallucinatory image of a final desolation is Sydney Carton's equally hallucinatory vision of the spiritual wasteland that is the underlying reality of the City of Man. Steegman has said that, through the Pre-Raphaelite feeling for parable and symbol, 'Hunt's *Scapegoat* was elevated from a platitude to something approaching tragedy'.[10] That does not seem quite right. Aristotle was careful to exclude terror from the legitimate responses to tragedy, and *The Scapegoat* is, in the full and proper sense of the word, terrible. The pictorial expression of the persistent Victorian nightmare of social, moral and spiritual wreck, it is an authentic image of despair.

In comparison with many other Pre-Raphaelite landscapes, William Dyce's *Pegwell Bay, Kent, a Recollection of October 5th 1858* (10)[11] is a visually simple picture. Remarkable for the clarity of its individual forms, it has a tight precision of registration that invites comparison with photographic effects. Yet there is a more-than-photographic quality about the painting, for Dyce deliberately eschews visual hierarchy. Even the foreground is distanced lest it should take on too much visual weight. No one pictorial element dominates: everything is there and everything is recorded with the same dispassion. Detail in *Pegwell Bay* does not have the intensity or the sense of violent fragmentation it has in other Pre-Raphaelite works. Although forms are as visually isolated – the one from the other – as they are in *The Scapegoat*, repose is engendered by evenness of working, by the distancing of the pictorial world, by the toning-down of local colour. Each objectively recorded, things rest in their solitude. Moreover, the suppression of visual hierarchy results in a seemingly random distribution of forms across the picture. 'The foreground figures, the pilings added behind them, and the lines of rock reaching into the sea provide precise punctuation in a manner that seems arbitrary.'[12] The reason for this seeming arbitrariness becomes apparent if, following Arnheim's technique, lines of maximum visual stress are superimposed upon a structural outline of the picture, as in Figure 11.1. None of the major pictorial elements relates, in any but

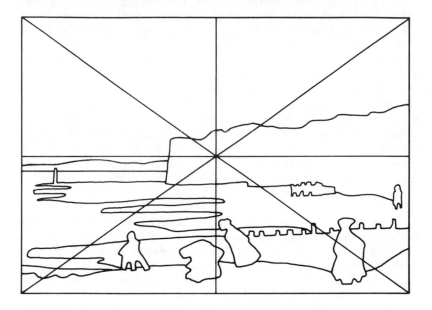

Figure 11.1

the most casual way, to the visual matrix imposed by the spectator's habits of perceptual organisation. Visual relationships within the picture are precise yet random. The foreground figures 'are a family group, and yet not a group, for they stand apart from each other, and nobody looks at anyone else'.[13] The unity of atmosphere, the suppression of any expressionist implications of colour, the scrupulously objective detail, the evenness of registration, the apparent chance distribution, all work to convince the spectator that this is what the world really looks like. The very signs by means of which reality is represented seem transparent, seem to have lost their interpretative function. Telling no story, recording no important event, the pictorial statement of *Pegwell Bay* is straightforward: here is reality, life is like *this*. Oddly enough, what confirms such an impression is the presence, just visible, of Donati's comet. A comet with full tail, visible in daylight, has ceased to be in the least miraculous. Far from being a significant focus of the painting, it is easy to miss it altogether; in the picture itself, only one background figure appears to notice it at all. The comet, traditional harbinger of catastrophe, has become just one more fact, as important or as unimportant as any other. The abolition of hierarchy has left an undifferentiated democracy in which everything is of equal value, or of no value at all, and everything is disconnected – not violently, but irreversibly – from everything else. The little boy has the same visual weight as the rocks that dot the seashore; the warning-post at the end of the reef constantly draws the eye, but with no discernible purpose. If the nightmare desolation of *The Scapegoat* is analogous to Carton's vision of a spiritual wasteland, then *Pegwell Bay* is an image of *Little Dorrit*'s world of nobodies. As in the novel, ironic reversals subvert the very notion of a social organisation. Dyce's painting is a realist depiction of a bourgeois excursion to the seaside, but this epitome of the everyday and the familiar occurs in a visual context from which the cues and tokens by which we are accustomed to organise the external world have been removed. The everyday world is estranged. The spectator's realist conviction that the people in the picture must be somebodies is contradicted by a perceptual conviction that they are nobodies. Undramatic, detached, meticulously accurate, *Pegwell Bay*'s image of a world that has lost itself quite irretrievably carries a powerful authority.

Contemporaneity was one of the basic demands of the European Realists of the nineteenth century; in Daumier's phrase, 'Il faut être de son temps'. It would be difficult to find a more obviously contemporary picture than Ford Madox Brown's *Work* (11).[14] Not only is it a painstaking record of Victorian urban life, its theme – the role of work in society – is also emphatically Victorian. The painting has generally been seen as a semi-allegorical paean lauding work in its different aspects and attempting to establish 'a new and relevant iconography with which to manifest the heroism of labour'.[15] The concept of the heroism of labour derives from Carlyle, who, with F. D. Maurice, actually appears in the picture: 'All work, even cotton-spinning, is noble; work is alone noble.'[16] Through the efforts of ethical popularists like Smiles and Tupper, the moral elevation of labour became established doctrine, part of the creed of *laissez-faire* and progress. In Carlyle's writings, however, it is the pendant to remorseless and often violent social satire; no matter how elevating the gospel of work, contemporary England followed the gospels of Mammonism and Dilettantism.[17] An entry in Ford Madox Brown's journal clearly indicates that he was equally conscious of something rotten behind the conventional propaganda, and equally savage about it. English Society is 'internally, a prey to snobbishness and the worship of gold and tinsel – a place chiefly for sneaks and lacqueys, and any who can fawn and clutch, or dress clean at church and connive'.[18] Too much criticism of *Work* has concentrated upon the navvies at the centre of the picture. Brown paints them as part of an epitome of society in which every class, from pauper to plutocrat, is represented. The picture must be seen in terms of the same distinction between inner and outer realities that is evident in the extract from Brown's journal quoted above. The ostensible subject of *Work* is given by its title; its real concern is with demonstrating the state of society. The visual arrangement of the picture, its overcrowding, its odd perspective and awkward juxtapositions, has none of the reassurance of its ostensible message. The theme is apparently harmonious labour, yet the spectator finds it impossible to harmonise the picture into a coherent structure. The immensely complex overlapping causes a breakdown of perceptual unity: people appear as a collection of dismembered parts. We recognise bits, not wholes. Similarly, the extraordinary detail throughout the picture identifies the individual object as isolated thing rather than as thing-in-context. As so often in Pre-Raphaelite art, the spectator is forced to recognise the intransigent individuality of each object in the physical world, its resistance to contextualisation. Each thing is itself alone. In *Work* the wholesale subversion of visual unity is an aesthetic analogue to Brown's sense of social disorganisation. Hilton remarks astutely that 'The workmen have just that posed amplitude of gesture . . . that belongs to the great decorators of the Vatican'.[19] This almost stagy posing of the central figures is part of a mannerist tendency in the whole. Individual gesture is heightened into idiosyncrasy. Each person in the picture seems totally self-involved, solemnly obsessed into the exaggeration of his own actions. Only the little beggar-boy grins wickedly as his sister pulls his hair, yet the effect of the whole picture is grimly comic. All the people in this great image of a unified society are solitaries; their very physical reality seems to be on the point of fragmenting around them, yet they remain seriously committed to their own private tasks in their own private worlds. Laughter is a great subversive and, in *Work*, Brown is guying the whole hopeful notion of a unified society working together for the common good. *Work* presents the characteristic social isolation of *Pegwell Bay* in satiric guise. Brown's own lengthy commentary on the picture reinforces this satiric mockery. The 'brain-workers', we are told, 'seeming to be idle, work, and are the cause of well-ordained work and happiness in others'.[20] Surely there is irony in that phrase 'seeming to be idle', and where is the 'well-ordained work' in the picture? The paramount impression is one of confusion. The whole range of social types comes in for the same sort of satiric deflation: the couple on horseback – 'These are the *rich*, who "have no need to work" – not at least for bread . . .'; the woman distributing tracts – 'This well intentioned lady has, perhaps, never reflected that excavators may have notions to the effect that ladies might be benefited by receiving tracts containing navvies' ideas!' 'In front of her is the lady whose only business in life is to dress and look beautiful for our benefit'.[21] In yet another part of the picture a policeman overturns an orange-seller's fruit-stall – 'I dedicate this portion of the work to the Commissioners of Police'.[22] This overt conflict dramatises the radical physical and social disconnection that the picture images. Brown's commentary remarks of 'the colonel' on horseback: 'could he only be got to hear what the sages in the corner have to say, I have no doubt he would be easily won over. But the road is blocked.'[23] Social groups are mutually alienated and the blocking of the road symbolises non-communication. The emphatic sense of non-communication between parts permeates the visual and semantic organisation of the whole painting, destructuring an image of society that – superficially and initially – appears to be unified. Comparisons with Dickens's novels are obvious both in terms of meaning and of imaginative method. Both Brown and Dickens use realist images, the stuff of the empirical world, to symbolise man's spiritual condition, and that condition is, for both of them, characterised by moral and physical confusion, by the tragi-comic isolation of the individual, by a sense of incipient social disintegration, the consequences of which are at once alarming and absurd. Carlyle's presence in the painting, ostensibly as the evangelist of work, takes on an ironic dimension, for he is also the satirical anatomist of society. In the background of the picture an election procession meanders up the dusty street, a motley collection of sandwich-boards advertising the merits of the candidate, none other than Carlyle's own Bobus, 'Sausage-maker on the great scale'.[24] Who else could be more suitable to govern – or, rather, not to govern – the society – or, rather, non-society – that *Work* depicts? Who else, indeed, would such a society be more likely to elect? 'The man gets himself appointed and elected who is ablest – to be appointed and elected. What can the incorruptiblest *Bobuses* elect, if it be not some *Bobissimus*?'[25]

The particular fusion of realism and symbolism found in Pre-Raphaelite painting is nowhere so clearly demonstrated as in Holman Hunt's *The Awakening Conscience* (12).[26] A careful disposition of forms establishes meaning at a primary structural level: Figure 11.2, a structural and visual map of the picture, makes this clear. Attention is drawn to the dramatic complex of gestures at the centre of the picture, the sense of pressure from the woman's hands contrasted to the relaxed ease of the man's open-handed gesture. Tension at this central point focuses the pressure felt all along the picture's horizontal axis. The line formed just below this axis by the table, the man's arm and the edge of the piano cuts the formal arrangement of the picture in half. Below the line is that random assemblage of physical lumber that is so recurrent a feature of Pre-Raphaelite realism: the unpleasing, niggling pattern of the carpet, the roll of music, the glove, the unravelled wool, the ornate table-leg, the repulsively slick texture of the piano's veneer, the intricate lace of the woman's dress. All the physical detail of middle-class opulence is there, depicted with intense mimetic conviction. This is the real world of Victorian materialism, rendered with the same terrible concentration as is the foreground of *The Scapegoat*, exemplifying the same disorder as it does in *Work*. The 'world of isolated integers, terrifyingly alone and unrelated'[27] that Van Ghent sees as being suggested by so much of Dickens's fiction is precisely the world that

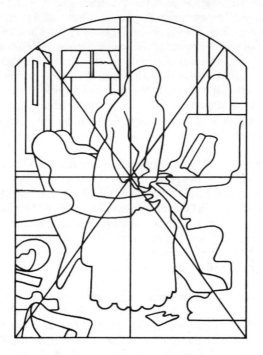

Figure 11.2

Hunt paints in *The Awakening Conscience*. Disorder is not merely the concomitant of such a world, but its inevitable condition: 'you cannot make "order" with an integer, one thing alone, for order is definitively a relationship among things'.[28] In the lower half of the picture, the absence of pattern or hierarchy gives to everything the same visual and existential weight: animate or inanimate, everything is reduced to just another object in a room of objects. The upper half of the painting is quite different. Although again reproduced with meticulous accuracy, the physical world is here visually organised. The lines of the piano-top, the mirror and picture-frames, the window and ceiling build a grid of horizontals and verticals, framing the image of life reborn, the spring blossom reflected in the mirror. The potential for order suggested by the upper half of the picture is in tense contrast to the evident chaos of the lower. The figures in the picture are aligned in terms of these two opposing visual contexts. The man's leg is stabilised along the top left to bottom right diagonal, but the top half of his body pulls away from it, his arms extended just below the horizontal axis. The effect is to force the figure of the man downwards. As is clear in Figure 11.2, the man seems to fall, physically, pushed away from the stability of the diagonal towards the disordered junk that fills the lower half of the canvas. The woman's alignment is quite different. Initially, her form is stabilised along the vertical axis, but her head and the upper part of her body move away, towards the visually powerful bottom left to top right diagonal, and towards the ordered space of the upper half of the painting. The moral awakening that cuts her away from her wealthy 'protector' is actualised through the pictorial structure: narrative drama is realised as visual drama. As Nochlin has pointed out, the core concern of this drama is not simply with sexual morality, but with the status of people in a materialist world.

> . . . for the Victorian lower-class woman, strict morality could be a liberating assertion of personhood, as opposed to objecthood, degradation and passing enjoyment in the hands of 'gentlemen' exploiters, and thus, the young woman who casts off the material fruits of her sinful existence is, in a sense, affirming her humanity by an act of decision, indicating her essential difference from the 'fatally new' things which she at once rejects, and, at the same time, in a single epiphanic gesture, differentiates herself from.[29]

The physical world takes on an aspect of menace, threatening to swamp the human world, to subvert and destroy the identity that separates people from things. Such a process is, of course, fundamental to Dickens's imaginative world: aggressive objects threaten Nell in *The Old Curiosity Shop*, junk swamps Mrs Jellyby and Krook's shop. The corollary of the process, the metamorphosis of people into things, turns Nell into ' "a wax-work child" ', Jane Murdstone into 'a metallic lady', and Mrs Merdle into a frigid bosom for the display of jewellery. The moral epiphany represented in *The Awakening Conscience* consists precisely in the woman's refusal to become a Mrs Merdle-like, purchasable object. In such a context, the portrayal of the threatening material world takes on – as it does so often in Dickens's novels – a hyper-clarity that, as Ruskin recognised, has a hallucinatory quality.

> Nothing is more notable than the way in which even the most trivial objects force themselves upon the attention of a mind which has been fevered by violent and distressful excitement. They thrust themselves forward with a ghastly and unendurable distinctness, as if they would compel the sufferer to count, or measure, or learn them by heart.[30]

The feverish intensity with which Hunt invests physical detail is here analogous to the sudden act of vision that the painting imputes to the woman. In Arnold's phrase, though not in his sense, she 'sees things as they really are'. Her 'seeing', simultaneously physical and spiritual, reveals to her – as the painting reveals to the spectator – a world that is both

13 Alfington, the rectory and church. Anonymous watercolour *c.* 1885. The Governors of Ottery St Mary Church.

14 Waresley church, tower buttressing and stair turret.

15 St Matthias, Stoke Newington, the tower and east end. Royal Commission on Historical Monuments.

16 All Saints', Margaret Street, exterior. Royal Commission on Historical Monuments.

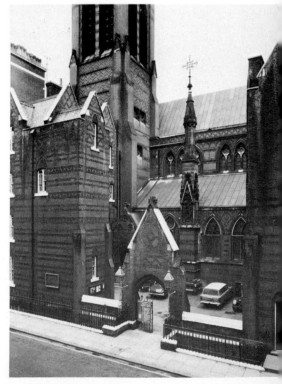

17 All Saints', Margaret Street, the porch. Royal Commission on Historical Monuments.

18 Blunsdon St Andrew church, west end.

19 Barley church, detail of south side of chancel.

20 St Alban's, Holborn, the tower and west end.

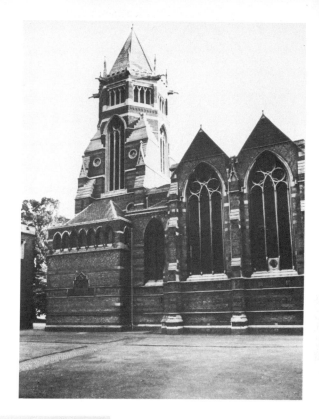

21 Rugby School, the chapel and tower.

22 Foxham church, the tower and west end.

23 All Saints', Margaret Street, interior. *The Builder,* vol. 17 (1859), p. 377.

24 Ottery St Mary church, Coleridge memorial transept.

25 St Matthias, Stoke
Newington, aisle window
tracery.

26 St Matthias, Stoke
Newington, aisle window
tracery.

27 All Saints', Margaret Street, the pulpit. Royal Commission on Historical Monuments.

28 Ottery St Mary church, the font.

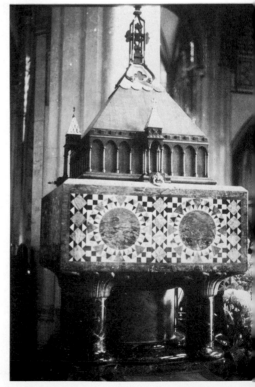

Baverstock church, chancel
ing.

30 All Saints', Margaret Street,
nave arcade. Royal Commission
on Historical Monuments.

31 St Alban's, Holborn, chancel arch decoration. *The Builder,* vol. 20 (1862), p. 443.

32 Keble College, Oxford, detail of the South Parks Road front.

33 Waresley church, south side of chancel interior.

34 Waresley church, detail of tiling on chancel east wall.

35 Waresley church, detail of tiling and mastic work on chancel north wall, showing patterns 1 to 3.

36 Waresley church, detail of
tiling and mastic work on
chancel east wall, showing
pattern variant 1a.

37 Waresley church, detail of tiling on
chancel south wall, showing pattern
variant 1c.

38   Yealmpton church, chancel arch and east end.

39   Milton Ernest Hall, south front. Royal Commission on Historical Monuments.

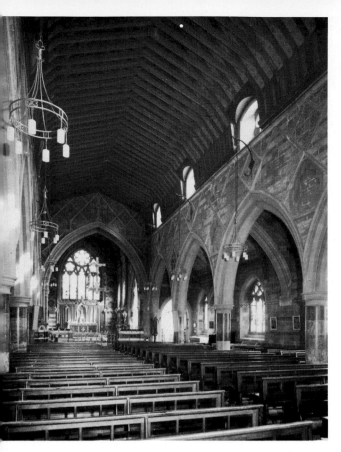

40 All Saints',
Babbacombe, interior.
Royal Commission on
Historical Monuments.

41 All Saints',
Babbacombe, exterior.
Royal Commission on
Historical Monuments.

42 All Saints', Babbacombe, the pulpit. Royal Commission on Historical Monuments.

43 All Saints', Babbacombe, the font. Royal Commission on Historical Monuments.

symbolic and materially actual. Moreover, the physical structure of the real not only exemplifies the antithesis between spiritual rebirth and spiritual disorder, but its constituent parts are also themselves emblematic. Detail functions semantically as well as mimetically: the cat torturing the trapped bird, the wallpaper, with its fruit 'preyed on by thievish birds',[31] the discarded glove, the unravelled and disordered skein of wool, the tangle of bindweed in the vase on the piano; all are parallels to the narrative situation that are also explications of that situation. Our sense of each entity as a material reality is coincident with our reading of it as a symbol. Moreover, because – as was said in discussing narrative paintings – paintings exist primarily in space, narratives in time, the symbolic realism of *The Awakening Conscience* takes on a quality of revelation. The symbolic patterns of the Dickens novel and the typological patterns of Carlylean history are understood diachronically, progressively emerging through narrative. Precisely because such a dimension is unavailable in a painting, the meaning of the symbolic realism of *The Awakening Conscience* is presented in a single moment of vision which the woman in the picture implicitly shares with the spectator. Hunt's painting thus dramatically realises a point of time at and in which the meanings contained in the fabric of the everyday world are suddenly made apparent. Its moment of vision is authentically visionary, an awakening to the true nature of the real. As such, *The Awakening Conscience* is directly responsive to Ruskin's call for a renewal of perception itself, a call that is paralleled in Carlyle's injunction, quoted earlier, 'Awake, poor troubled sleeper . . . look, see, behold it, the Flame-image; splendours high as Heaven, terrors deep as Hell'. Similarly, it can be compared to those moments in Dickens's novels in which the semantic structure carried in the physical and phenomenal world seems to crystallise: Paul Dombey watching the reflection of the river on the wall of his sick-room, David confronting the body of Steerforth 'thrown up' by the Yarmouth storm, Stephen Blackpool in Old Hell Pit, Carton's Christophanic identification with 'the glorious sun rising' over Paris. The Pre-Raphaelites' exploration of symbolic realism, focused in *The Awakening Conscience* but evident throughout their realist painting, leads in the same direction as does Carlyle's, Dickens's, and indeed Ruskin's: towards the revelatory remaking of reality itself.

PART THREE

PART THREE

12

'Functional and Mystical':
Architectural Meaning and Puginian Gothic

There are affinities – expressed most simply by Horace's *Ut pictura poesis* – between our experience of painting and our experience of literature that make comparisons like those made in the previous chapter an obvious possibility. Indeed, what is true in general is true in particular for Victorian literature and painting: affinities of mimetic intent, of narrative, of moral tone and theme throughout nineteenth-century painting and literature make comparison inevitable. No such inevitability attends a comparison between literature and nineteenth-century architecture: the difficulty lies, of course, in the problem of architecture's aesthetic status. As has been argued, both literature and painting are symbol structures that, sooner or later, either denotatively or connotatively are 'about' life, structurings of raw experience that confront a spectator as highly organised tools for the investigation of their experience, and as aesthetic objects, to be admired in their own right. No matter how strong one's stress upon the *necessity* of art, however, no poem, novel or painting *qua* poem, novel or painting is functional. Wilde was right: 'All art is quite useless.' A building, however, is a functional object, 'intended to provide for one of the three great wants of man – food, clothing and shelter'.[1] But a building is also an aesthetic object. Functionalist denials of 'style' – such as those by Alfred Loos or Walter Gropius – are illusory: the Bauhaus preference for concrete, steel, and simple form is as much a judgement of taste as is, for example, John Soane's preference for neo-classicism over Gothic. On the other hand, the opposition between aesthetic and functional values – particularly common in nineteenth-century criticism – is equally unsatisfactory.

> . . . no one would call the laws architectural which determine the height of a breastwork or the position of a bastion. But if to the stone facing of that bastion be added an unnecessary feature, as a cable moulding, *that* is Architecture.[2]

Ruskin's capitalisation of 'Architecture' gives the game away, lifting architecture into an empyrean of absolutes and abstracts above the prosy realities of common nouns. Architecture has no such Platonic status, nor is there a point at which 'an architectural experience' supersedes an experience of the building as building. Bad or uninteresting architecture is just that: to deprecate it as 'mere building' or 'mere aesthetics' just confuses the matter.

The traditional way of approaching architecture – from Vitruvius downward – is through the categories of form, function and technique. Charles Jencks, in *Meaning in Architecture*, provides some useful definitions. Architecture comprises 'a form (comprising such things as colour, texture, space, rhythm), a function (purpose, use, past connotations, style, etc.), and a technic (made up of structure, materials and mechanical aid, etc.)'.[3] These traditional categories seem dubious both theoretically and empirically. A buttress *functions* as support, a doorway *functions* as entrance; why should one be a part of 'technic', the other of 'function'? Both are surely two aspects of function, the first structural, the second operational. Similarly, both are aspects of 'technic' and both are components of overall 'form' that express 'form' in their own right. In a building, any one of the traditional theoretical triad implies – and even necessarily involves – the other two, and, if we do not murder, we seriously disfigure to dissect. Given that the traditional critical categories seem over-rigid, it is worth returning to the basic points made earlier. A response to architecture combines a sense of functional purpose with an experience of aesthetic identity. 'A building is a work of art, but at the same time it fulfils a specific function as a practical object in our life space.'[4] Such a definition, true as it is, still suggests a lurking dualism, a discomfort in the company of this bastard child of art and utility. Even if one regards a building as being, simultaneously, a functional structure and an aesthetic construct, the question of how those different structurings relate remains. Greenough's famous formulation, 'Beauty is the promise of function', is more helpful, suggesting some continuity between the two terms of the equation.[5] Moreover, by stressing the idea of a *promise* of function, Greenough draws attention to the relationship of building to spectator. Here again, our experience of architecture is significantly different from that of painting or literature: if these arts are *about* an experience *of* real life, architecture *is* an experience *in* real life. So, too, of course, is looking at a picture or reading a book, but we do not 'use' a book or a picture in the way we 'use' a building. Experienced both temporally and spatially, a building has three-dimensional existence round which, through which and in which we both live and move; more than an object in our life-space, it is a physical determinant of that life-space. Our sense of the practicality, the function, of a building is a consequence of the way in which that physical determination of life-space is arrived at. Where, then, aesthetics? Greenough's formulation is hardly adequate. Fourteenth-century Gothic tracery is not considered beautiful because it promises some sort of function, nor un-beautiful because it does not. This kind of traditional theoretical impasse is illusory because the terms within which it is stated are wrong. Too much of the argument about the relationship between utility and aesthetics has been conducted within the terms of Beauty and Function, both of which have, in consequence, been construed as definitive. Rather than being definable qualities possessed by a building, however, beauty and function are aspects of our experience of a building, and both our sense of architectural beauty and our sense of architectural function are affective responses consequent upon the perception of architectural meaning.

The experience of architecture is a semantic transaction, and all architectural forms are potentially terms in that semantic. Meaning is primarily generated by the precise way in which, to return to an earlier definition, a building physically determines our life-space. At its simplest, this is a matter of constructional identity and function combining in meaningful form. The 'meaning' of the brick box in Figure 12.1 is generated by its being a solid enclosure; the response of a spectator will come somewhere on an affective spectrum that ranges from Sense of Protection to Sense of Entrapment. If one wall is pierced with a window, as in Figure 12.2, then the situation changes – the inside of the box is accessible from the outside, space is allowed to flow through the wall. If the windows are enlarged and increased in number, as in Figure 12.3, the situation becomes more complex: do we experience the windows as piercing the box, or do we see the wall in which the windows are set as a framework for the free movement of space? In Figure 12.4 the walling has become simply a matrix that frames a completely fluid sense of space; the total enclosure of Figure 12.1 has become total access. In these examples, windows and walls function expressively, and what they express are different degrees of openness and closedness. Their 'meaning' lies, thus, in the way in which their manipulation determines the relationship between the finite space inside the box and the infinite space outside. Such expressive meaning has a symbolic quality: the arrangement of a window in a wall enables a spectator to grasp the dynamics of space penetrating solidity. In this sense, a specific architectural feature can be said to symbolise the operation of an abstract force. But this is not symbolism proper, for the specific feature is also an instance of the operation of that force. A buttress, for example, does more than symbolise support; it *is* support, direct and immediate, whereas symbolism is a mediatory process. What we have, of course, is exemplification, and it is worth quoting Goodman's definition again in this new context.

An object [e.g. buttress] that is literally or metaphorically denoted by a predicate [e.g. supporting], and refers to that predicate or the corresponding property, may be said to exemplify that predicate or property . . . all expression is exemplification . . . Exemplification is possession plus reference.[6]

The process of exemplification has been considered earlier in both literature and painting: fog in *Bleak House* both possesses opaqueness as an immediate attribute and refers to it mediately as a spiritual force; similarly, physical detail in Pre-Raphaelite realism has both the quality of disorder and refers to disorder as a spiritual condition. In precisely the same way, a buttress both possesses

148

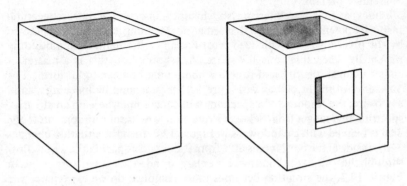

Figure 12.1

Figure 12.2

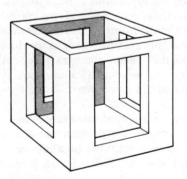

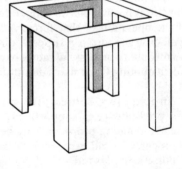

Figure 12.3

Figure 12.4

support as an immediate property and refers to it mediately as an abstract spatio-structural force. Because immediate possession and mediate reference have, by the nature of exemplification, been conflated, and because the range of properties that any architectural feature may exemplify may be – as Goodman suggests – both actual and metaphoric, aesthetic and affective meaning is as integral to architecture as is functional and structural meaning. Thus the properties of, say, mass and vertical thrust exemplified by a wall are no more integral to that wall than are properties of, say, protectiveness and safety. From this one can generalise: because architecture *is* the physical determination of our life-space, it is also – because of the nature of exemplification – co-existensively *about* that determination. For the spectator there is thus no gap between an experience of architectural being and an experience of architectural meaning. The synthesis of the real and the symbolic that I have discussed as a primary imaginative strategy in Carlyle and Dickens, Ruskin and the Pre-Raphaelites is innate to architecture.

A further aspect of functional suitability needs to be mentioned here – suitability to social or operational function, and symbolisation of that function. In the design for a country house, for example, because the function of the kitchen is distinct from that of the library, some registration of this distinction inside the house should be evident from outside. Similarly, where function is identical – as in the different offices of an office block – external appearance, so the argument goes, should be the same. The cry of 'Truth to Function', like the painter's cry of 'Truth to Nature', is a recurrent one. Victorian Gothicists attacked neo-classicism for imposing a regular facade that belied differences in operational function; modernist precursors like Sullivan and Frank Lloyd Wright criticised the Gothicists for designing from the facade into the plan, rather than allowing plan and operation to determine external form. Whatever the merits of individual cases, the principle of a referential relationship between the interior and the exterior of a building is obviously an important extension of architecture's semantic potential.

Constructional and formal exemplification, and the symbolisation of operational function – the two aspects of architectural meaning so far discussed – are *intrinsic*, generated from the visual and spatial configurations of the building itself. But there are also *extrinsic* meanings imposed upon the architecture by tradition and social usage.[7] Such semantic impositions are schemata, sets of visual expectations and association shared by the community within which a building exists. It is extrinsic meaning that carries populism into architectural semantics, that is ultimately the reason for architecture's being more than the art of functional space and form – exquisite perhaps, but in the end clinical. Intrinsic meaning may be construed synchronically, present in all buildings at all times and – if one agrees with Arnheim that it is an objective property – always the same. Extrinsic meaning is a diachronic phenomenon, the product of cultural tradition and experience, dependent upon comparison between historically previous or analogous forms. Thus the wall-piercing in Figure 12.5

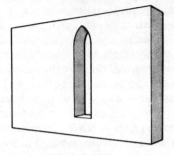

Figure 12.5

generates a certain set of intrinsic meanings because of its form, relationship to the wall surface and so forth. But, simple as it is, it is replete with extrinsic meanings when experienced within the tradition of Western European architecture, because its shape is that of a thirteenth-century lancet window. The remarkable growth of historical awareness evident in the architectural writings of the beginning of the nineteenth century guaranteed that such extrinsic meanings would be of central importance in the way that the Victorians not only thought about, but also actually perceived, architecture. Indeed, the historicist phenomenon of extrinsic meaning underlies the establishment of certain architectural paradigms in early Victorian England: Jacobethan for country houses; an Italianate style for town clubs; columnar neo-classicism, in various forms, for museums; and, of course, fourteenth-century Gothic for churches.[8] The reasons for these choices were aesthetically valid, a matter of appropriate form, of selecting a stylistic language with a semantic vocabulary that guaranteed the right extrinsic meanings.

Architectural meanings, all of them, are codified and ordered by convention, by a social consensus of expectation and taste, and this is one aspect of the phenomenon we label 'style'. This is not to ignore intrinsic meaning, but to recognise that it cannot exist in a pure state, unsullied by the more plebeian air of the extrinsic. The seventeenth-century porch of St Mary Magdalene, Oxford, for example, has a set of intrinsic meanings, but these can only be understood in the context of the stylistic harmonies and discords generated by the imposition of Baroque forms upon a Gothic body. The extrinsic experience of style – or of non-style, or of anti-style – sets the boundaries of meaning, establishes the universe of discourse, within which architecture's semantic transaction can take place. Without the common schemata that establish agreed boundaries, architectural meanings become uncertain. The early decades of the nineteenth century saw such a situation with the dissolution of that polite dictatorship of taste that had ruled eighteenth-century architecture. Out of the ruck of the resulting Battle of Styles the Gothic Revival emerged in a form very different from that which it had assumed in the eighteenth century, and supported by a new body of theory. As has already been suggested, the essentially semantic nature of our experience of architecture, and particularly the centrality of symbolism to that experience, makes comparison between architecture and the other arts feasible. The new theories of architectural meaning generated by the Gothic Revival make possible quite specific parallels with the symbolic realism that I have seen as so important in the literature and painting of the mid-Victorian period. The first formulator and constant champion of the new architectural semantic was Augustus Welby Northmore Pugin.

Pugin dedicated the prefatory plate of *Contrasts* to the architectural profession, or, to use his own term, 'The Trade'; it is probably the funniest piece of architectural criticism ever composed. Designated, with a ruthless unconcern for ironic subtlety, 'TEMPLE OF TASTE', the parodied neo-classicism of the façade is nothing but an enormous billboard, advertising, amongst much else, for 'DESIGNS WANTED'.

A MOORISH FISH MARKET with a Literary Room over/AN EGYPTIAN MARINE VILLA/A CASTELATED TURNPIKE GATE/A GIN TEMPLE in the Baronial Style/A MONUMENT to be placed in WESTMINSTER ABBEY A COLOSSAL FIGURE in the HINDOO STYLE would be preferred.[9]

Pugin was horrified by the architectural Bedlam which seemed to surround him, by the tasteless and grotesque incongruities of a stylistic free-for-all: 'Every linen-draper's shop apes to be something after the palace of the Caesars . . . every paltry town has a cigar divan stuck out to look Turkish.'[10] He saw a situation in which aesthetic standards had become entirely subjective, free of the restraint imposed by common criteria or schemata. 'Private judgement runs riot; every architect has a theory of his own, a beau ideal he has himself created.'[11] The cry is familiar, the same as Ruskin's and Carlyle's against the wilfulness of the individual imagination in painting and literature, the same as that echoed years later by William Butterfield: 'We are living in an age most terribly subjective and sensational.'[12] The reactionary stress of Pugin's criticism is, in its rejection of the subjective, an attack upon the autonomy of the individual artist. Like Ruskin's insistence upon the inviolability of 'fact', it attacks the very basis of Romantic aesthetics. The overthrow of the neo-classical rule of taste engineered by the Romantics and their precursors gave to the late eighteenth century the chance for stylistic experiment and innovation. The motives behind such innovations varied widely, from the bizarre aggrandisement of Beckford's Fonthill to the scholarly historicism of the Greek revival, from a desire for public monumentality to egotistical self-expression. By the 1830s no universally recognised authority determined stylistic practice. Such a situation placed Pugin in an ambiguous position. Although the erosion of authority had freed Gothic from the trammels of Enlightenment disapproval, it had freed it to become just one style in an undifferentiated democracy of styles. If Gothic was again received in polite society, so also were Chinese, Moorish and Egyptian. Pugin craved authority, an aesthetic dictatorship to eradicate the licentiousness of subjective taste; but it had to be the right sort of authority, the authority of a thoroughgoing revival of medieval Gothic. The alternatives, a reassertion of the neo-classical consensus or a triumph of the Greek revival, were for Pugin worse than anarchy. His central concern – and it is essential to realise this – was *not* just with the establishment of some kind of stylistic orthodoxy, but with the establishment of a specific architectural semantic.[13] Post-Romantic eclecticism may have been a chaos of irrelevant architectural meanings and downright inarticulacy; but neo-classicism was the positive establishment of a semantic system that, to Pugin, was irrational and ultimately immoral. A taste for the Classical was a 'mania for paganism',[14] no longer an expression of solidly social Vitruvian virtues, but of 'the revived Pagan Principle'. 'What madness . . . while neglecting our own religious and national types of architecture and art, to worship at the revived shrines of ancient corruption, and profane the temple of a crucified Redeemer by the architecture and emblems of heathen Gods.'[15] What is remarkable in Pugin's diatribe is that its terms are not obviously aesthetic. Classicism means Paganism and Gothic means Christian because *Contrasts* is concerned in its argument, almost exclusively, with extrinsic meaning, with an attempt to expose meanings long forgotten or submerged by usage. The meanings that emerged inevitably carried an ethical charge, because, for Pugin, aesthetics and morals were not independent systems but co-partners in the same system. 'Christian', 'Catholic', 'Pagan' were terms of aesthetic as well as ethical judgement. Pugin's extrinsic meanings are thus conjured into being intrinsic – ethical meaning and aesthetic being become co-extensive. What is true in theory of the exemplification and expression of intrinsic meaning becomes, in practice, true of *extrinsic* meanings: 'Connotation . . . approached denotation in the minds of contemporaries when they saw an early Victorian church.'[16] One might, quite justifiably, demur upon theoretical grounds, but historically the nature of Pugin's forcible extension of architectural semantics was of immense importance for subsequent critics and architects.

Puginian Gothic was Gothic with an entirely new architectural identity. For Pugin the playful Gothic of Strawberry Hill or the sentimental picturesque of the *cottage orné* was evidence of mere flippancy. Nor could Gothic be merely assumed – as it is in the rather fragile elegance of Georgian Gothic – or selected as stylistic cladding in the manner recommended to and by the Church Commissioners. 'Of an exterior . . . we may have either a Greek dress for the parallelogram or a Gothic dress, and we may adopt either the one or the other.'[17] Significantly, in terms of the Spirit of the Age, the same anti-

Romantic need for historical authority was the motive force of the Oxford Movement. The movement's arch-Toryism is analogous to Pugin's; where he feared architectual liberalism, the Tractarians feared the tolerant theology of Latitudinarian Protestantism. Where Pugin saw stylistic and therefore semantic chaos, they saw an anarchy of confused religious opinions. The irony of such anti-Romanticism lies, first, in that Tractarianism opposes the rationalism of eighteenth-century religious thought and expression in a thoroughly Romantic manner; second, in that the externalities of Tractarianism, and its later consequent ritualism – the 'enthusiasm', the esoteric worship, the predominant historicism – *seem* so Romantic. Similar ironies are implicit in Ruskin's adoption of the Romantic Sublime as part of a non-Romantic aesthetic, and Pugin's exploitation of the Picturesque in a context which claims to find such trivial manifestations of taste an irrelevance. Whether unconscious of such irony or, conceivably, because only too conscious of it, Pugin's demands for authority are uncompromising.

We *can never successfully deviate one tittle from the spirit and principles* of pointed architecture.[18]

We seek for *authority*, not *originality*, in these matters; for the establishment *of a principle, not individual celebrity*.[19]

Gothic, for Pugin, becomes what the inviolability of external nature and its meaning is for Ruskin; what the painstaking hyper-realism of their painting is for the Pre-Raphaelites; what symbolic realism is for Dickens and typology for Carlyle: a way of combating and controlling the apparent collapse of actuality and of art into subjective disjointedness, and, simultaneously, guaranteeing the objective irreducibility of one's own interpretative structures. In this context it is inevitable that the twin foci of Pugin's – and of a vast amount of subsequent – criticism and theory should be the definition and elaboration of architectural reality and architectural meaning.

Pugin's Gothic meaning could not be established simply by stylistic association. The 'Christian', 'Catholic' meaning of Gothic was to be dependent upon semantics in depth, upon, initially, constructional and functional meanings. Classicism was not only pagan; the style's manipulation of plastic elements robbed them of their functional identity. Of Soane's Bank: 'It appears to have been the aim of the architect to perpetrate as many unreal features as possible in a wall. Sometimes we have a row of *blank windows*; sometimes a blocked-up entrance, five feet from the ground.'[20] The key-word is 'unreal'. How can something so evidently, concretely 'there' as the Bank of England be 'unreal'? Obviously its unreality is not a matter of physical presence but of semantics. Certain types of intrinsic meaning were too important to allow of their being compromised by anything approaching Soane's cavalier mannerism. These meanings were those of an unequivocal expression of function and construction: '*there should be no features about a building which are not necessary for convenience, construction, or propriety*'.[21]

Construction is to be demonstrated: 'A buttress in pointed architecture at once shows its purpose'; Gothic, moreover, 'does *not conceal her construction but beautifies it*'. Architectural decoration is only valid when dependent upon the stern utility of construction: '*all ornament should consist of enrichment of the essential construction of the building*'. Construction must be expressive not only of its structural purpose, but also of its material: 'the construction itself *should vary with the material employed*, and the designs should be adapted to the material in which they are executed'.[22] Finally, all this expression of architectural truth must be legibly expressive of the building's purpose: '*the external and internal appearance of an edifice should be illustrative of, and in accordance with, the purpose for which it is designed*'.[23] Few twentieth-century architects would disagree with the functionalist philosophy of *True Principles*; it is one of the great programmes for intrinsic meaning. But, as we have seen, Pugin was peculiarly concerned with extrinsic meaning as well. Pugin's statement that 'The severity of Christian architecture requires a *reasonable purpose for the introduction* of the smallest detail'[24] is perfectly consistent with pure functionalism, but an earlier theoretical statement casts an interesting ambiguity upon the definition of 'reasonable purpose'. 'In pure architecture the smallest detail should *have a meaning or serve a purpose.*'[25] The distinction between meaning and purpose is suggestive. Intrinsic meaning is guaranteed by structural integrity, by subordination to 'purpose'; the other 'meaning' to which Pugin refers is the product of a new semantic that interpenetrates both the specific meanings of functionality and the associativeness of 'Catholic' style – the semantics of architectural metaphor, of an elaborately precise Christian symbolism.

The general stylistic properties of Gothic Pugin claimed as directly symbolic: 'The vertical principle, emblematic of the resurrection, is a leading character of Christian architecture';[26] church arrangement is allegorical, the nave representing the Church militant, the chancel the Church triumphant. Features specifically structural are, simultaneously, components of a semantic: a pinnacle has 'a double intention, both mystical and natural' for whilst it is functionally 'an upper weathering, to throw off the rain', it is also 'an emblem of the Resurrection'.[27] Such emblematism can be, indeed, the primary purpose of an architectural feature; thus the significance of a roodscreen 'must be sought for on profound mystical grounds'.[28] Pugin presents Christian symbolism as a categorical demand upon Gothic architects, constituted in the same terms as the imperative to construction and function, and holding the same status. As the general religious connotations of Puginian Gothic approach denotation, so also the complex meanings of Christian emblematics become as real for Pugin as the meanings of functionalism. The development of 'Gothic means Christian' – the co-extension of the aesthetic with religious sentiment – is Gothic means Christian theology – the co-extension of the aesthetic with doctrine. Emblematic meaning is a symbol system, uniting a building by its own immutable logic.

The symbolic associations of each ornament must be understood and considered . . . Altars, Chalices, Vestments, Shrines, Images, Triptychs, Lecterns, and all the furniture of a Catholic Church was formed after a Christian moral and idea: all spoke the same language.[29]

'Language' is right, but the full semantic situation is complex indeed, for it synthesises extrinsic symbolism and intrinsic meaning. Architectural features are to be 'read' as symbolising extra-architectural referents – in the same way as words symbolise extra-linguistic referents – *at the same time* as the *same* features are being read as the components of a specifically architectural semantic. Just as Ruskin asserts that meaning in nature has a real existence independent of the perceiver, so Pugin asserts that a Christian symbolic language is an objective property of Gothic. What complicates the situation, however, is that Pugin recognises that architecture – unlike Ruskinian nature – has a semantic structure belonging to it anyway, by virtue of its being an art – that no matter what it means as Christian symbolism it will always *mean* simply as architecture. Hence the stress upon the morally conceived – that is, extrinsic – importance of functionalist – that is, intrinsic – values. Architectural truth takes on a primarily ethical weighting. Hence, also, the stress upon architectural truth as 'reality'; like Ruskinian 'fact', an attempt to guarantee objectivity, but also implying that the unmistakable truth to construction, material and function in Puginian Gothic acts as assurance for the status of the religious symbolism: that one sort of reality guarantees reality elsewhere. Pugin's architectural semantic is, like the work of the other artists and theorists considered already, an instance of the desire to make physical reality and symbolic meaning co-extensive.

If, however, such a sophisticated symbolic scheme was to be introduced, Pugin early realised that a measure of specific stylistic consistency was necessary. Medieval Gothic covers an enormous stylistic range, and the whole question of the revival was for Pugin far too serious to allow of any confusion about *which* Gothic to build in. As any autocrat knows, people need to be told what is good for them. Pugin's choice, despite some earlier essays in Perpendicular, fell upon fourteenth-century English Gothic, the style labelled Decorated or Middle Pointed. Pugin's first essay in Decorated was the tiny church of St Anne, Keighley (1838). His complete conversion to Decorated was not immediate: St Wilfrid's, Hulme, Manchester, exactly contemporaneous to St Anne's, is, externally at least, a forcefully functional exercise in Early English. The transition is signposted by the little Decorated church in the foreground of the view of an English town in 1440 included in the second edition of *Contrasts*. St Giles's, Cheadle (1841–6), and St Augustine's, Ramsgate (1845–50), show Pugin's full adoption of Decorated, the style that was to become so absolute a monarch of Victorian ecclesiastical architecture. But why Decorated in the first place? A major reason, one may suggest, was the opportunity it gave for a decorative elaboration that had

neither the savageness of Romanesque nor the mechanical character of
Perpendicular. Pugin's criticism is studded with evocative descriptions of
a complex, crowded Gothic.

> . . . each window beams with sacred instructions . . . the pavement
> is a rich enamel . . . Every capital and base are fashioned to represent
> some holy mystery . . . the high altar blazing with gold and jewels
> . . . three unextinguished lamps . . . the gleaming tapers, the tombs
> of the faithful, the various altars . . . etc.[30]

The words and phrases rush along, gabbling across one another in sheer
enthusiasm. Such catalogues in Pugin's writings come to suggest,
uncomfortably at times, a super-real intensity in everything that fills his
dream of Gothic: 'the albs hang in the oaken aumbries, and the cope chests
are filled with orphreyed baudekins; and pyx, and pax, and christatory are
there, and thurible and cross'.[31] This is the litany of object-worship, of a
fixation with the talismanic power of the cult object. Pugin finishes this
particular incantation with a triumphant '*Ecce Habitaculum Dei cum
hominibus*'; more appropriately he might have written *Ecce Habitaculum
Dei cum rebus*. A similar attachment to sheer detail in things is obvious
in Pugin's designs. No small factor in the polemic effectiveness of the plates
in *Contrasts* is the elaboration of detail and chiaroscuro in the pictures of
Gothic architecture, as compared to the thinness of his illustrations of
modern architecture. Many of his early designs for furniture and metalwork
– ostensibly, it must be said, in a post-Decorated style – reveal an
extraordinary proliferation of detail and motif, a restless reduction of surface
to discrete decorative units.[32] Pugin's prodigious output of details,
ornaments, furnishings, for Barry's Palace of Westminster (1840–c.1865)
is perhaps the fullest expression of his love of decorative elaboration. But
examples are available from his more mature work as well – the jewel-like
enrichment of St Giles's, Cheadle, or the brilliant complexity of the tomb
recess in the Rolle Mausoleum at Bicton, Devonshire (1850). For Charles
Eastlake, this facility in decoration seems to have in some measure
disqualified Pugin as an architect: 'His strength as an artist lay in the design
of ornamental detail.'[33] Subsequent critics, particularly in the first half of
this century, have given similar verdicts. This is unfair for, at his best –
and one thinks of St Augustine's, Ramsgate – Pugin's handling of space
is both moving and entirely coherent. He was thus able to provide the
unified space that was essential for the control of his love of elaborated
detail. In larger theoretical terms the relationship between these two
elements of design, between decorative concentration and overall volumetric
organisation, is vital. Having jettisoned the prearranged proportions and
harmonies of neo-classicism, Victorian Gothic from its very inception opens
the whole question of the relationship between the meaning of parts and
the meaning of wholes. In this relationship, I would suggest, lies the

imaginative – rather than archaeological or religious – rationale behind Pugin's adoption of Second Pointed. The elaboration of elements possible within the style, with its resultant potential for planar disintegration and visual fragmentation, suggests an affective response to the proliferating complexity that I have seen as characteristic of the rapid expansion of early Victorian Britain. Pugin's response parallels those of Carlyle and Dickens, Ruskin and the Pre-Raphaelites both quantitatively, insisting upon the sheer amount of individual detail, and qualitatively, insisting upon the separable identity of each detail. Every element of the Pugin building is *true*, true to structure, to function, to material, to a religious meaning; above all, true to itself, its own isolable reality. For Pugin – and for the High Victorians – Decorated expressed the principle of individuation. 'There is an insistency about everything Pugin touched',[34] the same insistency with which Dickens and the Pre-Raphaelites register physical detail. But with this difference: Dickens, the Pre-Raphaelites, Carlyle even were symbolising realities outside the aesthetic contract, words and paint mediating between the audience and the real. Architecture is actual, and Puginian Gothic makes possible a synthesis of what the world *is like* in imaginative terms, with what it *is* in concrete terms. Further, Pugin's theoretical synthesis of intrinsic and extrinsic meanings makes it possible to interpret Pugin's architecture as an attempt to reunify fragmented realities both in and by overall functional and spatial organisation, and in and by the structure of a symbol system concerned not with what was, for Pugin, the poor humanism of aesthetic order, but with the divine order of the Christian dispensation.

To summarise: Puginian Gothic works semantically in three ways: it means intrinsically through structural and functional exemplification; it means symbolically through a general identification of Gothic with Christian, and through an elaborate emblematic system; it means affectively and imaginatively through the relationship between individuation and holism. It is easy to see how all three semantic constructs – each with its own peculiar mix of meaning and reality – could co-exist, if not co-extend, within the same architectural element. This extraordinary semantic complex, both theoretical and practical, was Pugin's legacy to the critics and architects who followed him.

13

'Making the Building Speak':
Symbolism and the Gothic Revival

The evolution of the Gothic Revival in the twenty years after the publication of *Contrasts* shows a remarkably logical working out of Pugin's central concerns. In architectural practice, Decorated becomes the leading article in any revivalist's faith; in critical terminology 'real' becomes the *sine qua non* of Gothic. The final establishment of Decorated was achieved by the Cambridge Camden Society.[1] High Anglican, deeply influenced by Tractarianism, advocates for ritualism, the Camdenians committed ecclesiastical architecture to Middle Pointed, relentlessly propagandised through their journal, *The Ecclesiologist*,[2] as the one style that expressed the Catholicity of Anglicanism. A review of J. L. Petit's *Remarks on Church Architecture* in the first volume of the *Ecclesiologist* gives the tone of the magazine. Petit's recommendation of a stylistically tolerant eclecticism is anathematised as 'a merely utilitarian view of the subject' with 'no reference whatever to any higher standard than that of mere *taste* in church-building, which is treated quite as a matter of trade, convenience, caprice, or of arbitrary arrangement'.[3] Throughout the 1840s the Camdenians pronounced, denounced, prescribed, proscribed, and emerged triumphant. Decorated, in the end, ruled supreme – or, rather, that phase of the style christened with solemn pedantry Early Late Middle Pointed. By 1850, with the kind of smugness that is so often such an irritating feature of the magazine, the *Ecclesiologist* could say of R. C. Carpenter's St Mary Magdalen, Munster Square (1849–51), 'the style, we need scarcely say, is Middle Pointed'.[4] Carpenter and his orthodoxy – both doctrinal and stylistic – were favourites of the Camdenians and, on its opening, St Mary Magdalene was pronouned 'the most artistically correct new church yet consecrated in London'.[5]

But there is more to Carpenter and to the churches produced by the antiquarian phase of the Revival than orthodox copyism. The 1840s churches of London architects with national practices – men like Carpenter, Benjamin Ferrey and Gilbert Scott – and of informed provincial Gothicists like John Hayward of Exeter share a common style with an aesthetic identity that is expressive of more than medieval precedent. There is a precision of cutting and moulding, a sharpness of spatial division and of light and shade, a clarity of line in the best of these early churches: they rejoice in hard edges and hard surfaces. In play against this there is a concentration of detail, not only in decorative carving or in the highly finished mouldings and geometrical tracery, but also in the ornaments and furniture of High Anglican worship. Such churches and their fittings seem to celebrate their own objecthood, their that material identity, and at the same time to celebrate the appropriation of the material identity for the purposes of the spiritual. These qualities derive from Pugin's Gothic rather than from the medieval Gothic to which the architects are ostensibly indebted. Authentically of their time in the particular use they make of the Gothic vocabulary, the churches of the 1840s anticipate and, indeed, prepare the way for the freedom from historical precedent that characterises the High Victorian Gothic of architects like George Edmund Street, William White and – in particular – William Butterfield. Their freedom resulted partly from their own demand for creative independence, partly from the development of the potentialities already apparent in revived Gothic, and partly from a liberalisation of the stylistic rule of Middle Pointed. This liberalisation was ensured, ironically enough, by John Ruskin.

In *The Seven Lamps of Architecture,* Ruskin demands adherence to stylistic rules with all the authoritarian insistence of Pugin.[6]

> . . . the architecture of a nation is great only when it is as universal and as established as its language. (8, p. 252)

> We want no new style of architecture . . . But we want *some* style . . . a code of laws . . . accepted and enforced from one side of the island to another. (8, p. 252)

> It may be said that this is impossible. It may be so – I fear it is so: I have nothing to do with the possibility or impossibility of it; I simply know and assert the necessity of it. (8, p. 255)

Yet, in the end, Ruskin prevaricates; rather than recommending one style he suggests four, with a fifth thrown in as a kind of stylistic yeast.

> The choice would lie I think between four styles: – 1. The Pisan Romanesque; 2. The early Gothic of the Western Italian Republics . . . 3. The Venetian Gothic in its purest development; 4. The English earliest decorated. The most natural, perhaps the safest choice, would be the last . . . perhaps enriched by some mingling of decorative elements from the exquisite decorated Gothic of France . . . (8, pp. 258–9)

Italian, French, English; Romanesque, Early Gothic, Decorated: there is a farcical, and really rather pathetic, discrepancy between Ruskin's demand

for authority and his inability to provide it. But Ruskin's vacillation heralds
a new Gothic eclecticism. Borrowing from European sources led to a stylistic
mixing that would have appalled Pugin, and that caused Ruskin to despair
of architecture altogether. Within a decade and a half of *Contrasts*, Decorated
had not only been established as the only permissible ecclesiastical style,
it had also been superseded. With its passing Victorian Gothic attains full
stylistic independence. In the same year that building started on Carpenter's
St Mary Magdalene, Butterfield was designing All Saints', Margaret Street,
the first major architectural statement of High Victorian Gothic.[7]

High Victorian Gothic has more than its stylistic roots in the
developments of the 1840s, however; it also has its imaginative and semantic
origins. As well as ensuring the promotion of Middle Pointed, the 1840s
also saw the wholesale development of the other major elements of Pugin's
programme: his theories of architectural meaning and architectural reality.
The Camdenians maintained Pugin's stress upon intrinsic meaning. As early
as 1841, however, the critical terminology that Pugin loosened – or
unloosed – in his attempts to inject fresh semantic potential into
architecture has become markedly ambiguous. Condemning St Paul's,
Cambridge, for having a tower but no chancel, the *Ecclesiologist* says:

> . . . if ornamental appendages are bad when anything real is given
> up for their sake, much more are they so when they are imitations
> of that which they really are not. Stucco, and paint, and composition,
> and graining, are not out of place in the theatre or the ball-room; but
> in GOD'S House every thing should be *real*.[8]

Unreality compounding unreality, it would appear; but different sorts of
reality are in question. A tower may be unreal, but its unreality is not the
same as that of stucco. Ambiguity in the use of 'real' is more or less
acceptable when its meanings can all be seen to cluster around a centre
of functionalism – although, in the passage just quoted, is the 'unreality'
of the tower a matter of architecturally intrinsic function, or of the rubrical
arrangement of a Christian church? The functionalist aspect of the Revival
did, however, continue throughout the 1840s, although a thoroughgoing
functionalist like Alfred Bartholomew was by-passed in critical discussion.[9]
It was Ruskin who formulated the mid-Victorian version of Pugin's doctrine
of architectural truth. The second chapter of *Seven Lamps*, 'The Lamp of
Truth', is, for the most part, a straight development of Pugin. There are
three main architectural deceits, structural and material – both Puginian
– and also operative deceit about the amount of labour involved in
decoration by the use of machine-made ornament: 'exactly as a woman of
feeling would not wear false jewels, so would a builder of honour disdain
false ornaments. The using of them is just as downright and as inexcusable
as a lie' (8, p. 83). Already the terms of 'truth' and 'reality' are extended
to include humanitarian ethics. But, if these three deceits are 'the principal

kinds of fallacy', there are also 'other and more subtle forms of it, against which it is less easy to guard' (8, p. 86). Thus, material deceit also includes denying the nature of a material – which for Ruskin seems to take on the nature of an absolute: medieval Gothic starts to decline when tracery bars begin to deny the rigidity of stone, when a non-malleable substance comes to seem malleable. But, even as Ruskin's warnings against unreality increase, his application of the terms 'real' and 'unreal' becomes increasingly indiscriminate. Having stated that architectural sculpture must imitate natural objects from the 'real' world – 'Never imitate anything but natural forms' (8, p. 175) – Ruskin claims, in a consideration of sculptural and architectural colour, that 'sculpture is the representation of an idea, while architecture is itself a real thing' (8, p. 176). Further, colour is necessary to architecture because it is, we are led to assume, 'real', and 'a reality ought to have reality in all its attributes' (8, p. 176). In all these cases, it is possible to work out the specific meaning of 'reality' from context. But when we come to a comparison of architecture with sculpture and painting in which Ruskin contrasts 'her realism' to 'the picturing of stories and of dreams' (8, p. 251) in the other arts one is entitled to ask why 'reality' should have become 'realism', and, in any case, *which* reality, or which combination of realities?

It is the same in *Stones of Venice*.[10] The first volume is a textbook of constructional method; everything in a building has a purpose, a discrete identity. But Ruskin's concept of the logic of structural reality has widened again: thus, he explains the addition of spurs to column bases.

> The changes are made, not for the sake of the almost inappreciable increase of security they involve, but in order to convince the eye of the real security which the base . . . *appears* to compromise . . . the props or spurs . . . are absolutely useless in reality . . . (9, p. 109)

'Reality', apparently, is not necessarily contradicted by some sorts of 'unreality'. In terms of one sort of 'reality', Ruskin defends the encrusted construction of St Mark's – plating is not a material deceit because there is 'no intention to deceive' (10, p. 95), which can only mean that a further determinant of architectural reality is intentionality. In terms of another 'reality' he condemns restoration because 'what is left . . . however fragmentary, however ruinous . . . is most always, the real thing' (10, p. 437). Obviously 'real', as a critical term, has come to attract a vast number of increasingly disparate connotations. By 1850 'real' is no longer a synonym for 'truthful'; it is more, even, than, in Pevsner's definition, 'truth and seriousness of purpose'.[11] Semantically, it is Legion. Yet this loss of semantic focus was predictable from the beginning; as soon as Pugin tried to institute a synthesis between the extrinsic meanings of religious symbolism and the intrinsic meanings of construction, function and material, the semantic precision of the word 'real' was under threat: if Puginian 'meaning' and Puginian 'reality' were co-extensive, were not the labels interchangeable? This sudden expansion of the semantic field of 'reality' as a critical label was nowhere more ruthlessly exploited than in the *Ecclesiologist*. Cutting a window from a single block of stone 'is a gross unreality';[12] Scott's use of Catholic Gothic for the Lutheran Nicholai-Kirche is condemned for its 'unrealness';[13] the sanctuary of Trinity College Chapel, Cambridge, 'is an unreality and is devoted to objects alien to its real destination';[14] family pews placed in a chancel are 'the crowning abomination, the climax of unreality and irreverence'.[15] Examples could be multiplied, but sufficient have been quoted to make the point: in each of these instances unreality is assigned to objects of adverse criticism on quite different grounds – stylistic, doctrinal, liturgical and devotional respectively. In only one case – that of the 'unreal' window – might those grounds be considered primarily aesthetic. What has happened is that the aesthetic debate about Gothic and the debate about the intrinsic meaning of architecture have been subsumed by a far wider debate about ethics – architectural and otherwise – and about the whole symbolic significance of ecclesiastical building.

The extension of the 'intrinsic-ness' possessed by certain architectural meanings into areas of semantics theoretically extrinsic – the kind of extension argued by Pugin – originated in religious, rather than architectural, practice. Puginian Gothic had at its base the liturgical needs of Roman Catholicism; the Anglican Gothic of the ecclesiologists took its *raison d'être* from the sacramental theology of the Oxford Movement. The result of this cross of High Anglicanism and architecture was the doctrine of Rubrical Planning – by Tractarianism out of Pugin. The ecclesiologists demanded churches that would both contain and express the newly elaborated forms of Anglican worship: aisles, a clear division of nave from chancel, a deep chancel, no pews, no galleries, none of the appearance of the hated Georgian 'preaching box'. The theoretical implications of this are far-reaching: if a building is to express its function, a church must be expressive of Christian worship. The function of a church having been defined in terms of an elaborate ritual, the building becomes a symbol of that ritual. Hence the attack upon St Paul's, Cambridge, quoted above – a chancel is a ritual necessity, a tower is not, therefore the inclusion of tower rather than chancel is ritually indefensible, therefore functionally 'unreal'. Once function has been defined in terms of ritual, the extension of symbolism into the doctrine which is the basis for that ritual is an obvious step. The function of a church then becomes not just to provide for worship but overtly to express specific doctrine: thus religious symbolism comes to be justified through a functionalist argument, and extrinsic meanings come to assume the status of intrinsic.

The Font was not put near the door by chance, for it was meant to

shew by this that Baptism is the door by which a child is brought
into the church.[16]

A Cross is of course the most beautiful form in which a church can
be built . . . the symbol conveyed by the Cross better adapted than
any other for a Christian place of worship . . .[17]

The co-extension of realist and symbolic values in contemporary literature
and painting is precisely paralleled by the Gothicists' insistence upon
symbolic meaning as an intrinsic part of architectural reality: where Dickens
and the Pre-Raphaelites have symbolic realism, the ecclesiologists have
symbolic functionalism. It proved irresistible. 'Ecclesiastical Architecture
is a language,'[18] said G. A. Poole with Camdenian fervour, and if Pugin,
the man who started it all, might have agreed with that, in the years that
followed he was soon out-symbolised and semantically out-distanced.

The form of font which has an octagonal bowl

. . . is in itself symbolical, according to the ancient method of
spiritualizing numbers, of the new birth in Baptism: for the seven days
creation of the natural world are symbolized by the number seven;
and the new creation by Christ Jesus by the number eight.[19]

The east window in Dunchurch church, Warwickshire, is a type of the
Trinity: 'Its *three* tre-foiled lights, its tracery of *three* tre-foiled *triangles* round
an *equilateral triangle* and its *three* tre-foils interspersed between these; what
else can they point to?'[20] In just one year, the *Ecclesiologist* details the
numerical symbolism evident in Chichester Cathedral – 'the *triplicity* which
pervades it is truly astonishing'; carries correspondence and articles on the
hagioscope as 'the symbol of the Wound in Our Blessed LORD's side';
publishes, with commendable scholarship, a treatise on the symbolism of
the church fabric translated from the twelfth-century Icelandic.[21] In Exeter
an enthusiastic, but unfortunately anonymous, member of the Diocesan
Architectural Society – a sister-society to Cambridge – is moved to verse.

> Before the range in goodly file
> Along the vista of the Pile,
> Two rows of Pillars, staunch and tall,
> On which uprear'd the lofty wall,
> Rises like that Communion,
> Built by the Lord of living stone,
> Which knit by faith and love's cement,
> Can never by the world be rent:
> These Piers that bear this Fabric up
> Are they who drank their Saviour's cup;
> Apostles, Prophets, Martyrs true,
> A noble host, Christ's retinue;

I see them all with glory crown'd
Their Capitals are foliaged round,
Anticipating that great Day
For which they wait so peacefully.[22]

Today it all can seem like a delightfully ingenious game – Hunt the Symbol perhaps; certainly it could fetch up in the realms of total fantasy, as in Lewis's account of the orders of moulding on the chancel arch at Kilpeck. 'The first or uppermost moulding is flat, so made to represent the label on which Pilate wrote the title and put it on the Cross . . . the second is the Crown of thorns. The third is a hollow moulding, shewing the interior is gone, given up.'[23] Ecclesiastical symbolism finds its most elaborate expression in Neale and Webb's long introduction to their translation of Durandus.[24] Modern churches are less satisfactory than medieval not because they are in need of associations or picturesqueness, but because 'the thing required [is] Reality' and reality is defined in functional and constructional terms plus symbolism. That reality 'must be Christian Reality, the true expression of a true ideal . . . This Christian reality we call SACRAMENTALITY'; 'Symbolism uses real personages and real actions [and real things] as symbols of the truth . . . Sacramentality is symbolism'; 'the material fabrick symbolizes, embodies, figures, represents, expresses, answers to, some abstract meaning'.[25] In *Stones of Venice* Ruskin adopts a similar semantic programme, similarly based upon the co-existence of the symbolic and the real – although the meanings he discovers have, even more, the air of personal inventions. A building should 'speak well, and say the things it was intended to say in the best words' (9, p. 60). Architecture symbolises social organisation: 'the great Christian truth of distinctive services of the individual soul is typified in the Christian shaft; and the old Egyptian servitude of the multitude . . . is typified also in that ancient shaft of the Egyptians' (9, p. 129). It symbolises philosophical abstractions: 'the Greek pediment, with its enclosed sculpture represented . . . the law of Fate' (9, p. 304). Ruskin defines the nature of Gothic architecture in terms of 'certain moral tendencies of the builders, legibly expressed in it' (10, p. 183). Ultimately, every architectural feature takes its identity from a fusion of ethics and aesthetics. Thus, in a discussion apparently concerned with construction, Ruskin refers to 'the awkward (moral or architectural) feature, the *corner*' (9, p. 311). Confronted with this kind of total synthesis – a synthesis that exists in the very way in which Ruskin experiences architecture – Steegman's remark that 'as if he himself were one of the Pre-Raphaelite Brothers, Ruskin was captivated by symbolism' is obviously appropriate.[26]

Ultimately, the redefining of 'real' and 'unreal' in terms of so many divergent semantics, so many different symbolic possibilities, leads to an almost entire loss of precision. As terms in the mid-century architectural debate they are swamped by a welter of connotations and associations. In

The English Cathedral of the Nineteenth Century 'reality' and 'unreality' flounder hopelessly, drowning words looking for any semantic straw to catch at. Beresford Hope criticises 'the trickery, the flimsiness, the unreality so common in modern art', a Puginian, constructional definition of 'real'; because of the Anglican tradition of worship, he regards the basilican model as 'unreal in our day', a Camdenian, rubrical definition; but the basilica is also 'less real and less appropriate to our present condition of society', a Ruskinian, sociological definition; an open spire contradicts 'its real elevation', a diminishing tower is 'too artificial', whereas a solid spire 'combines the truth and the beauty of architecture', all definitions in visual and spatial terms; the cathedral divisions of arcade, clerestory and triforium may be reintroduced, but one must always consider 'the feeling of reality',[27] whatever, by this stage, that might mean. However destructive of critical precision this swamping of 'real' may be, it is of the greatest importance for architecture itself. 'There are several reasons why the Gothic Revival was able in England, and almost only in England, to pass into a new and creative phase around 1850. One was the ethical emphasis of its doctrines . . .'[28] This 'ethical emphasis' was more than the specific emblematics of Pugin or the Camdenians; it was an emphasis that suggested the possibility of architecture's being used to symbolise and to express new areas of reality at the same time as it remained itself functionally, structurally, materially 'real'. Architects felt free to exploit all aspects of building for their newly found semantic potential. This semantic freedom affected the whole range of Victorian architecture, not just church-building, and a whole range of styles. It resulted in the extraordinary symbolic programme of Bunning's Coal Exchange (1846–9, now demolished); in Deane and Woodward's Venetian Gothic University Museum at Oxford (1855–9), with its 'inscriptions everywhere to make the building speak';[29] and, later in the century, in Waterhouse's Romanesque Natural History Museum (completed 1881), of which 'the façade is an open book, whereon are recorded, in a language which all can read and understand, the inexhaustible wonders of the world in which we live'.[30] It is in this context that the architecture of William Butterfield must be considered, for the synthesis of meaning and reality is the focus of that architecture, just as it is the focus of Pre-Raphaelite realism or of Dickens's novels of the 1850s. Butterfield is the first architect of the new semantic.

14

'Without Flow or Continuity':
The Architectural Semantic of
William Butterfield

Pugin, attacking what was to him the sophistical regularity of neo-classicism, stressed the functionally derived asymmetry of Gothic; Poole claimed that 'irregularity is a beauty purely Gothic';[1] Ruskin began his characterisation of Gothic with the qualities of Savageness and Changefulness. William Butterfield's first church group, at Coalpit Heath, Gloucestershire (1844–5), has a quiet, rather workmanlike church in Middle Pointed, but a parsonage that announces a no-nonsense functionalism – irregularly massed, structurally expressive, its component parts precisely defined by firm bounding-lines. Yet there is more than straight functionalism here. The angularity of the sharply pitched gables and the preference for abrupt juxtapositions of mass suggested by the way in which the chimney breast meets the sheer wall surfaces emphasise the separate identities of constituent forms and masses. The expression of structure and function is overstated, as it were, establishing a tendency to formal awkwardness. The school and house at Alfington, Devon (13), built in 1850, show clearly the direction of Butterfield's development from Coalpit Heath: 'subdivided into a great and confusing number of parts . . . the arrangement intends to show all individual rooms as individual entities from ground-level upwards'.[2] The suggestion of confusion does not seem quite right: Butterfield's technique sets up two different modes of perceptual organisation – one based upon a unity of functional expression, the other upon a principle of individuation of form. This technique Butterfield maintained throughout his career. The resultant preference for hard-edged masses brought forcefully together often leads to a visual effect in which the eye is forced to jump across related planes and masses: at Milton church, Oxfordshire (1854–6), the oblique surfaces of vestry roof, buttress chamfer, chancel roof, nave roof and squat tower relate in a jerky series of upward visual leaps: similarly at Waresley, Bedfordshire (1855–7), the harsh outlines of buttress, stair turret and nave assert formal individuation in counter-movement to the formal connections that are made by the eye (14). Such an effect is unsettling, an exploitation of harshness of outline that partly determines and partly emphasises awkwardness of juxtaposition. The gablings of the east end of St Matthias, Stoke Newington (1849–53), are uncomfortably sharp (15); E. A. Freeman, criticising the design, talks of 'the most unpleasant outline' and 'hideous nakedness'.[3] Balliol Chapel (1854–7) was similarly attacked:

'the thing stood out with a great staring strong roof, and a most awkward thing upon it'.[4] More precisely, the *Ecclesiologist* complained of the quasi-arch between choir and sanctuary at Balliol: 'the curve on each side changes abruptly into a straight line . . . This sudden mutation of outline gives a broken character to the whole member, and disturbs the proportion of the remaining chapel.'[5] 'Broken character' is important, for Butterfield not only individualises architectural units by hardness of outline and awkwardness of relationship, he also constantly allows line and form to be interrupted, broken into smaller units, each one of which lays claim to individuality.

The technique is present as early as All Saints', Margaret Street. The constricted site is brilliantly managed, and more; the courtyard is crowded round by closely packed, elongated masses, shouldering one against the other, dominated by the enormous spire (16). Processes of interruption and disturbance focus on the porch, forcefully placed where the wall of the aisle, the wall of the clergy house, the aisle roof and the spire all meet. Compounding this sense of collision, the porch is 'squeezed against the house on the left so that one side of its surround is cut off' (17).[6] 'Squeezed' is appropriate, for one has a sense of mass being extruded under pressure, outwards into the courtyard, from the base of the spire. All the sheerness and mass of the tower is concentrated at this corner; the force of its downward thrust, however, is broken at the point where it meets the horizontal junction of clerestory wall and aisle roof; downward movement along the roof's diagonal is checked again by the tower's angle buttress – with its own downward thrust – and split between the wall of the clergy house – already merged with the other angle buttress – and the steeply gabled porch, the roof line of which meets the aisle wall just below the junction of buttress, tower and aisle wall, and which becomes, oddly, a further buttress against the downward pressure of the tower. Diagonal movement across the porch roof eventually finishes in the emphatically stepped diagonal buttress set awkwardly against the corner of the porch. The whole dramatic complex works through what might be called visual pressure-points, foci of conflicting directions, pressures and masses. Disparate elements are forced together under an extraordinary tension: the result is a formalisation of architectural conflict that implies discord as a determinant of co-existence. Similarly, in smaller country churches, Butterfield organises plastic elements in sudden, dramatic clusters of disparate yet related forms, functionally determined but visually exploited. The tight grouping of buttress, doorway and vesica window at Blunsdon St Andrew (restored, 1864–75) further unbalances a west end of insistent asymmetry (18). Again at Barley Church (1871–3), window, drainage pipe, buttress and doorway are squeezed one against the other (19): the kinds of interaction set up by this Barley group are typical of Butterfield's technique. Together they form what is almost a digest of function – access, support, drainage and the provision of light, all focused at one moment, as it were, in one's experience of the wall. The sharpness of the stone cutting, the individuality of form, the depth of the window mouldings emphasise the three-dimensionality of the forms against the even texture of the knapped flint. Visual organisation moves in two directions. The elegant pointed arch of the window, the cylindrical pipe, the rectangular buttress, the triangular head of the doorway encourage visual organisation in terms of formal, geometrical separation. But formal echoes – the overall pointedness of window and doorway, the cusping of window and shouldered arch, the flint squares in both door-head and buttress – establish visual connections. Similarly, directional oppositions are stated, then reconciled. Vertical emphasis in window, pipe, buttress and doorway clashes with the horizontals of string-course and parapet moulding, but the stepped diagonal running from the window head to the base of the door synthesises and thus reconciles vertical principle and horizontal principle. This kind of effect is directly consequent upon a definition of architectural reality by absolute functional, structural and material integrity. Constituent elements are conceived as discrete, each one 'true' *in itself* to its material and to the different systems – functional and constructional – of the building, rather than as being subordinate elements in a visual hierarchy. An architectural democracy prevails, in which the claims of any one constituent are allowed free play against the claims of any other. A taut balance is generated as the assertiveness of one element neutralises the assertiveness of another, whilst, simultaneously, formal and visual correspondences suggest the rudiments of congruity.

Butterfield develops this technique in two ways. The one stresses the forcefulness of the bringing-together of elements. Thus, at St Alban's, Holborn (1859–62), windows, buttresses, stair turret and transepts are jammed together against the massive saddle-back tower (20), telescoped and thrust upwards as if under enormous pressure, the volumes themselves broken together. Such qualities are even more apparent in the tower of Rugby School Chapel (1870–2) (21), which Thompson describes in terms of a dramatic fracturing of volumes, pointing to 'the flattening of the face of the apse . . . the abrupt reduction of the square central tower to an octagon, and then to a stump of solid stone spire . . . the breaking of even the junction of square to octagon, and octagon to spire'.[7] Both St Alban's and Rugby are exercises in volumetric violence – a yoking together of disparate forms in a way which suggests positive coercion. The other development lies in the opposite direction: independent elements are freed from functional or structural logic. A simple example is the two west-end buttresses of Dropmore church, Buckinghamshire (1864–6), which, rather than standing in the line of the walls, 'are moved a few feet to one side, as if to emphasize their structural irrelevance'.[8] Similarly, the triple buttresses to the south transept of Yealmpton, Devon (1848–9), and the solitary tower buttress at Foxham, Wiltshire (1878–81) (22), assert their identity as structural elements, even as their structural role is seen to be perfunctory. The belfry of Holy Saviour, Hitchin (1863–6), is corbelled out on to an elongated pier; similarly the central corbel carrying the gable and gable window of the New Schools at Rugby (1867–70) is elongated into a pier, itself corbelled out at a point which interrupts the rhythm of the paired ground-floor windows. This kind of architectural mannerism is evident throughout Butterfield's career. Thus, the courtyard buttress of All Saints' is set off-centre, 'arbitrarily construed into a grand feature on cathedral scale',[9] independent of the forms around it and of any obvious structural function. It seems singularly appropriate that this buttress should carry a relief of the Annunciation for, in effect, it announces the central structural principle of Butterfield's architecture – the aggressive individuation of architectural elements. Obviously, analogies to both Dickens and the Pre-Raphaelites may be made. The prevalence, in Butterfield's work, of what I have called an 'architectural democracy' forces the spectator to register each constituent part as a distinct entity, claiming its independence from a larger whole. In *The Hireling Shepherd*, to take just one Pre-Raphaelite example, realist details have a similar independence. So also the details of the physical world in Dickens's novels are minutely and separately articulated and labelled, as in the description of Krook's shop: 'blacking bottles, medicine bottles, ginger beer and soda-water bottles, pickle bottles, wine bottles, ink bottles'.[10] The insistence that, as was remarked before, typifies Puginian details is heightened in the characteristic aggressiveness of Butterfield's work: 'ordinary Middle Pointed details smoulder away with an intensity and rigidity which would probably have astonished their thirteenth-century creators'.[11] Similarly, the sheer concentration with which Hunt and Millais depict external realities gives their art a more-than-real intensity that is also a characteristic of Dickens's registration of the physical world.

That the intensity with which Butterfield treats individual forms should be seen as deliberate ugliness is not surprising. Such 'ugliness' suggested, to his contemporaries, certain significant parallels.

> The architecture of All Saints' answers to the earlier 'Pre-Raphaelitism' of the sister art ... And curiously enough there is here to be observed the germ of the same dread of beauty, not to say the same deliberate preference for ugliness, which so characterizes in fuller development the later paintings of Mr Millais and his followers.[12]

'Ugliness' or not, the comparison between the angular awkwardness and apparent arbitrariness of Pre-Raphaelite forms, and the architectural forms of Butterfield, is obviously appropriate. But the parallels go farther, as Boase, in his account of All Saints', suggests.

> The frescoes, Dyce's saints in the east end, were painted on heavily gilt backgrounds; the windows . . . are unusually harsh and garish.

These violent contrasts were as bold and striking as those . . . of paintings by Millais or Holman Hunt; as bold also as the silhouette of the tower . . . and the awkward adjustment of the gabled porch . . .[13]

This is right, but needs amplification: Butterfield's colour is not a matter of frescoes and glass, but of constructional polychromy, the exploitation of contrasted colour in the very materials of a building. The connection between his structural and decorative scheme is not only visual but also actual. Butterfield's colour is as permanent, as 'real', as the structure itself, because it is part of that structure, a point made at the time by Beresford Hope: 'the present scheme is that of a church whose character and beauty shall arise from *construction* and not from superaddition'.[14] Hope's statement is revealing. 'Superaddition' implies impermanence, even superficiality, whereas constructional colour is ineffaceable, necessarily to be construed as integral to the actualities of structure and function. The High Victorian enthusiasm for constructional polychromy is a direct consequence of their constantly reiterated commitment to 'real' architecture.

Butterfield's decorative organisation should always be considered in terms of structural organisation; *ex hypothesi*, the one is integral to the other. Its prime feature – paralleling that of Butterfield's plastic forms – is its geometric precision of outline, its hard linear quality, and this remains true throughout his career. The external banding of All Saints' is as precise, as rigid, as is that of Keble College a quarter of a century later. Internally, the abstract tile patterns of All Saints' (23), executed during the 1850s, have the same sharpness of definition as the mosaic decoration of the Coleridge transept, Ottery St Mary (1878) (24), or of Harrow Weald church (1889–92) and St Mary sub Castro, Dover (1888–9). Similarly, Butterfield's tracery – important in this present context because of tracery's ambiguous status between decoration and construction – resists all fluency: constituent forms are rigidly separated and a preference shown, even, for awkwardness, for clashing form against form. The tracery of St Matthias, Stoke Newington – which Freeman stigmatised as 'hideous'[15] – is typical. The collision of forms is aggressive and may almost be considered sexual – the sharpness of the central light hard against the convex curve of the sextafoil in the window head (25), or actually penetrating it, forcing it to yield its form and to become a voluptuous but unbalanced quatrefoil (26).[16] Instead of movement from one form to another, there is movement of one form against another. It is this uneasy sense of in-built conflict – literally built into the structure – that underlines the *Ecclesiologist*'s criticism of the All Saints' tiling. 'The patterns in the nave and over the chancel arch seem to us abrupt, and disproportionate, and ungainly. They are without flow or continuity.'[17] This sense of staccato discontinuity is generated not only by decorative shape, but also by decorative material. Proposed in the *Ecclesiologist* as 'a practical example of what we are very anxious to see tested.

viz. constructional polychromy',[18] All Saints' gave Butterfield an opportunity to explore the visual and expressive qualities of the very material substance of decoration. That exploration becomes, with purposeful inevitability, a study in textural and material discontinuity that caused the *Ecclesiologist* to complain of 'the comparatively rude brickwork of the nave edging itself up . . . among the more costly materials of the chancel'.[19] The effect of conflict between the materials themselves is heightened by an intractability of surface: the pier shafts are of highly polished granite; matt surfaces are set with highly glossed tiles; the marble surfaces of the chancel screen are inviolably hard and smooth. Butterfield's stress upon the intractability of materials is a stress upon their independence, a stress analogous to the hard edge of his patterning and the individuation of his plastic forms. The actual textures of his surfaces repudiate any emotional warmth on the part of the spectator, any human contact with the constructional material: Hitchcock notes 'the curiously unsensual lushness of All Saints'.[20] This Butterfieldian characteristic is a development of similar qualities in earlier Victorian Gothic: the material, the surface, is objective, both in its repudiation of sensual response, and in its assertion of its own object-hood. It is the assertion of an independent reality. But, against surface as material, Butterfield plays surface as colour. From the point of view of the spectator, the objective 'otherness' of Butterfield's decorative material determines response in the direction of distance – the detachment of experiencer from the experienced object – but the subjective expressiveness of Butterfield's decorative colour determines response in the direction of involvement – the attachment of experiencer to experienced object. The one determines existential status in terms of isolability – the 'inwardness' of identity – the other in terms of reciprocality – the 'outwardness' of identity. Two different techniques for interpreting reality are suggested within the same experiental context, and a complex interaction of the subjective and the objective – more dynamically, an alternation between attraction and rejection – takes place.

Constructional colour must, however, be considered in terms of its companion structures of meaning and expression. Thinking of it in isolation has led to an extraordinary divergence of critical response. Summerson talks of 'the acid chords'[21] of All Saints', Thompson of its 'vivid enthusiasm, astonishing in its warmth and openness';[22] Butterfield's obituary claims that he 'had an insensitive eye for colour',[23] Hitchcock praises the 'delicate harmony'[24] of colours in Baldersby church (1855–7). The lack of critical consensus derives from the generally impressionistic way Butterfield's decorative colour has been described, and from failing to recognise the extent to which its expressive character is dependent upon the formal dispositions in which it occurs. Thus Thompson's description of the All Saints' pulpit (27):

. . . lumpish in outline, glittering in jewelled colour, Derbyshire fossil grey, autumn red Languedoc, Irish lime green, set on fat brawny pink granite columns which branch into waving seaweedy capitals, a triumphant display of the Victorian love for the colour pageantry of rocks and marbles.[25]

Eloquent as this is, it ignores the aesthetically determinant relationship between colour and form. Colour areas are rigidly demarcated; bounding-lines are hard and precise; patterns are formally self-sufficient; the different dappling of some of the marbles simply reinforces our sense of the tight control that prevents any movement towards texturing; surfaces are impenetrably smooth. Butterfield's designs are, in twentieth-century terms, those of a hard-edge abstractionist. The geometrical pattern-forms emphasise chromatic and tonal contrasts: rather than colours merging they abut abruptly upon each other. The abruptness with which transitions from colour area to colour area are made tends towards the break-up of visual coherence, a tendency which is in dynamic opposition to the restraint imposed by the rigid formality of the patterns and the integrity of the surfaces. Alike in Butterfield's relatively small designs – the All Saints' pulpit, the Ottery St Mary font (1849–50) (28) – and in his large decorative schemes – the chapels of Rugby and Keble – the vigorous relationship between colour and form both initiates processes of conflict and visual fragmentation and, equally forcefully, checks them. This kind of dynamic tension is reinforced by the constructional nature of Butterfield's polychromy, by the fact that his patterns are *built* rather than simply painted. In the chancel tiling at Baverstock, Wiltshire (1880–2) (29), for example, the main motif appears to be the product of a logical process of pattern-building, the product – as Thompson says – of 'superimposed triangles and squares'.[26] As soon as one tries to reconstruct the order in which such superimposition might have taken place, however, the hypothesis breaks down, for the *actual* construction of the pattern obstinately reasserts itself as what it is – a juxtaposition of coloured squares and triangles. The apparent logic behind the building up of the pattern is contradicted by the way in which it is really built.

The visual tensions and contradictions inherent to Butterfield's handling of pattern and colour are instances of a larger expressive technique: the exploitation of the potential conflict between the elements of construction and the elements of decoration, rendered all the more tense, of course, by the synthesis of the two in constructional polychromy. This conflict is more than simply collision. Hitchcock, describing the interior of All Saints', talks of 'an all-over composition of decorative flat patterns and then, cutting through this as if by accident, an almost unrelated arrangement of plastic architectural forms'.[27] He sees in this a working out of Ruskin's dictum, 'natural colour . . . never follows form'.[28] But Ruskin also claims that architectural colour, like natural, should be 'irregular, blotched, imperfect'.[29] This is certainly not true of the hard-edged, highly finished colour patterns of All Saints'; nor does their disposition have a truly Ruskinian randomness; the roundels of the nave tiling are balanced symmetrically in relationship to the arcade (30), tiling outlines the extrados of the nave arcade. Conflict is there, nevertheless, in the deliberately exploited clash between the continuity of a decorative scheme and the necessities of plastic forms. Butterfield will not relinquish the independent right of either: one system never quite subordinates the other. One reason for this is another non-Ruskinian feature of the church – the denial of hierarchy. Decorative hierarchy, visually determined, was a fundamental of Ruskin's sense of architectural order; against it he opposed 'democratic ornament, in which all is equally influential, and has equal office and authority; that is to say, none of it any office or authority, but a life of continual struggle for independence'.[30] All Saints' is just such a democracy: decoration is evenly stressed wherever it exists in relation to the building or the spectator, the lines and surfaces of its different systems vying in hardness, precision and visual independence with each other and with plastic elements. Thus the horizontal movement of the nave arcade tiling collides with the extrados tiling; the squeezing of the easternmost roundels against the chancel arch emphasises the coming together of chancel wall and nave wall; the insistent zig-zags above the chancel arch conflict with the decorative roundels and the *mandala* – the bottom of which is itself chopped off by a moulding; the rhythm of the clerestory clashes with that of the chancel arch zig-zags, its window-space colliding with dense brickwork. Hope remarked, spitefully, that Butterfield had 'spoilt his own creation with the clown's dress . . . spotty and spidery'.[31]

Despite adverse criticism, Butterfield continued to explore this clashing of decorative and structural systems. The *Builder* complained that the polychromy of Balliol chapel 'destroys the continuity of mouldings that are continuous', that the alabaster was 'so spotty and stained . . . as to hide all mouldings, patterns, or carving that may be introduced into it'.[32] At Yealmpton (decorations, 1863) the mastic diaper in the chancel collides with the window and archway surround, and the pattern of the aisle walls is arbitrarily chopped short by the west end. The chancel of Heytesbury (restored 1865–7) shows a similar collision of uncompromising pattern with unflinching plasticity. The chancel arch of St Alban's, Holborn, to judge from engravings, multiplied these conflicts.

> Over the chancel arch . . . the wall is enriched with ornamental brickwork arranged in diaper patterns which are intersected here and there by circular panels filled with the same material. These panels are disposed, apparently, without the slightest reference to the outline of the arch below, which indeed intersects them abruptly as if it had been cut through the wall at random.[33]

The *Builder* mentions 'the maiming of the patterns',[34] assuring its readers that 'our engraving . . . is a particularly careful representation' (31), lest they should think the 'maiming' the work of an incompetent engraver. St Augustine's, Queen's Gate (1870–7), ruthlessly clashes horizontals and verticals in the towering west front. Bumpus, wincing at St Augustine's, regretted that Butterfield should 'have chosen to be so painfully aggressive'[35] and wondered how much of the architectural conflict 'is due to conviction and how much to accident'.[36] At Keble College (1867–83), Eastlake found the black and white banding and diapering 'oppose each other so crudely . . . one can see nothing but stripes'.[37] Certainly, externally, they relentlessly challenge the distribution of windows and plastic features (32), whilst, inside the chapel, the banding oddly dismembers walling from wall-arcade – making any visual correlation of verticals and horizontals difficult – while, high above, arbitrary bands of colour, striped across the plastic membering of the roof, break up the continuity of the vaulting ribs. It is all too consistent to allow of Bumpus's suggestion of accident. The challenge to our response is systematic, the experience of structure and plasticity constantly at odds with the experience of colour and patterning, and what makes these conflicts so unavoidable, so integral to any experience of Butterfield's architecture, is the fact that the decoration is, in itself, structural: conflict is built into the building itself. Just as discord is exemplified in Dickens's presentation of the physical world – in the junk that fills *Bleak House* or in the physical labyrinth of *Little Dorrit* – and in Hunt's realism – in the chromatic collisions of *The Scapegoat* or the random bric-à-brac of *The Awakening Conscience* – so also, by the nature of architectural exemplification, is discord rendered as part of the intrinsic meaning of Butterfield's architecture.

But Butterfield's decoration is structured as well as structural, and structured – rather paradoxically – in a way that is consistent with the great principle of individuation: it is organisation generated from the very fact of disorganisation. Its processes are easier to appreciate in a relatively modest scheme. The chancel of Waresley church (33) is decorated with a pattern of squares and diamonds contained within mastic bandings; the colour is restrained: dark pink and bright green on off-white, with some buff and yellow. The consistent colour and continuous banding – which forms a kind of decorative matrix – link up the different parts of the scheme. The basic motif is the simple diamond that forms the pattern either side of the altar (34). This is repeated in vertical series on the side walls of the chancel, associated with other motifs. I have labelled the north wall series 1–3 (35), and it forms a set of pattern variations: 2 is formed by expanding the bounding-lines of 1 into buff-coloured ellipses, thus turning diamond into circle; the central pink squares of 1 remain, though now also the centre of a green cross figure, the arms of which are also elliptical. The whole pattern of 2 is ambiguous – is it a series of buff crosses varying against a series of green, or a superimposition of circle upon cross? – while 3 is another development: the square bounded by the mastic repeats the off·

white square of 1, and contains the same green diamond, but now with
a formalised leaf pattern at the centre of which is the elliptical cross of
2. These changes are not true variations; the different motifs vary without
any consistent plan – not illogically, but non-logically. Similarly the basic
form, 1, repeats in each of the four diamonds within the mastic trellis either
side of the east window (1*a*, 36), but for the colour sequence of 1 – pink,
off-white, green, pink – 1*a* has off-white, green, off-white, pink, a non-
logical variation. Form 1 varies again in the sedilia tiling: the sequence
of 1*b*, green, off-white, green, pink, though an inconsistent development
from 1, is consistent with 1*a* – though the pink cross containing the whole
form complicates any sense of ordered relationship. The most fascinating
of the mutations is that of 1*c* (37): this appears, at first, to be form 1 with
half a repeat, the sequence varied with additional triangles. It is nothing
of the sort, for the inversion of the lowest flanking triangles renders the
whole pattern developmentally inconsistent: as such it epitomises the
unsettling ambiguity of the Waresley scheme. Visual and chromatic
connections necessitate our reading the scheme as a decorative series, but
the special quality of serial relationship – that there should be a manifest
order of connection between parts – has been suppressed. The scheme
is a pattern *structure* constantly aspiring to be construed as a pattern *system*.
The same process is at work in Butterfield's treatment of plastic elements.
At Yealmpton the chancel arch is echoed in an arch lower set (38); at Stoke
Newington this repeat arch is dropped back into the sanctuary, where its
relationship to the chancel arch sets up surprising spatial ambiguities. The
gables that are so important to the skyline of Keble College are used
echoically, differenced by the treatment of masonry and brickwork; but gable
forms also appear as purely decorative elements at the bases of the chimney
stacks. Milton Ernest Hall (1853–6) shows a complex operation of the same
processes of variation and repetition. The south front (39), asymmetrical
as a whole, divides into four sections, each one of which is symmetrical
in itself. Window forms repeat across the four sections: the pairs of
shouldered windows in the westernmost gable, with their shallow brick
arches above, repeat at the other end of the front; the triple window grouping
of the main bay not only repeats upwards on the first floor and in the three
dormers, but all three tiers are squashed together and echoed in the elongated
bay window to the right of the centre.

The result of these echoic techniques is a structure comprising whole
series of architectural cross-references, not only *within* series, but also *between*
series: decorative elements connote plastic elements, structural features
repeat decorative motifs. At All Saints', Babbacombe (1865–74), the walls
above the nave arcade carry a pattern of diamonds formed by raised ribs
(40); the pattern continues over the chancel arch; the same ribbing continues
into the chancel and, arranged in smaller diamonds, fills the wall space
over the east window. On the exterior other diapers cover the top half of
the east end, the top section of the porch, and areas of the tower (41).

None of these external diapers is a repeat of another, though they all refer to each other. Internally and externally, one receives the odd impression of the building's being held in, restricted, even trapped. One set of forms snares another set: the diapers suggest restraining nets cast, seemingly at random, over different parts of the church, whilst the fat string-coursing of the tower suggests a rope binding the whole building together. The interior, in detail, reveals a whole series of imaginative variants upon the theme: the pulpit (42) exhibits the diaper again, whilst its thick marble stem is surrounded by two separate arcades as if to concretise the idea of enclosure; even more so, the font (43), where circular arcades seem to have been dropped, cage-like, over a central column. The diamond pattern of the nave arcade is repeated, for no apparent reason, in the tiling immediately in front of the chancel gate. The notion of reticulated forms is transferred to an uneasily ambiguous two-dimensionality in the inlaying of the marble floor of the chancel and in the basket-work pattern of the aisle ceilings. The spectator himself is trapped in an impalpable mesh of half-echoes, visual correlations he is almost allowed to make, architectural quotations he half-recognises. It is this extraordinary interplay of plastic forms and decorative forms that gives Butterfield's architecture its experiential unity.

Such unity, however, is replete with ambiguity. How is the spectator to 'read' such architecture? Are individual elements separate or subordinated to an overall scheme? Are motifs like the wall-web at Babbacombe to be seen as wholly decorative, or do they also refer – as Thompson has suggested[38] – to structure? Arnheim claims that 'ambiguity confuses the artistic statement because it leaves the observer on the edge between two or more assertions that do not add up to a whole'.[39] This is unnecessarily proscriptive. Ambiguity is undesirable when it frustrates a statement that tries to be unambiguous, but Butterfield's architecture seems to me to be deliberately concerned to make ambiguity a central issue. Yet Arnheim is right to suggest the difficulty of responding to ambiguity, and critics have tended to distort Butterfield's architectural statement by forcing it into an unambiguous mould. Thus Hersey sees a kind of deliberate free-for-all in the exterior of All Saints', Margaret Street, where the brick bands 'move up the building in irregular jumps . . . in disregard to floor levels and openings . . . the coordinates generated by the windows are quite different from those of the stripes'.[40] This is factually inaccurate. First, the banding is not irregular: one black stripe, comprising two layers of brick, is regularly paired by another stripe of two layers, with two layers of red bricks between; each pair is separated by five layers of red brick. Second, the bands are not independent of plastic features: on the clergy house to the left, the window ledge of the first window and the top of the window are both picked out by dark bands; the top of buttresses are marked by the first of the diapered dark bands, and so on. Yet Thompson's unproblematic view of All Saints' – 'the street front is sober . . . plain sash windows set in horizontal bands of brick'[41] – seems equally unsatisfactory. The association of plastic and decorative elements is there all right, but it is inconsistent. Why should the window ledge of the third tier of windows be marked by a diapered band, rather than the simpler form as elsewhere? Why should the *lower* of two bands mark the ground-floor window head, two bands *together* mark that of the first-floor window, and the *upper* band of a diapered pair mark the head of the second-floor window? To compound this sense of inconsistency, banding that may mark plastic features at one point of the building is continued so that it clashes *against* plastic features somewhere else. Hersey's collision of two separate systems, or Thompson's peaceful co-existence would both be far simpler aesthetic events. What in fact happens is what happens elsewhere in Butterfield's architecture – the ambiguous interaction of the decorative and the plastic. And so on throughout the church: the tracery form of a roundel in the spandrel formed by two arches was the basic motif of the original metal screen along the courtyard wall, and as such was repeated in the tracery of both aisle and clerestory windows, re-emerging as the dominant form in the nave arcade tiling; the roundel itself 'jumps' from the brick circle above the courtyard entrance, to the plastic circles above the porch, to the baptistry walls, to the panels of the pulpit, to above the chancel arch. Far from being 'wonderfully childish',[42] All Saints' is the product of a sophisticated structure of ambiguities – echo and half-echo, connection and disconnection, individuation and subordination – so that, finally, the presentation of fragmentation and conflict – Butterfield's infamous 'Victorian brutalism'[43] – is part of an ordered imaginative and aesthetic event.

Commenting on Butterfieldian 'brutalism', Kenneth Clark has seen 'a Dickensian need of cruelty in Butterfield';[44] Summerson has likewise seen in the creative arts of the mid-nineteenth century 'a singular attraction on the part of some painters, architects and writers towards ugliness'.[45] Such comparisons are suggestive but, couched as they are in psychological terms, too limited. Previous chapters have already stressed that the rapid expansion of Victorian Britain produced for contemporaries a world of unprecedented complexity, a world in which adequate strategies of response – and even psychic survival – were difficult to arrive at and difficult to maintain. It is in the exploration and attempted resolution of this complexity and its consequent conflict and difficulty that Butterfield's intimate association with contemporary art and literature lies. Just as discord and potential fragmentation – political, social, moral and metaphysical – are imaginatively central to and embodied in Carlyle's *French Revolution*, Dickens's fiction and Pre-Raphaelite realism, so also does the predominant principle of individuation in Butterfield's work exemplify conflict and disjunction, building them into the fact of his architecture. Furthermore, just as in their work symbolic structures, imaged as having independent reality within the world, both contain and explicate the elements of potential disintegration, so also Butterfield's use of echoic forms, of visual and structural cross-references, establishes a movement towards the reconciliation of conflict by ordering into similarity and congruence elements otherwise separate and dissimilar. The idiosyncrasy of Butterfield's architecture, its extraordinary and dramatic expressiveness – remarkable even in the context of an extraordinarily expressive style like High Victorian Gothic – leads one to seek to 'read' his buildings in a way that is, perhaps, unique. Ultimately Butterfield used architecture as a vehicle for symbolism. In doing so he was responding to the whole debate about architectural semantics that took place in the 1830s and 1840s. This debate allowed Butterfield to work in the context of a sudden – even if imprecise – expansion in the definition of architectural meaning and architectural reality. Indeed, it was the very imprecision of the new ideas of 'the real' that was so important. What was implicit – and sometimes explicit – in the whole debate, from Pugin through the Camdenians to Ruskin, was the availability of a free flow of meanings across areas of reality most usually thought of as distinct. Potentially, at least, the whole of extrinsic meaning, the whole symbolic spectrum from Puginian emblematics to Ruskinian social expressionism, was brought within the realm of architectural meaning, and then seen as part of what was semantically intrinsic. Goodhart-Rendel sees Butterfield's architecture as a direct attack upon 'what he regarded as a frivolous and self-indulgent age'.[46] This seems right, but only because Butterfield was able to find architectural equivalents for non-architectural realities, able to inject the intrinsic meanings of architecture with an expressionism essentially extrinsic. The functional, constructional and physical identity of architecture, its insistent – and, in terms of the Revival, insisted upon – 'reality', offered Butterfield an alternative to 'an age most terribly subjective and sensational', to repeat a remark of his quoted earlier. Gothic, for Butterfield, was congenial not for any antiquarian or sentimentally retrospective reasons, but because it gave him the chance to symbolise nineteenth-century social and metaphysical conflicts and uncertainties through a stylistic medium emphatically and ineluctably real, and to generate containing structures for those uncertainties actually from the symbolisation of them. Butterfield's view of his society, symbolised in his exploitation of architectural conflict, obtains to the condition of objectivity by being a part of intrinsic architectural meaning, meaning which is – *ex hypothesi* – co-extensive with architectural reality. The symbolic reconciliation effected by his technique of echoes and parallels exists at precisely the same level, as part of the real fabric of the architecture. In Butterfield's Gothic, the emblematic is fused in the actual: it is the architectural manifestation of symbolic realism. As in the literary and pictorial forms, the subjective gap between experience and interpretation is obviated and the apprehension of meaning becomes immediate, integral to the substance of the work of art – literary work, painting or building – itself. But with Butterfield, of course, symbolic realism reaches its final development: whereas Carlylean history, Dickensian fiction, Pre-Raphaelite painting are all concerned with the representation of the real world, architecture necessarily exists as a functional reality in that world itself. In Butterfield's architecture, symbolic meaning emerges, not as co-extensive with a historical, fictional or pictured reality but as an inherent part of the physical world we live in and thus as a determinant of our life-space.

Epilogue

We are symbols, and inhabit symbols
Emerson, 'The Poet', *Essays: Second Series*

Finally, then, what are we to make of the phenomenon of symbolic realism? H. P. Sucksmith sees in Dickens's fiction 'an introverted vision of a spiritual universe pervading the material world . . . all the more impressive in that Dickens does not try to deny or weaken our immediate perception of the tangible world but renders it with a remarkable verisimilitude'.[1] Such an infusion of the mundane with the values of the extra-mundane — of the Visible world, in Carlylean terms, with the Invisible — is far more robust than any incorporeal mysticism, for the meanings established by symbolic realism, whether positive or negative, are not located beyond the world of sense but are in it and inseparable from it. Erich Heller has argued that the synthesis of symbolism and reality — epitomised in the transubstantiation of the eucharist — was the fundamental imaginative and spiritual mode of the Middle Ages, and that the Zwinglian Reformation effected a severance of the symbol from the real. The post-Reformation world was, and is, left to cope with a semantic — and ultimately metaphysical — crisis. 'Robbed of its real significance, what did the symbol signify? Robbed of its symbolic meaning, what did reality mean?'[2]

The new-found rationalism of the Enlightenment, having cleared the way of 'metaphysical lumber', could conduct the serious business of reality by empirical science on the one hand, and by moral injunction and the truths of Universal Nature on the other. The symbol took up residence, sometimes in the realm of the aesthetic as the plaything of wit, sometimes in the realm of the social as the tool of satire. But the rationalist house, its foundations in the Cartesian dichotomy, was divided against itself: the philosophical scepticism born of empirical science made universals and general truths look increasingly chimerical. Rejecting ethical generalisations as vapid — 'To generalize', declared Blake, 'is to be an Idiot'[3] — and the Newtonian universe as a dead machine, the Romantics rediscovered meaning in the dynamic play of the subjective imagination upon the external world. The symbol was put to work as a primary agent in the subjective recreation of reality. Said Runge: 'we create symbols of our thoughts about the world's great forces'.[4] The uniqueness of the self, however, could turn the world into a fine but a private place, an incommunicable 'prospect in my mind'.[5] The symbol, equally, could become private property, an esoteric cipher, its meaning locked inside the individual psyche. The offspring and heirs of Rationalism and Romanticism — and of the strife between them — the late Georgians and early Victorians grew up in a society in which traditional patterns of life, both physical and psychological, were breaking down. The scope and sheer speed of expansion were, between them, effecting irreversible and unprecedented change – not least in the material appearance of the world itself.

The first necessity for an artist confronting such radical change and its characteristic social and spiritual disorientation was to find an appropriate and adequate language. Such a requirement, difficult enough to obtain, was rendered at once more difficult and more urgent by what Heller diagnoses as the peculiar 'hazard' facing modern literature in its attempt to communicate: 'the absence from our lives of commonly accepted symbols to represent and house our deepest feelings'.[6] That languages were found and that they were authentically of their time is self-evident in the extraordinary range and quality of the Victorian creative achievement, self-evident in the uniqueness of Carlylean prose, in the visual radicalism of Pre-Raphaelite realism, in the expressive vigour of Butterfieldian Gothic, in – above all – the sheer imaginative comprehensiveness of Dickens's fiction. That the price of failing to find such a language was the bafflement and ultimate defeat of the imagination itself is clear from Arnold's retreat into the abstractions of ethical idealism. In forging new languages, the artists considered in this book necessarily rejected or moved beyond the structures and strategies they had inherited from Rationalism and Romanticism. In so doing they also redefined the role and nature of symbolism. The sources for their symbols differed as widely as their languages: Carlyle went to the typological patterns of the Bible; Ruskin went to a divinely ordained natural world, the Pre-Raphaelites to a minutely detailed physical world; Pugin went to Christian emblematism, Butterfield to the intrinsic meanings of architecture; Dickens – again above all – went to the material and phenomenal fabric of the everyday, from the fog-hung alleys of the London maze to the clouds that dance at Little Dorrit's party.

Whatever the different sources and different strategies, however, the result of what almost seems like a common enterprise was nothing less than a semantic – and ultimately metaphysical – reordering of reality, a re-establishment of the bond between the symbol and the real. In terms of Heller's argument, it cannot be a coincidence that, at precisely the same time as symbolic realism was emerging in nineteenth-century literature, art and architecture, the theology of the Oxford Movement was stressing the sacramental nature of Anglican worship and asserting – more forcefully than any since the Caroline divines – the doctrinal mystery of the eucharist. By means of symbolic realism, what were seen as fundamentals of the contemporary world – its material and experiential complexity, its discord, the recurrent alienation of its inhabitants, the threat of social breakdown – could all be represented or registered as intensely and insistently real; but interpenetrating, co-extensive with this reality were symbolic structures that were inalienable from it and gave to it a shape and a meaning. The strategy of symbolic realism has perennial imaginative validity, for by it the subjective gap between perception and interpretation is closed, the self is united with the non-self and our apprehension of significance takes on the immediacy and authority of tangible reality. By regaining its place in the real world of our common experience, the symbol recovers its currency in our imaginative lives; reinvested with its symbolic dimension, the real regains its meaning.

Notes

Chapter 1

1 See W. B. Gallie, 'Essentially contested concepts', *Proceedings of the Aristotelian Society*, vol. 61 (1955–6), pp. 167–98.
2 Richard B. Ohmann, 'Prolegomena to the analysis of prose style', in H. C. Martin (ed.), *Style in Prose Fiction* (New York, 1959), pp. 8–9.
3 Nelson Goodman, *Languages of Art: An Approach to a Theory of Symbols* (London, 1969), p. 32.
4 David Lodge, *Language of Fiction: Essays in Criticism and Verbal Analysis of the English Novel* (London, 1966), p. 42.

Chapter 2

1 'On History Again', *Fraser's Magazine*, vol. 7 (1833): *The Works of Thomas Carlyle*, Centenary Edition, 30 vols (London, 1897–9), Vol. 28, pp. 167–76.
2 *Sartor Resartus*, originally published in *Fraser's Magazine* (1833–4), and as a separate volume in the United States (Boston, Mass., 1836) and in England (London, 1838): *Works*, Vol. 1.
3 *The Prelude* (text of 1805), ed. Ernest de Selincourt (London, 1933), bk 7, II. 679–91.
4 ibid., II. 701–4.
5 ibid., II. 598–606.
6 J. A. Froude, *Thomas Carlyle: A History of His Life in London*, 2 vols (London, 1884), Vol. 1, p. 54.
7 'Biography', *Fraser's Magazine*, vol. 5 (1832): *Works*, Vol. 28, pp. 44–61.
8 'State of German Literature', *Edinburgh Review*, vol. 46 (1827): *Works*, Vol. 26, pp. 26–86.
9 'Characteristics', *Edinburgh Review*, vol. 54 (1831): *Works*, Vol. 28, pp. 1–43.
10 'The Diamond Necklace', *Fraser's Magazine*, vol. 15 (1837): *Works*, Vol. 28, pp. 324–402.
11 *On Heroes, Hero-Worship and the Heroic in History* (London, 1841): *Works*, Vol. 5.
12 *The French Revolution: A History*, 3 vols (London, 1837): *Works*, Vols 2–4.
13 See, in particular, Herbert L. Sussman, *Fact into Figure* (Columbus, Ohio, 1979), and George P. Landow, *Victorian Types, Victorian Shadows* (London, 1980).
14 ibid., p. 54.
15 Scott's *Commentary on the Bible* was published in weekly parts between 1788 and 1792; thereafter, collected into book form, it went through numerous nineteenth-century editions.
16 Baron Jean Baptiste de Clootz was a member of the National Assembly, a supporter of the ideas of Rousseau and, according to Carlyle, an ardent advocate of human perfectibility. He took the name Anacharsis from the Greek sage of the sixth century BC who criticised Greek over-sophistication and advocated a return to nature.

Chapter 3

1 First published in weekly parts, *Master Humphrey's Clock*, vols 2–3, April 1840 to February 1841.
2 Tennyson, *In Memoriam AHH* (London, 1850), 1. 132: *The Poems of Tennyson*, ed. Christopher Ricks (London, 1969), p. 871.
3 Walter Bagehot, 'Charles Dickens', *National Review*, vol. 7 (1858), reprinted

in his *Literary Studies* (London, 1878): *Collected Works of Walter Bagehot*, ed. Norman St John-Stevas, 4 vols (London, 1965), Vol. 2, pp. 77–107; p. 85.

4 Dorothy Van Ghent, 'The Dickens world: a view from Todgers's', *Sewanee Review*, vol. 58 (1950), pp. 419–38; reprinted in Martin Price (ed.), *Dickens: A Collection of Critical Essays* (Englewood Cliffs, NJ, 1967), pp. 24–38; p. 29.

5 Robert Morse, '*Our Mutual Friend*', *Partisan Review*, vol. 16 (1949), pp. 77–107; reprinted in A. E. Dyson (ed.), *Dickens: Modern Judgements* (London, 1968), pp. 258–69; p. 262.

6 As Dickens, drawing Forster's attention to the passage, realised: 'I really think the dead mankind a million fathoms deep, the best thing in the sentence. I have a notion of the dreadful silence down there, and of the stars shining down upon their drowned eyes . . .': letter to Forster [4 October 1840], *The Letters of Charles Dickens*, ed. Madeline House, Graham Storey *et al.*, 5 vols to date (London, 1965–), Vol. 2, p. 131.

7 Shelley, 'Adonaïs: An Elegy on the Death of John Keats', 1. 462 (1821); *The Complete Works of Percy Bysshe Shelley*, ed. R. Ingpen and W. E. Peck, 10 vols (London, 1927), Vol. 2, p. 404.

8 Jean-Paul Sartre, *Nausea* (1938), trans. Robert Baldick (London, 1965), p. 227.

9 The New Oxford Illustrated Dickens has 'dim allusions' (70, p. 528); 'illusions' is the original reading in *Master Humphrey's Clock*, vol. 2 (1840), p. 201, which seems far more consistent with the developing sense of unreality that characterises Kit's journey.

10 T. S. Eliot, *Four Quartets* (New York, 1943), 'Little Gidding', 1. 14: *Collected Poems, 1909–1962* (London, 1963), p. 214.

11 T. S. Eliot, 'Andrew Marvell', *Selected Essays* (London, 1951), pp. 292–304; p. 301.

12 John Forster, *The Life of Charles Dickens*, 10th edn, 3 vols (London, 1872), Vol. 1, p. 190.

13 Aristotle, *On the Art of Poetry*, in *Classical Literary Criticism*, trans. T. S. Dorsch (Harmondsworth, 1965), p. 35.

14 W. B. Stanford, *Greek Metaphor: Studies in Theory and Practice* (London, 1936), p. 101; quoted by W. K. Wimsatt, Jnr, *The Verbal Icon: Studies in the Meaning of Poetry* (Lexington, Ky, 1954; London, 1970), p. 128.

Chapter 4

1 First published in monthly parts, October 1846 to April 1848.

2 Such a view has been suggested by Benedetto Croce, *Aesthetic*, trans. Douglas Ainslie (London, 1922); see ch. 2.

3 Nelson Goodman, *Languages of Art: An Approach to a Theory of Symbols* (London, 1969), p. 69.

4 T. S. Eliot, *Four Quartets* (New York, 1943), 'The Dry Salvages', 1. 15: *Collected Poems, 1909–1962* (London, 1963), p. 205.

5 ibid., 'Little Gidding', 1. 54: *Collected Poems*, p. 215.

6 It is neither accident nor oversight that there is no direct account of Walter's voyage. Jessie L. Weston, in *From Ritual to Romance* (London, 1921), makes clear the esoteric nature of the Grail quest; the indirect way in which we learn of Walter's shipwreck and survival carries just such a suggestion of mystery in the very nature of the voyage.

7 The quest motif in the form it assumes in the Grail legend and what have been subsequently identified as fertility myths occurs with great frequency in both Victorian literature and painting. Dickens's modernisation of the myth may be compared to the full-length medievalism of Tennyson's *The Holy Grail* (1869) or the highly effective gothicism of Browning's ' "Childe Roland to the Dark Tower Came" ' (1855).

8 First published in monthly parts, May 1849 to November 1850.

9 Dorothy Van Ghent, *The English Novel: Form and Function* (New York, 1953), p. 127.

10 David's mother's language is clearly echoed by Dora: ' "I am sure I am very affectionate" ' (41, p. 604); ' "It's better for me to be stupid than uncomfortable isn't it?" ' (43, p. 696). Parallelism is also suggested by the illustrations. Compare, in particular, Mrs Copperfield in 'Our Pew at Church' and Dora in 'I am married': as well as similar expression, tilt

of the head, and gesture, there is an ominous echo of the former's widow's veil in the latter's bridal veil.

11 George Eliot, *Middlemarch* (London, 1873), ch. 21.

12 W. B. Yeats, 'To a Child Dancing in the Wind', 11. 1–3, *Responsibilities* (London, 1914): *The Collected Poems of W. B. Yeats*, 2nd edn (London, 1950), pp. 136–7.

13 W. H. Auden, 'In Memory of Sigmund Freud', 11. 34–7, *Another Time* (New York, 1940): *Collected Shorter Poems of W. H. Auden, 1927–1957* (London, 1966), p. 167.

Chapter 5

1 First published in monthly parts from March 1852 to September 1853.

2 J. Hillis Miller, *Charles Dickens: The World of His Novels* (Cambridge, Mass., 1958; London, 1969), p. 171.

3 Nelson Goodman, *Languages of Art: An Approach to a Theory of Symbols* (London, 1969), pp. 52–3; my examples.

4 Miller, *Charles Dickens*, p. 166.

5 W. J. Harvey, 'Chance and design in *'Bleak House'*, in John Gross and Gabriel Pearson (eds), *Dickens and the Twentieth Century* (London, 1962), pp. 145–57; p. 152.

6 Ruskin certainly found the *Bleak House* toll of death and misery intolerably pessimistic; see 'Fiction, Fair and Foul', *Nineteenth Century*, vol. 7 (1880), p. 945: *The Complete Works of John Ruskin*, ed. E. T. Cook and A. Wedderburn, 38 vols (London, 1903–9), Vol. 34, pp. 271–2.

7 John Forster, *The Life of Charles Dickens*, 10th edn, 3 vols (London, 1872), Vol. 3, p. 24.

8 First published in serial form, *Household Words*, April to August 1854.

9 Suggestively, the description of Bounderby is similar to that of the corpse of a drowned man in 'Travelling Abroad', *The Uncommercial Traveller* (7, pp. 65 ff.).

10 In *Victorian Novelists and Their Illustrators* (London, 1970), J. R. Harvey traces this picture of Bounderby back to origins in 'figures of vastly exaggerated bloatedness' in the caricatures of Cruikshank and Gillray (p. 64); the sources are convincing, though they do not, of course, explain the way in which the image works in the novel itself.

11 The *Prelude* (text of 1805), ed. Ernest de Selincourt (London, 1933), bk 13, 1. 141.

12 *Past and Present* (London, 1843): *The Works of Thomas Carlyle*, Centenary Edition, 30 vols (London, 1897–9), Vol. 10, see particularly bk 3, ch. 2, 'Gospel of Mammonism'.

13 Harvey P. Sucksmith, *The Narrative Art of Charles Dickens* (London, 1970), p. 141.

14 F. R. and Q. D. Leavis, *Dickens the Novelist* (London, 1970); Penguin edn (Harmondsworth, 1972), p. 258.

15 Raymond Williams, *Culture and Society, 1780–1950* (London, 1958); Penguin edn (Harmondsworth, 1971), p. 97.

Chapter 6

1 Lionel Trilling, 'Introduction' to *Little Dorrit*, The New Oxford Illustrated Dickens (London, 1953), pp. v–xvi.

2 First published in monthly parts, December 1855 to June 1857.

3 Trilling, 'Introduction', p. vi.

4 Dickens to John Forster, quoted John Forster, *The Life of Charles Dickens*, 10th edn, 3 vols (London, 1872), Vol. 3, pp. 138–9.

5 Pancks's reference – as the capitalisation indicates – is to the anonymous devotional work *The Whole Duty of Man* (London, 1658). The original source is Ecclesiastes, 12: 13: 'Fear God, and keep his commandments: for this is the whole duty of man.' Pancks's ironic version closely echoes Dickens's satiric commentary in *Hard Times*, where the utilitarian and capitalist ethic of buying in the cheapest market and selling in the dearest is 'the whole duty of man – not just a part of man's duty, but the whole' (II, 1, p. 115).

6 The origins of the technique, both semantically and linguistically, are to be found in *Hard Times*, in the philosophy of Harthouse, who, Dickens tells us, was one of 'the fine gentlemen'

who 'having found out everthing to be worth nothing, were equally ready for anything' (II, 2, p. 124).

7   James R. Kincaid, *Dickens and the Rhetoric of Laughter* (London, 1971), p. 209.

8   'Nobody, Somebody and Everybody', *Household Words*, vol. 14, no. 336 (30 August 1856), p. 146.

9   See Forster, *Life of Dickens*, Vol. 3, pp. 51 ff.

10 Ferdinand here certainly seems to express Dickens's own political pessimism, a despair he came to feel at the complicity of the population in their own repression: 'I do reluctantly believe that the English people are habitually consenting parties to the miserable imbecility into which they have fallen, *and never will help themselves out of it* . . . I have no present political faith or hope – not a grain': letter to W. C. Macready, 4 October 1855, in *The Letters of Charles Dickens, 1833–1870*, edited by his Sister-in-law and his Eldest Daughter, 3 vols (London, 1880–2); revised edn, 1 vol. (1893), p. 379.

11 It is instructive to compare John Chivery's fate with the very definite denouements of the parallel subplots of Mr Toots in *Dombey and Son* and Mr Guppy in *Bleak House*.

Chapter 7

1   First published in serial form in *All the Year Round*, 30 April to 26 November 1859.

2   One of the personal accounts of the September Massacres that Carlyle quotes in *The French Revolution* is actually entitled *Résurrection*: *The Works of Thomas Carlyle*, Centenary Edition, 30 vols (London, 1897–9), Vol. 4, p. 32.

3   For a critical argument that sees Augustine's concept of the City of Man and the City of God as fundamental to all Dickens's novels, see Alexander Welsh, *The City of Dickens* (London, 1971). Curiously, Welsh has little to say about *A Tale of Two Cities*, the only novel in which, in my opinion, the concept really is fundamental.

4   Intriguingly, Carlyle provides the information that Controller-General Necker, the supposedly enlightened financial administrator of pre-Revolutionary France, had been 'once Clerk in Thelusson's Bank': *Works*, Vol. 2, p. 48. How far is the obvious echo in Dickens's Tellson's Bank a deliberate one?

5   T. S. Eliot, *Sweeney Agonistes*, 'Fragment of an Agon', in *Collected Poems, 1909–1962* (London, 1963), p. 133.

6   Ephesians, 6: 12.

7   Compare the similar reference in the final paragraph of *Hard Times* and Carlyle's several uses of the episode in *The French Revolution*.

8   G. M. Hopkins, 'Spring and Fall: To a Young Child', 1. 14; *The Poems of Gerard Manley Hopkins*, ed. W. H. Gardner and N. H. MacKenzie, 4th edn (London, 1967), p. 89.

9   John Carey, *The Violent Effigy* (London, 1973), p. 108.

10 Joseph Gold, *Charles Dickens: Radical Moralist* (Minneapolis, Minn., 1972), p. 237.

11 See, in particular, the beautifully managed frontispiece, 'Under the Plane Tree', and the later plate, 'Congratulations'.

12 T. S. Eliot, *Four Quartets* (New York, 1943), 'Little Gidding', 1. 80–1: *Collected Poems*, p. 216.

13 Romans, 6: 9. The Epistle to the Romans, particularly chapters 3–6, dealing with justification, death and resurrection, is basic to the religious argument of *A Tale of Two Cities*. Dickens's general emphasis upon New Testament sources is a revealing contrast to Carlyle's evident preference in *The French Revolution* for the Old Testament and retribution.

14 Romans, 6: 7.

15 Carey, *Violent Effigy*, p. 108.

16 The consciousness of mortality and sin that Dickens gives Carton/Christ has its theological basis in the Calvinist doctrine of the Atonement which asserted that Christ 'bore in his soul the tortures of a condemned and ruined man'. The Calvinist Heidelberg Catechism of 1562 expressly stated that Christ 'had borne the divine wrath during the whole period of his earthly life'. See K. R. Hagenbach, *Compendium of the History of Doctrines*, trans. C. W. Buch, 2 vols (Edinburgh, 1852), Vol. 2, pp. 336–44.

Chapter 8

1 G. M. Young, 'Portait of an Age', in G. M. Young (ed.), *Early Victorian England*, 2 vols (London, 1934), Vol. 2, pp. 413–502; p. 478.

2 First published in *Poems. A New Edition* (London, 1853): *Poems of Matthew Arnold*, ed. Kenneth Allott (London, 1965; 2nd edn, 1979), pp. 355–69.

3 *Culture and Anarchy: An Essay in Political and Social Criticism* (London, 1869): *The Complete Prose Works of Matthew Arnold*, ed. R. H. Super, 11 vols (Ann Arbor, Mich., 1960–77), Vol. 5.

4 ibid., p. 105.

5 Richard Jenkyns, *The Victorians and Ancient Greece* (Oxford, 1980), p. 265.

6 *Culture and Anarchy*, in *Complete Prose*, Vol. 5, p. 233 (preface of 1869), p. 91, ch. 1 title.

7 ibid., p. 146.

8 ibid., p. 163.

9 In his thirty-five years as a school inspector Arnold produced nineteen general reports to the Education Department on elementary education and three reports on education abroad. That so little of Arnold's energetic involvement in the struggle for popular education should find a specific place in his discussions of culture, society and religion seems a further indication of the divorce in Arnold's consciousness whereby the immediate and specific become the province of 'life' and the theoretical and general the province of 'literature'. The separation impoverishes both.

10 Raymond Williams, *Culture and Society, 1780–1950* (London, 1958); Penguin edn (Harmondsworth, 1971), p. 135.

11 *St Paul and Protestantism with an Essay on Puritanism and the Church of England* (London, 1870), in *Complete Prose*, Vol. 6, pp. 1–127; *Literature and Dogma: An Essay towards a Better Apprehension of the Bible* (London, 1873), in *Complete Prose*, Vol. 6, pp. 139–411; *God and the Bible: A Review of Objections to 'Literature and Dogma'* (London, 1875), in *Complete Prose*, Vol. 7, pp. 138–398.

12 *Literature and Dogma*, preface to Popular Edition (London, 1883): *Complete Prose*, Vol. 6, p. 146.

13 *God and the Bible: Complete Prose*, Vol. 7, p. 378.

14 *Literature and Dogma*, preface to Popular Edition, p. 146.

15 ibid., p. 144.

16 *God and the Bible*, p. 372.

17 *Literature and Dogma*, p. 175.

18 ibid., p. 182.

19 ibid., p. 189.

20 *God and the Bible*, p. 371.

21 *Literature and Dogma*, preface of 1873: *Complete Prose*, Vol. 6, p. 150.

22 Quoted G. W. E. Russell, *Matthew Arnold*, 2nd edn (London, 1904), p. 249.

23 *God and the Bible*, p. 396.

24 ibid., p. 397.

25 ibid.

26 'The Study of Poetry'; published in 1880 as the general introduction to *The English Poets*, ed. T. H. Ward, and reprinted in *Essays in Criticism. Second Series* (London, 1888): *Complete Prose*, Vol. 9, p. 161.

27 Basil Willey, *Nineteenth-Century Studies* (London, 1949), p. 91.

28 For Arnold's different uses of the phrase, see, for example: 'The Function of Criticism at the Present Time', *Essays in Criticism. First Series* (London, 1865), in *Complete Prose*, Vol. 3, pp. 258–85; and *Culture and Anarchy*, preface of 1869, in *Complete Prose*, Vol. 5, pp. 252 ff.

Chapter 9

1 John Guille Millais, *The Life and Letters of Sir John Everett Millais*, 2 vols (London, 1899), Vol. 1, p. 49.

2 *Pre-Raphaelitism* (London, 1851): *The Complete Works of John Ruskin*, ed. E. T. Cook and A. Wedderburn, 38 vols (London, 1903–9), Vol. 12, pp. 336–93. The prescription is Ruskin's own, taken from the first volume of *Modern Painters* (London, 1843).

3 Walter Bagehot, 'Charles Dickens': *Collected Works of Walter Bagehot*, ed. Norman St John-Stevas, 4 vols (London, 1965), Vol. 2, p. 84.

4 Hippolyte Taine, *Histoire de la littérature anglaise*, 4 vols (Paris, 1863–4); *The History of English Literature*, trans. H. Van Laun, 4 vols (Edinburgh, 1871), Vol. 4, pp. 129–30.

5 Linda Nochlin, *Realism* (London, 1971), p. 15.

6 Richard Wollheim, *Art and Its Objects* (London, 1970), pp. 33–4; for a full discussion of the Representation Is Resemblance argument, see Nelson Goodman, *Languages of Art: An Approach to a Theory of Symbols* (London, 1969), ch. 1.

7 E. H. Gombrich, 'Visual discovery through art', in James Hogg (ed.), *Psychology and the Visual Arts* (London, 1969), pp. 215–38; p. 219.

8 Rudolf Arnheim, 'Perceptual abstraction and art', *Psychological Review*, vol. 54 (1947), pp. 66–82; reprinted in his *Towards a Psychology of Art* (London, 1967), pp. 27–50; p. 33.

9 Goodman, *Languages of Art*, p. 33.

10 The anti-semiotic argument in England derives extensively from Pater, informing most of the criticism of, for example, Roger Fry. For a succinct statement of the position, see Richard Rudner, 'On semiotic aesthetics', *Journal of Aesthetics and Art Criticism*, vol. 10 (1951), pp. 67–77.

11 Rudolf Arnheim, 'Emotion and feeling in psychology and art', *Confina Psychiatrica*, vol. 1 (1958), pp. 69–88; reprinted in his *Towards a Psychology of Art*, pp. 302–19; p. 305.

12 See E. H. Gombrich, *Art and Illusion* (London, 1960).

13 Rudolf Arnheim, *Art and Visual Perception*, revised edn (London, 1967), p. ix.

14 ibid., p. 4.

15 Twelfth-century icon, School of Constantinople, Tretiakov Gallery, Moscow.

16 *c.* 1760, National Gallery, London.

17 1937, private collection, London.

18 All the periodical quotations that follow are from anonymous reviews of Royal Academy exhibitions for 1850 and 1851.

19 *Athenaeum*, 11 May 1850, p. 590.

20 *The Times*, 4 May 1850.

21 *Art Journal*, vol. 3 (1851), p. 158.

22 *The Times*, 3 May 1851.

23 ibid., 7 May 1851.

24 *Athenaeum*, 11 May 1850, p. 590.

25 Carlyle, 'Biography': *The Works of Thomas Carlyle*, Centenary Edition, 30 vols (London, 1897–9), Vol. 28, pp. 59–60.

26 *Modern Painters*, 5 vols (London, 1843–60): *Works*, Vols 3–7.

27 *Lectures on Architecture and Painting* (London, 1854): *Works*, Vol. 12.

28 *Works*, Vol. 5, pp. 201–20; although Ruskin's attack on the pathetic fallacy was not published until 1856, and thus too late to be a formative influence upon the Pre-Raphaelite Brotherhood, its argument is implicit in the first two volumes of *Modern Painters*.

29 C. K. Ogden and J. A. Richards, *The Meaning of Meaning*, 10th edn (London, 1956), p. 82.

30 Interestingly, Arnold quite specifically rejects Ruskinian symbolic realism. He quotes Ruskin's assertion, ' "There is not a moment of any day of our lives, when nature is not producing picture after picture and working still upon such exquisite and constant principles of such perfect beauty, *that it is quite certain it is all done for us, and intended for our perpetual pleasure*" '. Arnold comments: 'It is *not* quite certain, we have not a particle of certainty about it, and to say that it is certain is utterly fantastic' (*God and the Bible*, Preface: *Complete Prose*, Vol. 7, p. 385). That Arnold's rejection is right on any logical grounds seems to me to be undeniable; but that Ruskin himself *was* certain seems also undeniable, and he conveys his certainty with far more imaginative force that Arnold can muster for its rebuttal.

Chapter 10

1 William Holman Hunt, *Pre-Raphaelitism and the Pre-Raphaelite Brotherhood*, 2 vols (London, 1905); hereafter as *PR & PRB*.
2 *PR & PRB*, Vol. 1, p. vii.
3 ibid., p. 48.
4 ibid., p. 82.
5 William Holman Hunt, 'The Pre-Raphaelite Brotherhood: a fight for art', *Contemporary Review*, vol. 44 (1886), pp. 471–88, 737–50, 820–33; p. 478.
6 See, for example, the letters that Rossetti wrote to his brother and to James Collinson during his tour of France and Belgium in 1849: *Letters of Dante Gabriel Rossetti*, ed. O. Doughty and J. R. Wahl, 4 vols (London, 1965), Vol. 1.
7 *PR & PRB*, Vol. 1, p. 49.
8 ibid., p. 134.
9 John Guille Millais, *The Life and Letters of Sir John Everett Millais*, 2 vols (London, 1899), Vol. 1, pp. 52–5.
10 *PR & PRB*, Vol. 2, pp. 363–4.
11 Virginia Surtees, *The Paintings and Drawings of Dante Gabriel Rossetti: A Catalogue Raisonné*, 2 vols (London, 1971), Vol. 1, p. 69.
12 See W. M. Rossetti, 'Reminiscences of Holman Hunt', *Contemporary Review*, vol. 98 (1910), pp. 385–95.
13 Published in parts, 1883–4: *The Complete Works of John Ruskin*, ed. E. T. Cook and A. Wedderburn, 38 vols (London, 1903–9), Vol. 33, pp. 255–408.
14 *Nineteenth Century*, vol. 4 (1878), pp. 925–31, 1072–82, reprinted in *On the Old Road* (London, 1885): *Works*, Vol. 34, pp. 145–74.
15 1850, Ashmolean Museum, Oxford.
16 1849–50, Tate Gallery, London.
17 1849, Tate Gallery, London: Surtees, *Catalogue*, no. 44, plate 29.
18 Salvador Dali, 'Le surréalisme spectral de l'éternel féminin Préraphaélite', *Minotaure*, no. 8 (1936), pp. 46–9; p. 46.
19 1859, Tate Gallery, London: Surtees, *Catalogue*, no. 117, plate 179.
20 1864, Tate Gallery, London: Surtees, *Catalogue*, no. 168, plate 238.
21 1872, City Art Gallery, Manchester: Surtees, *Catalogue*, no. 229, plate 330.
22 *The Art of England*: *Works*, Vol. 33, p. 271.
23 F. G. Stephens, 'English painters of the present day – William Holman Hunt', *Portfolio*, vol. 2 (1871), pp. 33–9; p. 34.
24 This remains true, I think, despite Rossetti's professed indifference to the medium of stained glass; see Martin Harrison, *Victorian Stained Glass* (London, 1980), pp. 40 ff.
25 J[ohn] B[allantyne], 'The Pre-Raffaelites', *Art Journal*, vol. 3 (1851), pp. 185–6.
26 Letter to *The Times*, 13 May 1851: *Works*, Vol. 12, p. 321.
27 Francis D. Klingender, *Art and the Industrial Revolution* (London, 1947), revised edn (London, 1972), p. 154.
28 *PR & PRB*, Vol. 1, p. 176.
29 ibid., p. 315.
30 Heinrich Wölfflin, *Principles of Art History*, trans. M. D. Hottinger (London, 1932), ch. 1.
31 ibid., p. 45.
32 ibid., p. 22.
33 1849, Tate Gallery, London.
34 'Old Lamps for New Ones', *Household Words*, vol. 1, no. 12 (15 June 1850), pp. 265–7; p. 266.
35 1851, City Museum and Art Gallery, Birmingham.
36 1849, Collection of Lord Sherfield.
37 1850, Guildhall Art Gallery, London.
38 1855, City Museum and Art Gallery, Birmingham.
39 1853–9, City Museum and Art Gallery, Birmingham.
40 1862, Tate Gallery, London. Even more extraordinarily minute is Martineau's *Kit's Writing*

Lesson of 1852, also in the Tate Gallery. Painted under Hunt's tuition, its choice of subject-matter from *The Old Curiosity Shop* is suggestive.

41 1852–4, Collection of HM the Queen.
42 1849, Walker Art Gallery, Liverpool.
43 *Lectures on Architecture and Painting: Works*, Vol. 12, p. 146.
44 Ballantyne, 'Pre-Raffaelites', p. 186.
45 An effect even more pronounced in a preliminary drawing for the painting illustrated in Mary Bennett's catalogue, *Millais — An Exhibition at the Walker Art Gallery, 1967* (Liverpool, 1967).
46 Ballantyne, 'The Pre-Raffaelites', p. 186.
47 Peter Conrad, *The Victorian Treasure-House* (London, 1973), p. 130.
48 For a discussion of perspectival gradients, see Rudolf Arnheim, *Art and Visual Perception*, revised edn (London, 1967), pp. 268 ff.
49 1851–2, Tate Gallery, London.
50 1852, Tate Gallery, London; also known as *Strayed Sheep*.
51 Allen Staley, *The Pre-Raphaelite Landscape* (London, 1973), p. 13.
52 Robin Ironside and John Gere, *Pre-Raphaelite Painters* (London, 1948), p. 13.
53 'Preparing for the Worst', *Punch*, vol. 22 (1852), p. 169.
54 1851, City Art Gallery, Manchester.
55 1853, Tate Gallery, London.
56 1862, Walker Art Gallery, Liverpool.
57 1863, Walker Art Gallery, Liverpool.
58 Staley, *Pre-Raphaelite Landscape*, p. 148.
59 1878, Walker Art Gallery, Liverpool. For an account of Victorian historical narrative painting, see Roy Strong, *And When Did You Last See Your Father? The Victorian Painter and British History* (London, 1978).
60 1857 and 1859, private collection, the latter also known as *'Not Guilty'*; for discussion and illustration, see *Great Victorian Pictures*, Arts Council exhibition catalogue (London 1978), pp. 74–5.
61 1864, private collection; for discussion and illustration, see Hilary Guise, *Great Victorian Engravings* (London, 1980), pp. 31, 135.
62 1877–8, private collection; for discussion and illustration, see ibid., pp. 116–17, 165–6.
63 1882, Baroda Museum, India; for illustration and a discussion of Frith's life and work, see Aubrey Noakes, *William Frith: Extraordinary Victorian Painter* (London, 1978).
64 For a discussion of this typology, see Herbert L. Sussman, *Fact into Figure* (Columbus, Ohio, 1979), pp. 47 ff. Sussman's argument does not consider the complex and subversive relationship between the typological semantic in the picture and the semantic generated by the painting's formal organisation.
65 1856, City Art Gallery, Manchester.
66 'Academy Notes, 1856': *Works*, Vol. 14, pp. 66–7.
67 1857, Lady Lever Art Gallery, Port Sunlight.
68 'Academy Notes, 1857': *Works*, Vol. 14, p. 109.
69 First version, 1853, Keble College, Oxford; second version, 1857, City Art Gallery, Manchester; third version, 1903, St Paul's Cathedral, London. For a history of the picture and discussion of the relative merits of its three versions, see Mark Roskill, 'Holman Hunt's differing versions of *The Light of the World*', *Victorian Studies*, vol. 6 (1962–3), pp. 228–44.
70 G. F. Waagen, letter to *The Times*, 13 July 1854.
71 Roskill, '*The Light of the World*', p. 240.
72 *PR & PRB*, Vol. 1, p. 174.
73 John Carey, *The Violent Effigy* (London, 1973), p. 106.

Chapter 11

1 1854, Lady Lever Art Gallery, Port Sunlight; for the account of Hunt's experiences while painting the picture, see his 'Painting *The Scapegoat*', *Contemporary Review*, vol. 52 (1887), pp. 21–38, 206–20.
2 *PR & PRB*, Vol. 1, p. 474.
3 See 'Academy Notes, 1856': *The Complete Works of John Ruskin*, ed. E. T. Cook and A. Wedderburn, 38 vols (London, 1903–9), Vol. 14, pp. 65–6.
4 And, in fact, mythically: the picture's setting is Oosdoom, on the shore of the Dead Sea, traditionally identified with the destroyed city of Sodom.
5 Peter Conrad, *The Victorian Treasure-House* (London, 1973), p. 97.
6 Arnold, 'Dover Beach', ll. 35–7, written 1851, first published, *New Poems* (London, 1867): *Poems of Matthew Arnold*, ed. Kenneth Allott (London, 1965; 2nd edn, 1979), p. 256.
7 Tennyson, 'The Epic [Morte d'Arthur]', ll. 201–2, in *Poems* (London, 1842): *The Poems of Tennyson*, ed. Christopher Ricks (London, 1969), p. 594.
8 Robert Browning, ' "Childe Roland to the Dark Tower Came" ', l. 53, *Men and Women* (London, 1855): *The Poetical Works of Robert Browning*, 16 vols (London, 1888), Vol. 5, p. 197.
9 James Thomson, *The City of Dreadful Night*, ll. 209–10 and ff, *National Reformer* (1874): *The Poetical Works of James Thomson*, ed. Bertram Dobell, 2 vols (London, 1895), Vol. 1, p. 132.
10 John Steegman, *Victorian Taste* (London, 1970), p. 129.
11 1859–60, Tate Gallery, London.
12 Allen Staley, *The Pre-Raphaelite Landscape* (London, 1973), p. 167.
13 Timothy Hilton, *The Pre-Raphaelites* (London, 1970), p. 129.
14 1852–65, City Art Gallery, Manchester.
15 Linda Nochlin, *Realism* (London, 1971), p. 130.
16 *Past and Present*: *The Works of Thomas Carlyle*, Centenary Edition, 30 vols (London, 1897–9), Vol. 10, p. 153.
17 See ibid., bk 3, chs 2 and 3.
18 Ford Madox Brown, Journal, 5 October 1854: *Pre-Raphaelite Diaries and Letters*, ed. W. M. Rossetti (London, 1900), pp. 51–202; p. 136.
19 Hilton, *Pre-Raphaelites*, p. 157.
20 Brown, 1865; the text of the commentary is printed in full in Ford Madox Hueffer, *Ford Madox Brown: A Record of His Life and Work* (London, 1896), pp. 190–5; p. 190.
21 ibid., p. 191.
22 ibid., p. 194.
23 ibid., p. 193.
24 *Past and Present*: *Works*, Vol. 10, p. 31.
25 ibid., p. 32.
26 1853–4, Tate Gallery, London; called *The Awakening Conscience* at the RA exhibition of 1854, Hunt later altered the title to *The Awakened Conscience*.
27 Dorothy Van Ghent, *The English Novel: Form and Function* (New York, 1953), p. 127.
28 ibid., p. 126.
29 Nochlin, *Realism*, p. 201.
30 Ruskin, letter to *The Times*, 25 May 1854: *Works*, Vol. 12, p. 334.
31 *PR & PRB*, Vol. 1, p. 474.

Chapter 12

1 James Fergusson, *The Illustrated Handbook of Architecture*, 2 vols (London, 1855), Vol. 1, p. xxix.

2 Ruskin, *The Seven Lamps of Architecture* (London, 1849): *The Complete Works of John Ruskin*, ed. E. T. Cook and A. Wedderburn, 38 vols (London, 1903–9), Vol. 8, pp. 28–9.
3 Charles Jencks, 'Semiology and architecture', in Charles Jencks and George Baird (eds), *Meaning in Architecture* (London, 1969), pp. 10–25; p. 17.
4 Rudolf Arnheim, *Art and Visual Perception*, revised edn (London, 1967), p. 139.
5 Horatio Greenough, 'Relative and independent beauty', in *Memorial of Horatio Greenough* (New York, 1853); H. A. Small (ed.), *Form and Function* (Berkeley, Calif., 1947), p. 71.
6 Nelson Goodman, *Languages of Art: An Approach to a Theory of Symbols* (London, 1969), pp. 52–3; my examples.
7 The terms are taken from Jencks, 'Semiology and architecture'.
8 The paradigms of Early Victorian architecture were first suggested and discussed by Henry-Russell Hitchcock, *Early Victorian Architecture in Britain*, 2 vols (London, 1954).
9 A. W. N. Pugin, *Contrasts: or A Parallel between the Noble Edifices of the Middle Ages and Corresponding Buildings of the Present Day* (London, 1836; 2nd edn with additional plates, London, 1841).
10 A. W. N. Pugin, *The True Principles of Pointed or Christian Architecture* (London, 1841), p. 57.
11 A. W. N. Pugin, *An Apology for the Revival of Christian Architecture in England* (London, 1843), p. 1.
12 Butterfield to the Warden of Keble College, 20 January 1873, quoted Paul Thompson, *William Butterfield* (London, 1971), p. 33.
13 In this he differs from many later critics, like Fergusson, who longed for almost any kind of stylistic conformity, and from a practitioner like Sir George Gilbert Scott, who could talk of Gothic with a pragmatism that seems almost cynical by the side of Pugin's heady exhortations: 'If we had a distinctive architecture of our own day . . . I should be content to follow it; but we have not . . .' (*Remarks on Secular and Domestic Architecture, Present and Future* (London, 1857), pp. 188–9).
14 Pugin, *Contrasts*, p. 9.
15 ibid., p. 18.
16 Hitchcock, *Early Victorian Architecture*, Vol. 1, p. 397.
17 Archdeacon Wollaston to Jenner, 23 August 1819, quoted M. H. Port, *Six Hundred New Churches* (London, 1961), pp. 52–3; as Port rather grimly remarks of Commissioners' Gothic, 'Cost was the governing factor' (p. 56).
18 Pugin, *True Principles*, p. 9 n.
19 A. W. N. Pugin, *The Present State of Ecclesiastical Architecture in England* (London, 1843), p. 108.
20 Pugin, *Apology*, p. 16.
21 Pugin, *True Principles*, p. 7.
22 ibid., pp. 1–4.
23 ibid., p. 42.
24 ibid., p. 18.
25 ibid., p. 1.
26 Pugin, *Present State*, pp. 17–18.
27 Pugin, *True Principles*, pp. 8–9.
28 Pugin, *Present State*, p. 69.
29 A. W. N. Pugin, *The Glossary of Ecclesiastical Ornament* (London, 1844), pp. iii and vi.
30 Pugin, *Contrasts*, pp. 4–5.
31 A. W. N. Pugin, *Some Remarks on the Articles which Have Recently Appeared in 'The Rambler'*, Relative to Ecclesiastical Architecture and Decoration* (London, 1851), p. 24.
32 See A. W. N. Pugin, *Gothic Furniture in the Style of the 15th Century* (London, 1835), *Designs for Gold and Silversmiths* (London, 1836) and *Designs for Iron and Brass Work in the Style of the 15th and 16th Centuries* (London, 1836).
33 Charles L. Eastlake, *A History of the Gothic Revival* (London, 1872), p. 152.
34 T. S. R. Boase, *English Art, 1800–1870*, Oxford History of English Art, Vol. 10 (London, 1959), p. 196.

Chapter 13

1 Founded in Cambridge in 1839 by two undergraduates, J. M. Neale and Benjamin Webb; after some internecine struggles about religious allegiance in the mid-1840s the Society was reconstituted in London as the Ecclesiological (late Cambridge Camden) Society in 1846. For the Society's history, see J. F. White, *The Cambridge Movement* (London, 1962).

2 The *Ecclesiologist*, bibliographically, is horribly confusing: nos 1–36 run from November 1841 to September 1844; a new series, nos 1–12, runs from January 1845 to July 1846; the first series then again continues, nos 49–189, from July 1846 to December 1868. Volumes 1–3 run from 1841 to 1844; a new series begins at Volume 1 again in 1845, but each subsequent volume is also numbered from the original sequence. In my references I have retained this last convention.

3 *Ecclesiologist*, vol. 1 (1842), p. 91.

4 ibid., vol. 10, NS vol. 7 (1849–50), p. 353.

5 ibid., vol. 13, NS vol. 10 (1852), p. 167.

6 Some minor criticisms aside, the *Ecclesiologist* reviewed *Seven Lamps* with enthusiasm, finding it 'an eloquent and deeply instructive volume': *Ecclesiologist*, vol. 10, NS vol. 7 (1849–50), pp. 111–20.

7 The church was begun in 1849 as a Camdenian Model Church and eventually finished in 1859. The motive force behind the church was A. J. Beresford Hope, and the history of its building is confused by bickering between him and Butterfield: see Hope, *All Saints' Church, Margaret Street*, open letter of 13 June 1854 (London, 1854): the story is retold by Paul Thompson, 'All Saints Church, Margaret Street, reconsidered', *Architectural History*, vol. 8 (1965), pp. 73–94.

8 *Ecclesiologist*, vol. 1 (1842), p. 12.

9 See George C. Pace, 'Alfred Bartholomew, a pioneer of functional Gothic', *Architectural Review*, vol. 91 (1942), pp. 99–102.

10 *The Stones of Venice*, 3 vols (London, 1851–3): *The Complete Works of John Ruskin*, ed. E. T. Cook and A. Wedderburn, 38 vols (London, 1903–9), Vols 9–11.

11 Nikolaus Pevsner, *Some Architectural Writers of the Nineteenth Century* (London, 1972), p. 126.

12 *Ecclesiologist*, vol. 6, NS vol. 3 (1846), p. 43.

13 ibid., vol. 5, NS vol. 2 (1845), p. 184.

14 ibid., vol. 7, NS vol. 4 (1847), p. 84.

15 ibid., vol. 7, NS vol. 4 (1847), p. 123.

16 Cambridge Camden Society, *A Few Words to Church Wardens on Churches and Church Ornaments* (Cambridge/London, 1841), p. 9.

17 Cambridge Camden Society, *A Few Words to Church Builders* (Cambridge/London, 1841), p. 6.

18 G. A. Poole, *The Appropriate Character of Church Architecture* (Leeds, 1842), p. 18.

19 ibid., p. 71.

20 Cambridge Camden, *Church Builders*, p. 14.

21 *Ecclesiologist*, vol. 8, NS vol. 5 (1847–8): 'On the ecclesiology of Chichester Cathedral', pp. 1–9, p. 4; 'On vulne symbolism', pp. 166–71, p. 167; 'Icelandic homily for a festival of the dedication of a church', pp. 216–20.

22 'Church symbolisms', *Transactions of the Exeter Diocesan Architectural Society*, vol. 2 (1847), pp. 67–76; pp. 72–3.

23 G. R. Lewis, *Illustrations of Kilpeck Church, Herefordshire* (London, 1842), pp. 31–2.

24 J. M. Neale and B. Webb, *The Symbolism of Churches and Church Ornaments: A Translation of the First Book of the 'Rationale Divinorum Officiorum' written by William Durandus Sometime Bishop of Mende* (Leeds, 1843).

25 ibid., pp. xix, xxvii, xxv n., xxvi.

26 John Steegman, *Victorian Taste* (London, 1970), p. 87.

27 A. J. B. Hope, *The English Cathedral of the Nineteenth Century* (London, 1861), pp. 42, 142, 189, 243, 215.

28 Henry-Russell Hitchcock, *Architecture: Nineteenth and Twentieth Centuries* (London, 1958), p. 177.
29 *Builder*, vol. 17 (1859), p. 401.
30 E. Ingress Bell, 'The new Natural History Museum', *Magazine of Art*, vol. 4 (1881), pp. 358–62, 463–5; p. 361.

Chapter 14

1 G. A. Poole, *The Appropriate Character of Church Architecture* (Leeds, 1942), p. 91.
2 Stefan Muthesius, *The High Victorian Movement in Architecture, 1850–1870* (London, 1972), p. 59.
3 *Ecclesiologist*, vol. 11, NS vol. 8 (1850), p. 209.
4 *Builder*, vol. 20 (1862), p. 476.
5 *Ecclesiologist*, vol. 19, NS vol. 16 (1858), p. 242.
6 Nikolaus Pevsner, *London*, 2 vols, The Buildings of England (Harmondsworth, 1952), Vol. 2, p. 326.
7 Paul Thompson, *William Butterfield* (London, 1971), p. 285.
8 ibid., p. 160.
9 John Summerson, 'William Butterfield; or the glory of ugliness', *Architectural Review*, vol. 98 (1945), pp. 166–75; p. 170.
10 *Bleak House*, ch. 5, p. 49.
11 Ian Nairn and Nikolaus Pevsner, *Sussex*, The Buildings of England (Harmondsworth, 1965), p. 374; the account is of St Mary Magdalene, West Lavington (1849–50).
12 *Ecclesiologist*, vol. 20, NS vol. 17 (1859), p. 185.
13 T. S. R. Boase, *English Art, 1800–1870*, Oxford History of English Art, Vol. 10 (London, 1959), p. 243.
14 Hope to Henry Tritton, 6 August 1850; quoted Paul Thompson, 'All Saints Church, Margaret Street, reconsidered', *Architectural History*, vol. 8 (1965), p. 76.
15 *Ecclesiologist*, vol. 11, NS vol. 8 (1850), p. 209.
16 For an account of High Victorian Gothic that sees it primarily in terms of combined sexual and – rather oddly – mechanical metaphor, see George L. Hersey, *High Victorian Gothic: A Study in Associationism* (London, 1972).
17 *Ecclesiologist*, vol. 20, NS vol. 17 (1859), p. 186.
18 ibid., vol. 10, NS vol. 7 (1849–50), p. 432.
19 ibid., vol. 20, NS vol. 17 (1859), p. 186.
20 Henry-Russell Hitchcock, *Early Victorian Architecture in Britain*, 2 vols (London, 1954), Vol. 1, p. 598.
21 Henry-Russell Hitchcock, 'High Victorian Gothic', *Victorian Studies*, vol. 1 (1957–8), pp. 47–71; p. 53.
22 Thompson, *Butterfield*, p. 236.
23 *Building News*, vol. 78 (1900), p. 292.
24 Henry-Russell Hitchcock, *Architecture: Nineteenth and Twentieth Centuries* (London, 1958), p. 117.
25 Thompson, 'All Saints', p. 85.
26 Thompson, *Butterfield*, p. 245.
27 Hitchcock, *Early Victorian Architecture*, Vol. 1, p. 591.
28 *The Seven Lamps of Architecture: The Complete Works of John Ruskin*, ed. E. T. Cook and A. Wedderburn, 38 vols (London, 1903–9), Vol. 7, p. 177.
29 ibid., p. 179.
30 *The Stones of Venice*: Works, Vol. 9, pp. 302–3.
31 H. W. and I. Law, *The Book of the Beresford Hopes* (London, 1925), quoted p. 177.
32 *Builder*, vol. 24 (1866), p. 337.

33 Charles L. Eastlake, *A History of the Gothic Revival* (London, 1872), p. 257.
34 *Builder*, vol. 20 (1862), p. 442.
35 T. R. Bumpus, *London Churches, Ancient and Modern*, 2 vols (London, 1908), Vol. 2, p. 273.
36 ibid., p. 309.
37 Eastlake, *Gothic Revival*, p. 262.
38 See Thompson, *Butterfield*, pp. 332–3.
39 Rudolf Arnheim, *Art and Visual Perception*, revised edn (London, 1967), p. 31.
40 Hersey, *High Victorian Gothic*, pp. 107–8.
41 Thompson, *Butterfield*, p. 79.
42 Summerson, 'William Butterfield', p. 170.
43 John Gloag, *Victorian Taste* (London, 1962), p. 70.
44 Kenneth Clark, *The Gothic Revival* (London, 1928); revised edn (London, 1962), p. 174 n.
45 Summerson, 'William Butterfield', p. 172.
46 H. S. Goodhart-Rendel, 'Rogue architects of the Victorian era', *Journal of the Royal Institute of British Architects*, vol. 56 (1949), pp. 251–9; p. 255.

Epilogue

1 Harvey P. Sucksmith, *The Narrative Art of Charles Dickens* (London, 1970), p. 345.
2 Eric Heller, *The Disinherited Mind: Essays in Modern German Literature and Thought* (Cambridge, 1952; new edn with additional material, London, 1975), p. 268.
3 William Blake, 'Annotations to Reynolds' *Discourses*' (*c*.1808): *The Complete Writings of Blake*, ed. Geoffrey Keynes (London, 1966), 1974 edn, p. 451.
4 Philipp Otto Runge, letter to his brother Daniel, 9 March 1802: Lorenz Eitner (ed.), *Neoclassicism and Romanticism, 1750–1850*, 2 vols (Englewood Cliffs, NJ, 1970), p. 148.
5 William Wordsworth, *The Prelude* (text of 1805), ed. Ernest de Selincourt (London, 1933), bk 2, 1. 371.
6 Heller, *Disinherited Mind*, p. 282.

Index

Titles of literary works are given under author's name, paintings under artist's name; figures in italics indicate plate numbers.